PRAISE FOR *EVA*

"Inspired by a collection of keepsakes, Metz unearths a chapter of her mother's hidden past, deftly navigating between two spheres: her family's harrowing escape from the Nazis, and her own present-day world—one steeped in research and introspection, and replete with political red flags weighed against those of the Third Reich. A timely and deeply layered investigation."

—Georgia Hunter, *New York Times* bestselling author of
We Were the Lucky Ones

"Three generations of women—grandmother, mother, daughter—illuminate how history is lived and worlds overlap, filtered through families and passed down from one era to the next. Metz writes, with great insight, about how her mother's escape from Nazi-occupied Vienna to New York City—full of unexpected twists and turns—has echoed through her own life and her daughter's, down to the present moment. This journey of discovery and reclamation could hardly be more timely and resonant."

—Adrienne Brodeur, bestselling author of
Wild Game: My Mother, Her Lover, and Me

"Julie Metz's *Eva and Eve* is a beautifully written ode to her mother, who escaped the Nazis as a child in Vienna in 1940. With an artist's eye for detail and a detective's tenacity, Metz brings to life four generations of her family with great sensitivity and intelligence, and offers a timely meditation on political power gone awry."

—Helen Fremont, national bestselling author of *After Long Silence*

"*Eva and Eve* maps a wide arc, pulling a Jewish family's past in wartime Vienna into the present era with vivid and dramatic detail. The story of political repression, terror and dissolution, then arrival and retrieval in a new country, is full of astonishing and unlikely twists of fate, showing again that individual destiny may be the greatest mystery of all. Metz's journey to recover the past offers a model for connection and self-understanding—as well as a testament to the strengths of an America that is just and fair to all."

—Dani Shapiro, *New York Times* bestselling author of
Inheritance: A Memoir of Genealogy, Paternity, and Love

"Keeping secrets was a virtue for many in the Silent Generation and they died without ever revealing themselves to their puzzled, frustrated children. With a combination of dogged research and emotional archeology, Julie Metz has uncovered a nearly lost world, and in doing so, she has found the Viennese childhood that formed her mother's character."

—Mary Doria Russell, *New York Times* bestselling author of *The Sparrow*

"Interweaving past and present, blending research and imagination, Julie Metz's memoir crafts a portrait of an elusive mother with a bifurcated life. In her search for the threads of half-told stories and hidden treasures, Metz discovers an absorbingly complex family legacy. An illuminating and textured book."

—Elizabeth Rosner, author of *Survivor Café: The Legacy of Trauma and the Labyrinth of Memory*

"Using intrepid detective work and inspired imagination, Metz immerses the reader in interwar Jewish life and culture as it intertwined with Viennese society. She skillfully weaves a poignant family history of loss, escape, and refugee life as she evokes the sights, smells, and tastes of her mother's lost childhood."

—Marion Kaplan, author of *Hitler's Jewish Refugees: Hope and Anxiety in Portugal*

"Weaving together a lyrical exploration of her maternal family history—first as persecuted Jews in Austria, then as struggling immigrants in America—with poignant meditations on her own personal growth and trauma in an era of resurgent, reactionary nationalism, Metz illustrates the persistence of old, human evils, and the inspiration we can find for our own battles in the stories of resilient forebears."

—George Prochnik, author of *The Impossible Exile: Stefan Zweig at the End of the World*

"*Eva and Eve* is a beautiful memoir about all the ways history shapes a family. Metz's meditation on her mother's escape from Nazi Vienna, and the world of her ancestors that was left behind, is an important exploration of the past, but also a warning for the future. This is a devastating and important book, one that should be required reading."

—Danielle Trussoni, bestselling author of *Angelology* and *The Ancestor*

"With a historian's scrupulous research and a novelist's inventive power, Julie Metz has delivered a gripping and moving account of her mother's narrow escape from the Nazis. It is an indelible story of both what was gained and what was lost in the exodus from Vienna to New York."

—Professor Samuel G. Freedman, Columbia University Graduate School of
Journalism, author of *Breaking the Line* and *Who She Was*

"Julie Metz's *Eva and Eve* is a touching homage to her mother, who escaped the terror of Nazi Austria as a child, creating herself anew as an American in the United States. This is a work of startling eloquence and beauty, in its archeological excavation of four generations of a Jewish family and its literary depiction of how the broad sweep of history is threaded into the intricate drama of ordinary human lives."

—Lan Cao, author of *Family in Six Tones* and *Monkey Bridge*

"Equal parts beautifully-wrought memoir and mystery, *Eva and Eve* is the spellbinding intergenerational story of what it means to survive the trauma of impending tragedy and to keep it from the people you love most in the world. Julie Metz has pieced together the story of her beloved late mother's childhood in and escape from Nazi-occupied Austria, her own place in the story they shared as mother and daughter, and what it means to go to any length to save one's family in the face of unspeakable xenophobic horror. A masterpiece that I couldn't put down."

—Elissa Altman, author of *Motherland*

"In this beautifully woven personal history, Julie Metz plumbs how her mother's flight from Nazi-occupied Vienna shaped not only the woman who left, but the women who came after. An essential feminist memoir of women's lives, *Eva and Eve* explores how the trauma of demagoguery and losing one's nation reverberates through generations and how small, even random acts of goodness can rescue the worlds to come."

—Sarah Wildman, author of *Paper Love: Searching for the Girl
My Grandfather Left Behind*

Also by Julie Metz

Perfection: A Memoir of Betrayal and Renewal

EVA AND EVE

A SEARCH *for my*

MOTHER'S LOST CHILDHOOD

and what a WAR *left behind*

JULIE METZ

ATRIA PAPERBACK

New York   London   Toronto   Sydney   New Delhi

ATRIA
PAPERBACK

An Imprint of Simon & Schuster, Inc.
1230 Avenue of the Americas
New York, NY 10020

First Atria Books Paperback edition May 2022

ATRIA PAPERBACK and colophon are trademarks of
Simon & Schuster, Inc.

For information about special discounts for bulk purchases, please contact Simon &
Schuster Special Sales at 1-866-506-1949 or business@simonandschuster.com.

The Simon & Schuster Speakers Bureau can bring authors to your live event. For
more information or to book an event, contact the Simon & Schuster Speakers
Bureau at 1-866-248-3049 or visit our website at www.simonspeakers.com.

Interior design by Erika R. Genova

Manufactured in the United States of America

1 3 5 7 9 10 8 6 4 2

Library of Congress Cataloging-in-Publication Data is available.

ISBN 978-1-9821-2798-5
ISBN 978-1-9821-2799-2 (pbk)
ISBN 978-1-9821-2800-5 (ebook)

To my parents, Eve and Frank,
who gave me this life

For the Viennese golden age in its ultimate florescence was peculiarly a creation of that Jewish society: a society of outsiders, who, for all too brief a time, had become insiders.

—Peter Hall, *Great Cities in Their Golden Age*

The future keeps mocking the past. The past, in eerie resilience, keeps shadowing the present.

—Frederic Morton, *Thunder at Twilight*

Children are detectives of their parents, who cast them out into the world so that one day the children will return and tell them their story so that they themselves can understand it.

—Patricio Pron, *My Father's Ghost Is Climbing in the Rain*

Contents

Eva, at Nine

I'VE NEVER MET this sweet child who smiles at me with the confidence of a well-loved daughter. She is pretty, well-groomed, well-fed. Her dress, purchased or perhaps sewn at home for winter family celebrations, is of a floral material, with puffed sleeves and large round buttons, trimmed in white lace at its high ruffled collar. Her dark, shiny hair is cut short, above her chin, her bangs neatly pinned to one side. If I visited her school I'd see an entire classroom of nine-year-old girls who part and pin their hair the same way. She poses on her own in a comfortable sitting room, but in her easy gaze I sense the presence of other people: parents, siblings, aunts, uncles, cousins, family friends, and the unknown photographer. Behind her, a few hints of the room's décor—rounded backrest of an elegant wood chair, sideboard decorated with a lacy cloth, door framed in carved molding against a patterned wallpaper—all recede in layers of gauzy focus.

What is it about this girl? She seems at once so innocent, yet so knowing. Her plump cheeks are incarnadine, like a morsel of blush-tinted marzipan, yet something about the intensity of her dark eyes tells me she is fiercer than her sweet presentation.

She will need that fierceness.

In two months this girl's country will be taken over by a cohort of extremists led by an authoritarian germophobe who hates people of her kind. He sees them as filth, vermin, contamination. In truth there have always been people in her country who hated her ethnic group, but now their views will be fully validated and normalized.

In six months this well-appointed sitting room will be ransacked and most of the remaining possessions that aren't shattered or stolen by an emboldened police force will be sold off so that the family can survive for the next two years.

The girl's parents will spend those two years in a struggle against a mighty bureaucracy as they attempt to get out of a once-beloved city whose majority population now sees them as enemies of a new empire. Having lost all rights, the family will now be stateless.

Across the ocean, the latest incarnation of the xenophobic, isolationist America First movement is in full sway. Immigrants are suspect, even those who have thrown off most of their traditional customs in an effort to assimilate—to become Americans. People like this girl's family are reviled for their mysterious religion, olive skin, and prominent noses. They cannot shake off their reputation as anti-Christian money-hoarders. They speak the language of America's enemy and surely are spies, however desperately they and their political advocates plead for safe haven from persecution. America First is about protecting jobs from immigrants who will steal employment from true American citizens. America First means resisting engagement in the conflagration that threatens to engulf faraway lands. Let those foreign countries fight their own battles. Let some other place take the great masses of the persecuted and unwashed.

The girl looks at me intently and I meet her gaze. Eighty years have passed since a camera captured her face in the midst of a gentle winter afternoon. Now the gyres of history have revolved. Promoted by another would-be authoritarian and obsessive hand washer, America First is back, emblazoned on posters, T-shirts, and red baseball caps. Different immigrants from the east and south, just as desperate, just as feared and reviled for their dark skin, language, dress, religion, and all-round Otherness, plead for entry and are refused, in the name of national security. In the sweltering days of midsummer, parents and children are separated at the border or deported even as American farmers struggle to hire enough workers to pick fruits and vegetables. America has retreated from its European alliances and the walls of isolationism rise up like the wall an American president wants to build with taxpayer dollars. In an effort to stem the tide of immigrants, right-wing politicians have persuaded fearful British voters to leave the European Union. Other European governments teeter into anti-immigrant conservatism and authoritarianism. Ironically it is Germany's chancellor who continues to uphold the postwar European order of liberal democracy.

I flip the photograph. On the reverse side a diligent family archivist has written "January 1938" in soft pencil. The nine-year-old girl in the frilly dress lived in Vienna, Austria, where a world of safety and comfort was about to end. Her name was Eva, and she was my mother. I knew her as Eve.

———

ON THE WINTER mornings of my childhood, crystalline waves of frozen condensation would cover the windowpanes of our city apartment like lichen on rock, blocking the street six floors below. When I pressed a warm fingertip to the frost, a tiny clearing appeared, like the porthole of a miniature ship. If I made enough of these ovals I could begin to make out a wavy image of the street through the veil of melted ice. This for me is the challenge of memory and memoir writing: we create small vistas from what we remember, and if we can create enough of them, we can begin to piece together a story from what we see. But the vistas, like those my finger made in the frost, can close up again. They might very well remain sealed for a lifetime.

When I first found a keepsake book way in the back of my mother's lingerie drawer I thought I was looking only at a sentimental artifact from her childhood—something about which I knew too little.

Later, I remembered a high school history teacher who had pressed us students to consider the political, economic, and social implications of whichever event we were examining in class. To that end, I had subconsciously started thawing small portals long before I even understood that the keepsake book was part of something larger than my mother's childhood, or our family history. It would take years and a political sea change for me to fully unravel its meaning.

THE REAL MIRACLE, one that kept me up at night during my childhood and into adulthood, is that they got out of Vienna at all, let alone with visas to the United States. Years after my mother's death, the story still troubled me, that her life, and therefore mine, hung on such a slim thread of good fortune, one that was denied to so many equally worthy people deported to extermination camps. The luck of my family's survival wasn't entirely comforting, as it depended on the generosity or intervention of people I could never know: the employees at my grandfather's printing factory, who produced an item of paper packaging vital to the Third Reich war effort; relatives in the United States who vouched for the Singer family and helped with the cost of boat tickets to America; a mysterious vice-consul at the United States consulate in Vienna who granted a visa; and perhaps even some Nazi officials who were open to negotiation or bribery.

My mother's keepsake book felt like a challenge, as if she were asking me to tell our family's story to those people of her adopted country, people who may have forgotten that we are a nation of both adventurers and reluctant refugees, and that there could be quiet greatness in following one woman's journey from one name to another—from Eva to Eve.

PART ONE

PART ONE

Ending and Beginning

I N THE SUMMER of 2006, urgent orchestras of cicadas wailed in the trees of Brooklyn, where I lived with my ten-year-old daughter, Liza, and Clark, my boyfriend of two years. The insects, their life's work complete, dropped out of the branches one by one onto the sidewalks, fragile brown wings folded against bodies desiccating in the Indian summer heat. Across the East River, in Upper Manhattan, my mother, Eve, was dying in the bedroom of our family apartment on West End Avenue.

Until she took to her bed that August, my mother was the force of nature that ran our family. She was a decade retired from a thirty-four-year career at Simon & Schuster as a designer, then art director, of trade book interiors. My father had spent his equally long career as the trailblazing art director of Simon & Schuster's trade book jackets. The result of this unusual arrangement was that my parents ruled over the aesthetics of any book published by the company during those years. My father—indomitable, blunt, uncompromising, a thorn in the side of not a few editors and feared by their assistants—ran his department like an impenetrable castle where many young designers and junior art directors, mostly women fresh out of art school, thrived. My mother's experience was more complicated. While she earned the respect of her many colleagues, it took longer for her to receive the validation of a vice president corporate title. She was certainly paid less than she deserved.

My mother's working world was mostly a mystery to me as a child, except for the rare school holidays when she would bring my brother and me to her office. We had fun cutting up scrap paper from the galleys of page proofs, followed by a tuna salad sandwich plus milkshake at Schrafft's, one of a chain of now-extinct coffee shops.

Later, when I was a teenager, my parents arranged a summer job for me researching photographs for an editor, one of those gigs that would now be called an internship. During those few months I had my first glimpse of their workday routine as we rode the number 5 bus down Riverside Drive and onward into the land of midtown office towers. I would sit between my parents. My father divided the *New York Times* in half—the Gray Lady was the only paper that mattered to our family—reaching across me to hand several sections to my mother. Both immediately buried themselves in that morning's news. About halfway through the journey, in wordless choreography, they simultaneously refolded their sections and exchanged them over my head in an arc of rustling newsprint. The world of ink and paper was the raw material of their work lives, and so it became mine as well.

In old family photos my mother, Eve, was a striking young woman, petite and curvy. Her dark hair, styled in voluptuous 1940s waves, large dark eyes, aquiline nose, and expressive full mouth brought to mind several English movie actresses of Hollywood's golden age—Vivien Leigh, in particular. By midlife, and until her retirement, my mother presented an elegant figure at work, her salt-and-pepper hair coiled in a bun at her nape, five foot two inches in tailored suits and one of her many pairs of polished Ferragamos.

She was at home in the most faithful audiences of Carnegie Hall and the Metropolitan Opera House, or the galleries of the Frick. You could find her test-pinching plums in the fruit bins outside Fairway Market on Seventy-Fourth Street and Broadway, sniffing a round of funky-smelling triple-crème cheese at Zabar's, or ordering smoked salmon and sable at Murray's Sturgeon Shop (*I'll take six bialys with that and a tub of scallion cream cheese.*) She was a New Yorker: steely, savvy, thrifty, pragmatic.

During her working years, my mother "did it all," but of course no one called it "leaning in." She returned home from a full workday to cook meals that were both simple and ambitious. She paid the family bills and prepared tax forms. She ironed my father's shirts and cotton handkerchiefs. If my brother or I needed money for a school trip, she opened her wallet, if only just a crack. Whether you wanted them or not, she always had opinions, increasingly unwelcome as I passed from childhood into adolescence into adulthood.

It was never easy with us. As a child growing up with my parents and younger brother, Simon (named after a grandfather, not the company), in our New York City apartment, I loved her and sometimes feared her. Later, as a teenager, I loved and feared and hated her with an intensity that separated us like ripped tendons that even the most skillful surgeon could not repair. We fought almost daily then. Some nights my voice went hoarse from screaming. Doors slammed and invisible walls rose up. My childhood friends described my mother as severe, "a hard nut," "scary," "cold." I don't think she consciously wanted to be that way. As a child she'd toughened herself in the face of real danger. The sky could fall again at any time. Be prepared. Don't go soft.

As an adult I tried to love her, but at a distance. One close friend observed that when she saw me with my mother I became more child-like and eager for approval. By then I tried to avoid conflict. My mother and I embraced when we saw each other, but without the full abandon we probably both craved. Sometimes when I was with her my disappointment—that we could not seem to find a path to a less freighted love—overwhelmed me. Tears would come later, when I was safe in my own home.

———————

IN A FEW years I would begin to understand my mother's predicament when my own daughter turned into a teenager, seemingly overnight. Yet during that summer of 2006 my mother and I were still where we'd been for years, in a state of delicate truce. We'd talk once a week or so, and I visited for holidays and family dinners. After my husband's sudden death from a pulmonary embolism in 2003, she did not console me much, nor did she intrude as I made my way as a newly single mother. My parents liked my boyfriend, Clark, who, born and raised in Wisconsin, was a transplant to New York. Clark and my father bonded over their shared love for the Green Bay Packers, a singular intersecting point that always made me smile. On my best days I was careful around my mother, often running lines of dialogue in my head like an actor imagining how to play a scene. On not-so-good days, I got through shared meals reminding myself how much my parents loved their only granddaughter. Though my mother wasn't exactly the cuddly grandma type, she called Liza "kitten."

UNTIL THE SPRING of 2005, our emotional lives unfolded in separate worlds. Then, a few months before my mother turned seventy-seven, she called me one evening to deliver the news—without fanfare—that she had cancer. I'd never heard of mesothelioma, a slow-growing, always-fatal rarity caused by exposure to asbestos. In her case, it was likely the result of having inhaled airborne fibers during an office renovation decades earlier. Fortunately, my father had not been exposed, as his office was elsewhere in the building.

My father told me later that during the worst of the chemo, when she could do nothing more than doze in a chair, she asked him, *What did I do in my life to deserve this misery?* Follow-up tests after the chemo showed that the tumors weren't shrinking. I was grateful when she told me she'd decided to stop treatment. *I've had enough of this game*, she said with her trademark sarcasm. An unexpected brief period of rejuvenation followed. Her ashen cheeks flushed and I watched her eat meals with gusto, as if she were making up for the months of nausea and exhaustion.

While she was still well enough, my mother began teaching my father how to manage tasks that would make his future life without her possible. She was in a race against an unknown but imminent deadline to transfer all the information she had stored in her head during the fifty-plus years of their marriage. Even after she no longer got out of bed, her brief periods of wakefulness were devoted to this very task.

One day, I contemplated my impending motherless state on the long subway ride home from my parents' apartment. I understood that my loss would be a devastating absence of change. Nothing *would* change. My life would go on. I'd been living too separated from my mother to grieve the empty place I'd filled with friends and a therapist. The subway was a terrible place to cry, but I was overwhelmed and let down my usual guard. A few kindly onlookers watched as I wiped my nose with napkins from Starbucks.

Beginning in August, two capable nurses traded days and nights caring for my mother at our family's apartment. Jeanette and Carol, strong Jamaican women who laughed easily. When I visited, I smelled the fried chicken or Chinese takeout they brought in for their meals, laid out on the same round table in the kitchen where I'd eaten so many breakfasts, lunches, and dinners. They lifted my mother when she needed to use the toilet, bathed her, and dressed her in clean nightgowns. And then, as time passed, they changed her diaper, because it came to that. My mother accepted their care with a serenity that surprised me: she had always directed her life and ours.

September 2006 brought a final reckoning as her body continued wasting. This was particularly unsettling because the physical resemblance between us had always been striking. All the women on her side of the family looked alike. During adolescence I had recoiled from the evidence of my mother's middle age, one that one day might be mine, and now as I looked at her in bed, I comprehended another possible future that terrified me. Once, she had been curvy and buxom, then her weight had dropped to one hundred pounds, and now I was afraid to guess. I'll look like that one day, I mused as I sat by her bed, offering her apple juice with a straw. Something will get me and there I'll be, bones overdraped with skin, just as she is now—the fate of millions that her family somehow escaped during the war.

At times, her wasting was less terrifying, as if she were being gradually liberated from her failing body. When she was awake, she often stared into the distance, as if she were peering through a window at a landscape invisible to us, the living. Her hospice doctor said it was unusual for mesothelioma patients to linger this way. She was willing her body to hold on a bit longer. *I don't want to go*, she said to me one day, *but I am ready to go.*

DURING THIS TIME my father and I often went to a local restaurant so he could get out of the apartment for a while. For the first time as an adult I felt useful to him. Over dinner he told stories I'd never heard before, about his Depression-era childhood in Philadelphia—the good times, when his family lived in a house in a middle-class Jewish neighborhood, and then the years after 1932, when his father's business failed, the car and refrigerator were repossessed, and their house was foreclosed upon. The family moved to an apartment over a taproom, accepting food and money from relatives who still had jobs. His most vivid childhood memories were connected to food, or more accurately, a longing for it. As he continued his stories, week after week, I could see his childhood and his sometimes food-stricken time as a soldier in Patton's Third Army unfold like a film with a voice-over. No wonder he had fallen in love with my beautiful, intelligent mother, a gifted home cook, the daughter of a late-in-life restaurant manager and pastry chef.

One evening, on the walk back to his apartment (I'd already started thinking of my childhood home as "his" rather than "theirs"), my father pointed up to a bay window that popped out of a corner building on 104th Street and Broadway. "That's where your mother lived when I met her," he said. "That was the living room window right up there." We stopped to look at that window, one I'd walked by many times in my life without knowing its significance. "It was a revelation when I first met her parents. Everything was so serene. They were always gentle with each other. My parents weren't like that at all. Your grandfather Julius was quiet, but Anna was much more outgoing, always a laugh and a smile. They had a cat; he didn't like me much. Blackie. What a brute. But the food!" He paused his story as if to catch a whiff of a dinner from all those years ago. I loved how he stored the memories of his life in meals he'd eaten. "What a cook she was, Anna. Fantastic baker. And they were running the restaurant then, so whenever I showed up it was always *Frank, the future son-in-law!* The schnitzel, the strudel." He sighed. "I felt appreciated. Needed."

———————————

MY MOTHER DIDN'T seem to need me in the place where she was now. Where did she travel during the long hours of sleep? Sometimes I would move up close to her to make sure she was still breathing. The box containing the morphine that her hospice doctor had provided remained unopened in the refrigerator. On a few occasions I took the box out to read the label, wishing I could rip open its seal and drink the vial down to dull the pain of watching my mother disappear. She never asked for the morphine. "I've seen it go this way before," Carol said. "Where they just fade away. Let's be grateful and thank the Lord that she isn't suffering." I wasn't a believer, but I was intensely grateful for this one blessing.

One afternoon, as I waited for her to open her eyes, I investigated the blond-wood, midcentury dressers my parents referred to as the Delicatessen. There were two identical dressers, topped with a glass-fronted case that I could imagine stocked with an array of lamb chops and trussed chickens, but that was instead packed with photos, books, and curios of unknown origin. Gently I pulled open my mother's top drawer, admiring again the 1920s-era jewelry she'd inherited from her mother, who had been young and beautiful during the interwar years in Vienna, half a world away from New York. A small red cardboard box, still bearing the label of a jeweler on Vogelweideplatz held a Jewish pendant and another inscribed "Evie." Near the jewelry was a soft leather pouch containing a bone-handled folding fork and spoon that had belonged to my grandfather. In another red cardboard box I found a tiny compass. I knew that my grandfather had been an avid mountain climber, and these pieces were the surviving souvenirs of his camping gear. Tucked underneath the jewelry were the dull green Third Reich passports my mother had saved from their journey. I had only peeked at them a few times in my life, as they exuded a force field of horror. But now I leafed through the pages, looking closely at the grandparents I'd never met. On the last page was an American visa, stamped and signed. I picked up a familiar framed wedding photo of my young parents—my father, a bit sheepish with his lopsided smile and horn-rimmed glasses, nestled against my beautiful mother. There had been no grand wedding—though my father's family had offered to pay for one—just a simple service in a rabbi's office. My mother's bobbed curls framed her large eyes, the prominent Singer family nose and the painted lips, curved upward in the posed smile of a 1940s Hollywood starlet. She wore one of her expertly home-tailored suits rather than a white dress. I tried to take in the details of her face like a biographer. I knew so little about her young life, only sketchy memories of a lost happy childhood and what had always seemed like improbable stories of her family's escape in 1940. Too late to ask for details now.

———————

A DAY IN mid-October. I sat at the foot of my mother's bed, feeling useless. A week, maybe two, said her hospice doctor. I realized I wasn't prepared for life without a mother, even one with whom I hadn't shared my inner life in a long time. There were so many questions I hadn't asked and now it was too late to ask them. A wave of loneliness washed over me, and I started weeping. My mother watched me. She didn't speak much anymore; it was too much physical effort.

No crying, she said, just louder than a whisper, but I heard her. I stopped, just like that, because she had asked as much and I didn't want to disappoint her, not this late in the game.

October 21. My mother could no longer speak, so what turned out to be our last conversation was one-sided. No confessions, no tender parting words of love or advice. We were not a religious family, so there was no talk of meeting on the other side, where I sensed my mother already had more than a toehold.

"Are you in pain?" I asked.

She shook her head no. We had never opened the bottle of morphine.

"Are you worried about leaving Daddy?"

She nodded yes. I sighed. So this was why she'd hung on, as if she could still do anything for anyone now.

"Please don't worry. Simon and I will take care of everything. There's nothing left to do. It's time to go." I hoped she was still listening to me. I left that afternoon wondering if I would see her alive again, yet her will to live had surprised us all, for months now. A week more, I thought. At least.

———

THE FOLLOWING EVENING, my brother invited my father and me over to dinner in Brooklyn. Simon and his wife, Mary, had no children, just two adored cats, so their home was always calm and orderly. Their long dining table with multiple leaves had become the setting for family gatherings. This brief weekly meal had become another way to get my father out of his apartment.

We were all at the table, platters of grilled chicken and vegetables making solemn rounds, when the phone rang.

"It's Carol," my brother said. "She says it's going to be soon."

Moments later we were speeding up the West Side Highway in a taxi. We arrived at my father's building and the doorman held the doors so we could rush in. Upstairs, in front of the apartment, I fiddled with my key, struggling to find the sweet spot in the old lock. You had to jiggle it just so.

"She's just passed," Carol said as we burst in. My father was stricken. My brother took him aside. I asked Carol to tell me what had happened.

"Not even fifteen minutes ago," Carol said. "She was lying in bed and I thought she was sleeping. She seemed to have some trouble breathing. Then she opened her eyes very wide, like she was looking out somewhere. She opened her mouth, as if to say something, and then she was gone. Don't worry yourself. It was very fast and we see it like this a lot, where they wait till everyone's out of the house. Some folks, they just want to be alone when they go."

My father, brother, and I approached the bedroom, where my mother's body lay covered with a sheet. I knew I had to pull back the sheet, to fully comprehend what had happened. My mother lay still and gray, mouth open. I looked for a long hard moment, until I was no longer shocked.

"My angel," my father cried, standing in the bedroom doorway. He was so upset, I hurriedly replaced the sheet over my mother's face.

The hospice doctor had given us instructions to call the funeral home as soon as my mother died. Two men arrived speedily, as if they'd been waiting outside the apartment door. They removed my mother's jewelry—a bracelet of braided gold and a ring of twisted gold wire. I placed these items carefully in my mother's jewelry box—my inheritance now. The men wrapped her body in a gray blanket, placed it on a stretcher, and carried her away, so thin and unsubstantial that the blanket appeared to conceal nothing at all.

———————

AFTER THE FUNERAL came a new rhythm of tasks in my mother's absence. My father told me he couldn't face living with my mother's belongings still around. She'd owned a closet full of fine suits, trousers, skirts, blouses, and at least thirty boxes of Ferragamo shoes (alas, all one size too large for me). Her clothing from thirty-four years in an office didn't suit my freelancer life, where my commute was ten feet from the kitchen to my desk, often still in my pajamas. Mary offered a solution—donating everything to an organization that collected clothing for disadvantaged women entering the workforce. "Someone will be glad to have them," she said. It would be a relief to pass everything onward as quickly as possible so that my father could feel at ease in his new life.

Mary and I began right away. I saved the sweaters my mother had knitted (so many stitches!), and the cashmere cardigans she cared for meticulously, some dating back to the 1960s. I kept the sweater I'd given her for her last birthday, knowing then that it would soon become a keepsake. It still smelled like her favorite perfume, a gust of rose. I packed up a retractable tape measure, a gift from a printing company decades earlier. There was also a small rolling tool called a copy counter, used to paginate galleys from typed manuscripts. The logos on both looked to be from the 1960s. How like my mother to save such utilitarian analog vestiges from her years of work. I packed up the leather pouch that contained my grandfather's folding fork and spoon, the compass, my mother's jewelry collection of pearls and antique cameos, amber beads, gold bracelets, the necklaces that had belonged to my grandmother Anna. I slipped the twisted gold ring my mother was wearing when she died on my bare right pointer finger, swirling it round and round as Mary and I placed folded clothes into black plastic bags. The ring was a comforting presence until the shocked moment when I realized that my finger was naked again: I had lost it. I rummaged frantically in the black bags until, overcome with the futility of the search, I retreated to the back hallway near the service elevator, where I wept over the loss, cursing my carelessness and wishing I had a cigarette, even though I hadn't smoked one in fifteen years. *It was just a ring*, I told myself. I stepped back inside the apartment, hurriedly washed my tear-blotched face with cold water from the kitchen sink, mumbled an unconvincing "All right" as my dad passed me and asked how I was doing. Then I returned to work.

I found a pebble in the pocket of one of my mother's winter coats—soft and black, with a shiny patina that suggested long use as a comfort against worry. I placed it in my own coat pocket. We have that in common, I mused, both of us pebble collectors, though I had piles to her single one.

IN THE BACK of the drawer where my mother kept her perfume-scented silk slips and nightgowns, I found a small book, bound in coffee-colored linen. Pasted in the center was a lithograph of two kittens with red-and pink-ribboned collars. The word *Poesie* was stamped on the linen in faded gold ink.

Inside were handwritten notes, all in German, addressed to "Eva" or sometimes "Evie," with dates from November 28, 1938, to March 24, 1940, the day before my mother and her parents left Vienna for the United States.

My father came into the room and I held out the book. "Have you ever seen this? Do you know what it is?" He said he'd never seen it before, not once during all the decades of their marriage.

Mary had studied German and was able to decipher some of the old-fashioned script—messages of love and farewell from childhood friends and older relatives, sometimes accompanied by famous verses from the poet Goethe. One page was filled with girlish drawings of hearts and colorful stickers of children in traditional Austrian costume. *Do not forget me, your loving friend, Sylvie.* On one spread from 1939, a girl named Renate had copied the characters from Disney's *Three Little Pigs* from a movie advertisement in colored pencil. Across the spread she'd lettered the line "Who's Afraid of the Big Bad Wolf?" There was, indeed, a terrifying Big Bad Wolf in Vienna by January 12, 1939. His name was Adolf Eichmann, one of the architects of Adolf

Hitler's Final Solution, which would nearly obliterate European Jewry by the time the Nazis surrendered in 1945.

My father looked over my shoulder, voicing what I suspected: some, perhaps most, of the people who had signed this keepsake book, those who did not get out of Vienna by October 1941, when the German government forbade emigration, must have perished. By the time my mother left with her parents, it had been almost too late.

Who were all these people? Aunts and uncles, family friends, teachers, other girls who may not have reached adulthood. As I turned the fragile pages, I was saddened but not surprised that my mother had never shared this most private journal with her family. Eva had escaped and lived. She had become Eve. She'd found love, married, worked, created a family. She had become an American. But how had her family gotten out? Had she felt guilt for surviving?

———————

SOME WEEKS LATER I visited my father at his apartment. My brother had taken him shopping for a new bed. My father had moved back into the bedroom after many months in the living room and was already in some process of evolution. I could tell he was lonely. He'd had a partner for over half a century and now he was in new territory.

I sat heavily on the new mattress, wondering how it would feel to be alone after so many coupled years. My father handed me a small scrap of ruled paper, no bigger than a Post-it note. I recognized the quivery handwriting on it as my mother's, its former grace much altered by her illness.

"This was the last thing she wrote," he said.

It took me a moment to decipher the words, instructions for mixing fertilizer to feed her beloved roses in the garden of their weekend place in rural Connecticut. When I was about six, my parents had bought five acres of land sloping down from a granite ledge to swampy woods and had built a small home, at first unheated. They'd immediately set about taming their land, clearing away some of the poplar and shad-blow to make space for a pond. There, Simon and I gathered up viscous clumps of frog eggs, watched them hatch in plastic bags, dumped the pollywogs back into the pond, and then hunted for the adult frogs, grasping their slimy bodies for a moment before they wriggled away. In newly cleared land surrounding the pond, my parents planted flowers, while Simon and I built wigwams with discarded branches. Gardening was rough-going at first, given the granite substrate. If you pressed a shovel into the soil you were guaranteed to hit rocks, obstacles later repurposed as garden ornaments. Within a few seasons, perennials were established, as well as a vegetable patch, and a bed of hardy roses. As I grew older I discovered the satisfaction of weeding. Later, I, too, became a gardener.

My mother talked to her plants. As she propped up a drooping peony or a trailing rose branch she spoke to them firmly. She was strict with us, her children, and with her plants. *Now you. Stand up now. None of that flopping around.* And the plants did answer in their way. My mother, outside in T-shirt and jeans, tangled hair wrapped in a ban-dana, a schmear of loamy earth across her sweaty cheek. I never saw her happier than when she was digging in the garden or a tiny bit tipsy at one of the dinner parties my parents hosted for their friends.

It was late October when she died. The roses were dormant. The autumn gusts had carried off the withered petals and tossed away the leaves. During those somnolent bedridden hours of her last weeks, she must have imagined the roses flowering again the following June, knowing that she wouldn't see the fragrant blooms of New Dawn and Betty Prior. But my father would—as long as he remembered to feed them. Her roses were finicky: the correct ratio of water to fertilizer made all the difference. There was something so tender in these practical instructions, an acknowledgment of the years of effort they'd put into their garden, a manifestation of their worldview that, with unflagging effort, order could be created from chaotic wilderness. In this moment of reading her last note to my father, I understood that she was truly gone.

THE KEEPSAKE BOOK remained, a vault of secrets from my mother's past. I brought it home and looked through its pages, wondering about the Eva I had never known, a child of nine who spent what little pocket money she had saved to buy this book, making sure that all her beloved people signed it before she left Vienna. I didn't know then that many other Jewish girls in Germany and Austria had done the same, that there were archives filled with *Poesiealbums* just like this one. All I knew then was that this book had been important enough to my mother that she had held on to it, though it was too charged with painful memories to share with anyone.

Like many Jews of my generation, I'd grown up under a dark cloud of memory. Now I wanted to pierce the cloud and understand the Vienna my mother knew as a child, the terrifying years under National Socialism, and then her life as a wartime refugee and immigrant—to immerse myself in a way I hoped I could bear. I began tentatively melting small portholes, wondering what I could still uncover and piece together so many years later.

Meanwhile, anti-immigrant rage was exploding in America, elevated by a 2016 presidential candidate who at first appeared to represent only a harmless fringe. With his buffoonish pompadour and face tan it was hard to take the man seriously. As an openly racist blowhard, he'd been ranting in New York City tabloids since the 1980s, but now he emerged onto the national scene as a megaphone for Americans who knew him as the star of a reality series, where he'd played the role of a successful businessman. According to him, Mexicans were rapists and criminals. Muslims fleeing oppression in their home countries were guilty by association because of 9/11 and should be banned from entering the United States. Stunningly, he revived the slogan "America First," a xenophobic isolationist idea with a long history, reclaimed in the 1920s by a resurgent Ku Klux Klan and later endorsed by the aviator Charles Lindbergh, who often expressed his anti-Semitism and

Fascist sympathies as a member of the America First Committee. Too many Americans in 2016 had no idea that this slogan was a dangerous retread.

The keepsake book sat on my desk, its aging paper fragrant, exuding a force that pulled me back to a past my mother had tried to forget. Now I had other documents, too—the Third Reich passports my mother had saved and family photographs of long-gone relatives. I studied these artifacts with the intensity of a stargazer on a moonless night, when the eye's focus on one sidereal point inks over the other billions and trillions of distant sparkles.

As I sifted through papers and peeled away layers to reveal the past, I wished like hell I'd asked my mother more questions about her childhood, her family, and her immigration experience when she was alive. But it turned out that she'd left clues for me to follow. Almost from the beginning, my search felt like a séance, a conversation she and I never had when she was alive. A collaboration with a ghost.

A Visit to the Old Country

I'D LEFT HOME for college, a three-hour bus ride from the apartment on the Upper West Side. I had new friends and had found a home in the art building, where I spent many all-nighters in the studios supercharged with sour coffee and solvent fumes.

The apartment back in New York felt far away, until my mother would call me, once a week. I'd take the call on the hall phone. Too quickly, too easily, we slipped back into our tangle of arguments, and soon I'd be fighting with her about something, and one of us would hang up, and I'd sit on the hall carpet feeling crushed and bitter. During my sophomore year it became clear to me that three hours wasn't enough distance. I applied for a study abroad year in Paris. My French was only so-so, even after many years of high school and college courses. I'd never been to a country where I couldn't communicate. I'll learn, I told myself. My parents agreed to the year abroad. My painting professor begged me not to go. Your work will suffer, she said, insisting that the art school in Paris was too old-fashioned. I have to, I said. I have to get away from here. I could feel her disappointment, and wondered if she might be right. I weighed the future against the present. I had to go. And while I'm there, I thought, I must somehow get to see the mysterious Vienna my mother spoke about, her long lost home.

MY BIRTHDAY, JUNE 22, 1980. I was twenty-one and in Vienna with Michelle, my travel companion of a few weeks. Michelle had an adorable short crop of honey-brown curls and wire-frame glasses. Our shared Jewish heritage perhaps explained her willingness to join me on this afternoon visit to my mother's former apartment at 22 Weimarer Strasse.

I knew Michelle from New York, one of a larger circle of women friends. I had spent the past year in France as an exchange student: a month in Aix-en-Provence and the remainder of the academic year in Paris. The year had not gone smoothly, especially the beginning in Aix. But I had pushed on through the worst of it, and now I felt at ease in Paris, even with my still-wobbly French. I was not looking forward to returning to New York. Michelle had written to me during the rain-soaked Paris spring. She wanted to travel in Europe during the summer and proposed that we spend a month together. I liked her and her itinerary of places I hadn't yet seen: Bruges, Amsterdam, Copenhagen, Munich. She wanted to visit the former concentration camp at Dachau and I agreed. I asked if she'd be up for a trip to Vienna, and she said yes. We had set about buying Eurail passes and making our plans. And now, so far, we'd had an excellent few weeks.

When I told my mother that we planned to travel to Vienna, she named the famous cafés we should not miss, with a sense of nostalgia she was clearly trying to tamp down. *Café Demel*, you must go there. *And Café Mozart, for their famous Sacher Torte.* Though we were not able to speak about her lost childhood openly, I sensed her sorrow and heartbreak, papered over with bitterness. Like a lover who has moved on with effort after the sad end of an affair, my mother wanted an apology from Austria that, even if it had been offered freely, would never have been enough.

In the summer of 1980, the Austrian government was still a long way from any formal acknowledgment of their active participation in the Holocaust. Despite her enthusiastic recommendations, I could hear her familiar refrain: *The Austrians were worse Nazis than the Germans.*

In Vienna, Michelle and I found an inexpensive hotel in the university district. Our double room had eiderdown-covered mattresses—so wonderfully fluffy—and the first night there we bounced up and down on the beds like two little kids. Apple strudel for breakfast was a fine thing, indeed. Veal schnitzel, as crispy and as satisfying as my mother's, overhung our plates. I understood soon enough what a plump lady I would have been if I'd grown up in this city. Michelle and I worked off some of our meals walking through museum galleries and ambling through St. Stephen's Square and the Habsburg Palace. Everywhere we went, I saw tall blond people, who were, I presumed, the children and grandchildren of Nazis.

Vienna was beautiful, but that day was not about seeing the sights. I was on a mission. We made our way to 22 Weimarer Strasse—an evocative street name, with its nod to empire and glory.

My mother had frequently told a story of her first postwar trip to Vienna with my father in 1956. Sixteen years had passed since she had fled with her family and she was then a twenty-eight-year-old married woman. She and her mother had already tried, and failed, to seek restitution for the family's financial losses as a result of the Nazi takeover. An official at the Austrian consulate in New York had rebuffed her, protesting that the Austrians had also been victims of Hitler. Despite the misgivings she had about her former home, she had cultivated a correspondence with a woman who had cared for her father during an illness in his younger years.

In many ways the trip must have been heartwarming. As soon as they arrived in the city she knew her way around the center and took my father to one of the famous cafés. They visited my grandfather's nurse. They bought tickets for the opera. The State Opera's theater had been bombed during the war and was still being rebuilt piece by piece, so the evening's performance of *The Marriage of Figaro* was staged in a grand room in the Habsburg Palace, which had been spared. Afterward, they strolled to the Café Mozart for a late supper and a slice of the dense chocolate torte for which the place is famous.

But one excruciating memory lingered from this trip: while returning from a day trip outside the city, my mother desperately redirected a taxi driver when she realized that the car was approaching her old street. She did this in her Viennese dialect, surprising the driver, who imagined that he was transporting two American tourists.

I heard about this taxi ride often enough that it lived in my mind like a scene on film. During those retellings I couldn't understand how a building could still exert such power over her, but as we stood in front of the door, which was guarded by a fierce gargoyle, I imagined this place had entered her dreams in the way of all emotionally weighted places in our lives. This had been her home, from the innocent years of her early childhood until her family's hurried departure in March 1940 when she was not quite twelve.

The street was hushed. I wanted to see the inside, but who would be home at this hour? I hadn't planned this well. I scanned the labeled buzzers, then lost my nerve. At first glance the great wooden front door appeared to be locked, but a vertical sliver of light hinted otherwise. When I pushed gently, it opened with a groan, like the entry to a fairy-tale castle, revealing a white marble lobby draped in white canvas drop cloths. A crew of painters perched on ladders barely glanced at us as I quickly led Michelle to the stairway coiled around an ancient ornate cage elevator. I took a moment to admire the handiwork and wondered if my mother had used this elevator or, in the way of energetic children, had dashed up and down the marble stairs, racing her two older brothers. I had no idea which apartment my mother had lived in (stupid, I thought then, that I'd forgotten to ask; odd that she'd never told me). I took the stairs with purpose, as if I knew where I was going. Michelle followed behind. On the landings I edged toward each apartment door, straining to hear any sound at all. No muffled bark of housebound dog, mewl of lonely cat, scrabble or chirp of caged bird. No chatter of humans. It was midday on a weekday in summer. Even mothers would be outside with their children in nearby Türkenschanzpark, where my mother had once played as a girl.

Michelle looked at me for direction as we reached the top floor. I told her that simply being in the building was enough—and I tried to believe it. *Dayenu*, the Jewish Passover prayer refrain, *it would have been enough*. Had He taken us through the Red Sea to dry land and not fed us manna in the desert for forty years, *dayenu*. But I felt the sting of disappointment as we walked back down the stairs, slower this time, around and around the elevator shaft, my palm grazing the velvety wood banister. On the first landing I stopped. There was music coming from one of the two doors, the left one. Stepping closer, I heard a melody of classical violin and piano, perhaps Schubert. My father always played a game with us as we ate breakfast to the accompaniment of one of New York City's classical radio stations. If we could guess the name of the composer he promised us a new Mercedes or a Porsche. *No German cars for me*, my mother would say. Sometimes I guessed right. I smiled now, recalling all the undelivered cars I'd won over the years.

"I'll knock," I said.

Michelle laughed nervously. She'd agreed to be my translator if someone were home, as my German was limited to *Wo ist der Bahnhof?* (Where is the train station?) and a few other tourist phrases I'd learned to pay for food and hotel rooms. My decent pronunciation confused shopkeepers, who expected me to continue in more fluent sentences. I'd absorbed something from listening to my mother speak with her elderly Onkel Theo and Harry the butcher when I was a child. I regretted now that she hadn't taught my brother and me to speak her first language, but in wandering the streets of her city, populated with the descendants of the people who'd forced her family to leave, I wasn't so surprised that she'd put such distance between herself and the German language. Our early years at a Waldorf school in Manhattan gave us a rare taste—we had learned the Friedrich Schiller lyrics to Beethoven's "Ode to Joy"—but nothing more that I could now recall.

I rapped softly on the door. The music stopped abruptly. Whoever was inside was playing an instrument, not listening to a radio or stereo. Footsteps approached the door, and the lock unlatched.

A modestly built man of late middle years stood in the doorway: wiry build, a mussed spray of gray hair swept back from a speckled forehead. A sun lover with a friendly face. He looked Jewish to me. What were the odds in this city that had so successfully—*and enthusiastically, worse than the Germans*—purged its Jewish population? Remote, less than nil, I thought. Michelle approached, ready for translation duty. She began bravely, describing me as the daughter of someone who had once lived in this building before the war.

The man smiled. "You can speak English," he said in New Yorkese, just a gentle stretch on the vowels revealing his Viennese upbringing. He introduced himself as Mr. Weiss. Yes, he was Jewish, he had grown up in Vienna, fled with his family to New York and lived for most of his life in Greenwich Village, but after retirement he'd decided to return to this city of his birth.

An actual Jewish person in Vienna. Until that moment I'd felt so uneasy with my outrage, as if there were a sign on my chest: *Curses upon you, children of wartime Fascists, may the God of the Israelites strike you dead with a strong hand and an outstretched arm!* I was a Jew-ish Jewess who forgot to light Hanukkah candles by the fifth night of eight, whose attachment to Passover hinged on my love of gefilte fish, my mother's fluffy matzo balls, and chocolate almond flour torte. Okay, there was a psalm at the end that moved me deeply. *The mountains skipped like rams, and the little hills like lambs.* It was an image from a children's story. As Michelle and I walked through crowds on the streets of Vienna, I often felt an urge to grab strangers by the collar and remind them of the crimes of their parents and grandparents. One afternoon as Michelle and I stood on a corner eating delicious gelato (the Viennese worshipped this Italian import), I began weeping with the frustration of it all. This beautiful city would have been my home. Nurtured on schnitzel and stews, strudel and poppy seed cakes, I might have married, borne children, achieved contented zaftigness, and lived out my days here, perhaps even running my grandfather's printing factory alongside my brother. I was an art major. My brother had inherited my mother's gift for numbers. She said that her father could multiply three-digit numbers in his head.

It wasn't so hard to imagine this scenario, given that both my parents now worked in the publishing business. The heady smell of ink, book pages, and glued bindings perfumed our apartment. When my

mother first explained four-color process printing, handing me a mag-
nifying loupe to examine the tiny dots of cyan, magenta, yellow, and
black, I thought my head would explode with this new understanding of
how our colorful three-dimensional world could be translated onto a flat
white page. My grandfather's printing factory had produced wrappers
for soaps. Beautiful wrappings, my mother told us kids, with ornate label
designs created on heavy lithography stones. And some kind of patented
packaging for powdered medicine made of folded waxed paper. She
would try to describe what it looked like, but I never could get a clear
visual. Something like a paper fan. That packaging was important to the
Nazis, my mother said, and saved her father, Julius, from being deported
to Dachau. The power of folded paper. At college I'd already become
infatuated with the printmaking room: the smell of ink, the pliability of
dampened rag paper, the satisfying feeling of cranking the press over
inked plates. It should have been ours, the printing factory, and this city.

Now Mr. Weiss guided us into a sunny living room, where he introduced his adult daughter, who was putting away her violin. It was their
duet we'd interrupted. She left briefly, returning with glasses of water and
chocolate Manner wafers. I'd never had one before. As the wafer dissolved
on my tongue, leaving behind the creamy chocolate filling, I looked around
the room, startled by its resemblance to the living room in the apartment
where I'd grown up. The same midcentury, blond-wood Scandinavian
furniture. And in the corner, a baby grand piano draped with an embroidered fringed shawl, woven in silky shades of green and russet. The near
twin of this shawl was back home—the bedspread in my college dorm
room. It had once covered the Singers' piano in their apartment, somewhere in this building. Mr. Weiss looked to be just about my mother's age.
I wondered about their parallel lives as I nibbled wafers and Mr. Weiss told
us about his childhood and his years in New York. He'd lived for years
in a still-bohemian Greenwich Village, just down the street from a good
friend of ours. I could imagine him in a book-filled apartment, shopping
for cheese at Balducci's, or sipping coffee at the Caffe Reggio on MacDou-
gal Street. A tingle of recognition electrified the top of my head.

As Michelle and I prepared to leave Mr. Weiss's apartment, with many thanks for his warm welcome and the wafers, I remembered then that my grandfather's printing factory had been located behind the building. When we returned to the lobby, we made our way down a dark hall to an open rear courtyard. There was an industrial-style building with tall windows and skylights, similar to ones I'd seen in similar rear courtyards during my school year in Paris. A sign outside the door indicated that it currently housed a cosmetics company.

It was my first birthday so far from home. I was relishing my independence, but also missing my mother's dense chocolate birthday cake with coffee-flavored icing and longing just a bit for the security of the apartment on the Upper West Side.

As Michelle and I stepped out of number 22 onto Weimarer Strasse, I thought only about home. Late that June evening in 1980, dinnertime in New York City, we stopped at a phone booth and I placed a collect call. My mother answered the phone, and as my words were priced by the minute, I rushed into a description of our visit. But she had questions.

Is the factory building still in the rear courtyard? It is, I replied, mentioning the cosmetics company.

And did you see the inside? I described the marble lobby, the painters, the ancient elevator, the graceful staircase.

She began telling me a story I'd heard before, about the family that had lived across the hall from hers, how their son was the reason it became imperative to get her older brothers safely away in 1938. *This son failed his exams for the second time, but Fritz passed. The son joined the Hitler Youth right after the Anschluss and started telling everyone in the building that he would see to it that Fritz and Dolfi were deported to a camp. Herr Mazura, the building porter and the foreman of my father's factory, he warned my father, and my brothers went away to London that fall. But I stayed behind.* Why had she stayed behind? I wondered again, as I had many times before. And why had her parents let her stay, with such clear danger all around?

Then I told my mother about Mr. Weiss.

Which apartment was it?

I felt that tingling in the top of my head again.

"First landing, on the left," I said.

That was ours, she said. Just as I knew she would.

"Mr. Weiss is Jewish," I told her.

She marveled that a Jew would return to Vienna.

"He seems like a nice guy." I described the living room with the midcentury furniture and the piano with the embroidered shawl. "Maybe you could visit here again, and see your house," I ventured.

She sighed, and I thought I could hear her smiling at the thought of her childhood home safely in the hands of Mr. Weiss.

For all her traveling years I hoped that my mother would visit the apartment at 22 Weimarer Strasse, but she never could do it, though she and my father made two more trips to Vienna before she died. They enjoyed the museums and the opera, and drank coffees in the beautiful cafés, ate schnitzel and goulash, but they carefully avoided her old neighborhood. My uncle Dolfi did travel to Vienna and paid a visit to Mr. Weiss. When I spoke to Dolfi about it, I could tell there was something profoundly reassuring in the idea that a Jew had been able to return home, to their home. The apartment had been taken from them, along with most of their possessions, and nearly their lives, but in this small way some of what had been lost was returned. My mother could only receive this gift from the universe at a safe distance.

I knew that those last two years that Eva spent in Vienna after her brothers were sent away to England in 1938 must have been filled with terrifying days, the memories of which made her push away so much of her childhood and her city, and finally even her childhood name. What names the assimilated Austrian Jewish Singer progeny had been given: Siegfried (known as Fritz), a Wagnerian hero, and then Adolf and Eva, the same names as the Führer and his doomed mistress. By the time my father met my mother, seven years after her arrival as an immigrant in New York City, she was an American citizen and her name was Eve.

A Cassette Tape

IN 2004, MY mother and my uncle Dolfi responded to an interview request from the Leo Baeck Institute in New York City. As part of its work as a research center for German-speaking Jewry, the institute sent young non-Jewish German and Austrian interns to interview Holocaust survivors, and these interviews then became part of an archive of personal narratives. My mother told me about her interview, and I listened without asking what the experience had meant to her. I wanted to engage, of course, but I was always hesitant to pry into her past. And during that time I was still preoccupied with the aftermath of my husband's sudden death the year before. My fatherless daughter, then eight years old, was the necessary focus of my life.

My mother did give me a cassette tape of her interview. In 2004, I still owned a tape deck from circa 1985, so I gave it a listen, but the sound quality was so poor that after struggling part of the way through I gave up. I didn't want to tell my mother that I hadn't listened to such an important recording; any further conversations about the interview would involve more white lies than I wanted to attempt. I'd tried to reform my relationship with her since my lying teenage years to avoid even well-intentioned fibs. My apparent lack of curiosity must have disappointed her. Two years later she was gone.

I often thought of my trip to Vienna, wondering why I'd never been back, or why I had never gone there with her. Her last trip to Vienna was with my father in 1996. I wondered if I might have been able to persuade her to visit her home at 22 Weimarer Strasse. If only. Now I was left with the keepsake book, her jewelry, her father's folding utensils in their soft leather pouch, photographs, and the other paper documents—all of them filled with too many mysteries. Time passed in a swirl of family life and work. Liza left grade school for middle school and then high school.

———

IN THE SUMMER of 2010, Clark and I moved into a new Brooklyn apartment, and in the purge of relocation I unloaded my tape deck. My mother's cassette was now a historical artifact, part of a landscape on the shelf above my desk: pens, tape dispenser, a box of staples, photos of Liza, notebooks, and reference books. Soon veiled in a layer of the fine black dust that coats windowsills and all other stationary objects in New York City, the clear plastic case took on a cloak of invisibility— that is, until one day more than a year after our move my eye settled upon it. A friend with access to a professional editing suite offered to transfer the recording to CD. She improved the sound quality enough that I could finally listen to the interview from beginning to end.

The first thing I noticed was her accent. I'd always thought of my parents as quintessential New Yorkers. They talked like New Yorkers, interrupting each other, finishing each other's sentences. This was how any family conversation progressed, in volatile spurts and non-linear tangents, for we were all quick-tempered. My father had long ago tossed off his native Philadelphia singsong for the cadence of Manhattan, peppered liberally with Yiddish. I would have described my mother's voice as the American English of an educated woman from the Upper West Side, with some elongation of vowels that hinted at her European background, but so subtle it would've taken Professor Henry Higgins to correctly map her origins. Yet the first thing I heard on the recording was her melodic Viennese accent. Had she always spoken like this? Had her accent been more pronounced in the interview because she was talking to a young Austrian man? Had she intentionally called it forth to remind the young man, no doubt the grandson of National Socialists, what his ancestors had done to her family? As a child I'd wanted her to be like all the other mothers of my classmates; perhaps I'd simply heard what I wanted to hear.

The interview included the stories my mother had always told us, but there were new details that I'd never heard. The unnamed young man who interviewed her was patient, allowing her to unfold her narrative.

For the first time since my mother had given me the cassette tape I read the fine print on the box and contacted the Leo Baeck Institute. Michael Simonson, one of their archivists, invited me to visit their library. When I described the keepsake book, he smiled and told me that the archive held many *Poesiealbums* like the one my mother had hidden in her drawer. I listened to a number of recordings made by other refugees, including my uncle's, all of which began to create an impression of what life had been like for Viennese Jews before the Nazis seized power in March 1938, and the terrifying changes that quickly followed.

Michael gave me a long reading list and email addresses at various archives in faraway Vienna, including a high-placed administrator at the Austrian State Archives named Dr. Hubert Steiner, the head of the *Vermögensverkehrsstelle*, or Jewish Property Transfer Office. Michael said that Dr. Steiner would be able to provide information about my grandfather's paper goods business, the factory located behind the residential building at 22 Weimarer Strasse that had produced the mysterious item made of folded paper my mother had described so often.

It was early April 2012 when I wrote to Dr. Steiner, requesting information about the business and bank accounts the Nazis had taken from my grandfather Julius as part of the "Aryanization" of Jewish property following the Anschluss. I also requested copies of similar documents for Julius's best friend, Jakob Altenberg. My mother had told stories about him and, in fact, she had mentioned him several times during her interview for the institute. Julius and Jakob had met during their service in the First World War, and following the armistice they had made a transformative journey on foot from the Italian Alps to the Austrian Tyrol. I wondered if this was when Julius had bought the folding camping utensils. Jakob ran several successful art and framing galleries in Vienna. According to family lore, confirmed in Brigitte Hamann's *Hitler's Vienna*, Altenberg had taken several paintings on consignment made by a young Adolf Hitler, before the would-be artist gave up on bohemian life, left Vienna, moved to Germany, and began to reinvent himself as a political figure. As reported by Hamann,

> Around 1910 his ten-year-old daughter Adele occasionally helped out in the store and later remembered Hitler's "unkempt appearance," "but also his shyness and his manner of lowering his eyes and staring at the floor when talking with someone." Once he delivered a political monologue when he was with her father—we do not know on what subject. Altenberg, however, shut him down rigorously.

Two replies came from Vienna, sooner than I expected. The first, from Dr. Hubert Steiner's official Austrian State Archive email address, was a formal acknowledgment of my inquiry. My request would be filled as soon as possible, he wrote, allowing for the huge backlog. My grandfather's file number was 32144.

The second reply came from Hubert Steiner's personal email address. In stilted but curiously poetic English, he described his struggles over the twenty-five years of his career to get the Austrian government to fully acknowledge and address the past crimes of National Socialism. He wrote that he would personally photocopy and mail the documents I'd requested, as the bureaucracy involved in doing otherwise would have resulted in many months of delay. He told me how beautiful Vienna was in spring, with cherry trees in bloom. He hoped that I would visit and reacquaint myself with my mother's city.

He said that sometimes he felt a need for outside correspondence, as the work he was doing at the archive weighed heavily on him. Would I be agreeable to a correspondence? I read his email many times, trying to parse the tone. Guilt? Frustration? Loneliness?

His email closed: *Dear greetings from springlike Vienna sends you.* With the verb at the end, as in a German sentence, the disordered English syntax reminded me of an e. e. cummings verse. The email was signed, *Hubert.*

Soon a heavy cardboard box that had originally held reams of Austrian photocopy paper arrived at my Brooklyn apartment, containing precisely—according to a follow-up email from Hubert—843 pages related to Julius Singer's printing factory, "Adolf Eisenmann und Sohn," and Jakob Altenberg's gallery. An official letter was enclosed with the documents on the letterhead of the Austrian State Archives.

I leafed through the pages. I couldn't read most of the text, but I could figure out the gist: the transfer of bank accounts and insurance policies, the forced sale of his company. The dates were all from July 1938, just months after the Anschluss. This same ritual of choreographed bureaucracy had been happening all over Vienna with breathtaking efficiency. It was important to the Nazis that the "Aryanization" of Jewish property had the appearance of legitimacy rather than the theft that it truly was. Julius Singer had penned his elegant signature on each document.

So much paper.

After Julius signed away his business in the summer of 1938, what had the Singer family had left to live on during the time between mid-1938 and March 25, 1940, the exit date on their passports? I knew that my two uncles, seventeen-year-old Fritz and fourteen-year-old Dolfi, had been sent to live with relatives in London in September of 1938. I asked my uncle Dolfi if he'd heard much from his family between 1938 and 1940. He said that my grandmother Anna had written frequently, trying to downplay any worries. Dolfi said that he didn't recall writing home very often, in the manner of many teenage boys. In any event, correspondence would have been more limited after 1938.

Those missing two years haunted me. There was no one left who could tell me what that time must have been like for my mother, Eva, a young girl, from ages nine to eleven.

Dear greetings from springlike Vienna sends you. It was now late April. The cherry trees in Prospect Park were wrapping up their yearly spring display, scattering miniature pink tutus over fresh green lawns. One morning, I opened the box again, flipped through the pages as I'd done so many times, and I knew right then that I needed to return to Vienna.

Another Visit to the Old Country

JUNE 2012. LIZA and I were on an evening flight to Vienna via Austrian Airlines, per my father's recommendation (excellent service, food more than edible), though I knew this choice would have been troubling to my mother, who never wanted to purchase anything made by the country that had expelled her. I'd arranged this week as a research trip, with plans to visit several Jewish historical archives and to walk the streets of my mother's city again. I was most curious to meet Hubert Steiner, my mysterious correspondent at the Austrian State Archives.

Liza was fifteen. We were sullen travel companions. I'd told myself I was bringing her along to show her our family history. Her summer school vacation had already begun, long days without structure until a summer art class in July. After more than two decades as part of the administration of the Cooper Union, Clark was now in the midst of career reinvention as part of the fallout from the 2008 recession and needed workday time to focus.

A trip together had seemed like a good idea in April, but I could see already that I hadn't planned this well.

As we prepared for takeoff, Liza and I were not speaking. What had begun as a mother-daughter brushfire in the morning had burned hot and out of control by midday, gobbling up the plentiful fuel of resentment left over from previous fights over curfews and allowance. Even as the tension had escalated, I could not remember how it had all started. Despite my nagging, she would not fill her suitcase (I was an anxious traveler, she knew that). She'd even threatened to stay behind. I'd actually considered that option, though it would have meant forfeiting both her airfare and the hope I'd had of some kind of bonding experience in the old country. At last, with Clark's guidance, we reached a wary truce.

Clark escorted us to the waiting taxi and we rode in silence to JFK. As we shuffled through security, I smiled at the gray plastic bin holding Liza's ragged black Converse high-tops as it jerked along the conveyor belt and into the belly of the scanner. Those sneakers perfectly captured her current aesthetic: most of her clothing was black and had at least one hole in it. How my mother had hated my similar phase of tattered Army Navy clothing. She repeatedly threw out one of my favorite shirts, and I would fish it out of the trash and wear it the next day. I'd promised myself I would never comment on Liza's clothing. There was plenty of other stuff for us to fight about, especially late-night hanging out in Prospect Park in an area where kids drank illegally purchased cheap liquor and smoked a lot of weed. Clark and I knew we only had the dimmest idea of what was really happening, despite attempts to track her phone (she caught on to that quickly). Mothering a teenager felt so stupid and futile. Despite my best attempts, I feared I was turning into my mother.

A ghostly image of her sneakers appeared briefly on-screen, fully detected, inspected, ejected. As we hustled toward our gate, Liza declined my admittedly pathetic attempt to win her over by offering her a Starbucks chai latte. As soon as we were seated she popped in her headphones.

Squished next to the window as far away from me as the narrow space would permit, Liza let me know that she would have been happy to stay in Brooklyn. Message received, loud and clear. I felt sorry already about the fight we'd had earlier in the day. Her black Converse sneakers, tossed on the carpeted floor, seemed to be laughing at me for even trying to understand my daughter and her teenage misery. As I thought back to the morning, I saw now how a few ill-timed judgy words from me had sent a tense moment into overdrive. We were both stubborn as hell. On good days I was proud of her self-determination. On days like today, I felt like an abject failure. It had been just like this when I was Liza's age, fighting with my mother over clothes and curfews, a fact that made me cringe. I pretended to read a magazine as I attempted to remember what had even caused this latest fight. I tried to stay calm, determined to repair the damage during the next precious week.

I hated when I felt like I was turning into my mother. Hated it.

Liza and I had traveled together to Europe eight years earlier, the June following her father's death. She had still been a child then, one who was never bored and could find delight in so many things, despite the loss that had upended our lives. This was when travel had become stressful for me, where once it had been all adventure, but she was happy to be with me and forgave my schedule snafus, my anxious fumbling for tickets and passports. On the plus side: she relished the endless ice creams and fancy meals in Paris and Florence. But now Liza was a teenager. Time spent with her mother was occasionally a source of delight (mani-pedis!), but mostly a battle of wills.

I thought about my mother as we lifted off into the night sky and the sparkling towers of New York City faded under a mauve blanket of summer haze. My mother deserved a sincere apology, wherever she was now.

I also thought about the joint wrapped in two layers of tinfoil, hidden in a medicine vial, camouflaged among my toiletries: tufts of bud from my last season's modest crop, raised beneath branches of prickly rosebush and clematis in my Brooklyn backyard. Why had I planted weed in my garden? Because I was tired of fighting with my weed-smoking kid, tired of pretending that I hadn't done the same when I was her age. According to my teenage diaries, which made for a humbling reread, I had gotten stoned almost every miserable day of high school. The plants in my garden were like a white truce flag. Turned out, Liza's sense of rebellion was contagious.

———————

MY MOTHER AND I had never attempted a trip together. But as I flipped a page of the in-flight magazine featuring must-visit new restaurants in Paris, I remembered the time she'd visited me there for a week in late March of 1980, during that academic year I'd spent in France, just a few months before I traveled to Vienna with Michelle. It was a big deal for my mother to travel alone, after so many years of traveling with my father. She spoke just a few phrases of French. Our two overseas family trips had been to English-speaking Ireland and Scotland, with stops in London to visit my uncle Fritz and his family. Her travel agent had found a hotel near the apartment where I was living and all plans were in motion. Just a week together. What could go wrong?

She landed in Brussels just in time for one of France's many worker strikes, this time the railway employees. *La grève* was one of my first new French words upon arriving in the country the previous summer, and during my first months in Paris I'd endured a two-week sanitation workers' strike. To make my way up what had once been a flight of stairs from the underground tracks of the Métro to the street, I grasped the railing, pulling myself up a stinking slope of crumpled newspaper, greasy food wrappers, and crushed cigarette butts like a mountain climber. Paris, the most gorgeous city I'd ever seen, quickly became more squalid than the dirtiest streets I'd ever encountered in New York.

I guessed that the strike that had stranded my mother in Brussels would likely end in a day or two at most, but after she called me in tears, even I began to worry that she would spend the entire week in an airport hotel in Brussels. By the next day, however, *la grève* had ended and soon enough she'd called me from a pay phone at the Gare du Nord train station in Paris. She sounded terrible—exhausted and vulnerable. She needed me.

This was not our usual dynamic.

It was a gloomy day, misty rain shimmering the streets. This was winter in Paris, weeks of gray, no crisp blue sky after a snow-fall. I missed New York keenly on days like this. I dashed from my apartment up the hill to the Étoile Métro stop, counted the minutes till a train arrived, then willed the train to move faster as it crawled through stations, packing in and discharging shoppers and workers. I bolted from the train and raced into the Gare du Nord station. When I recognized my mother in the crowd, she looked small and forlorn—yet never happier to see me.

My mother loved my hostess, Mme Péry d'Alincourt, a willowy woman of aristocratic pedigree in her sixties—white-blond chignon, cream silk blouses, slim Chanel suits, Charles Jourdan pumps, trail-ing a floral gust of No. 5—who was in the last years of an advertising career. Mme Péry lived in the largest bedroom of an expansive apart-ment in the 16th arrondissement and rented two rooms out to foreign students from my college study abroad program. She had joined the French Resistance during the Second World War and had survived time in a concentration camp. She'd shown me the number tattooed on her arm, and she showed it again to my mother. In spite of the language barrier between them, they bonded in franglais over a shared hatred of fascist Germany and Austria. *The Austrians were worse Nazis than the Germans*, my mother told Mme Péry. *And the Germans, they were bad enough*, Mme Péry replied.

There was a restaurant near Mme Péry's apartment, a place I'd walked by a hundred times, salivating over the menu offerings, lamenting the prices. Now settled in her comfortable hotel, with a day at the Louvre and the Jardin de Tuileries already packed in, my mother offered to take me there for dinner. Inside, it was smaller than I'd expected, dark and intimate with no more than ten small tables. A rotund man of middle years and evident means sat at one table with a much younger African woman so painfully beautiful I can still see her face in my mind's eye. She was dressed as if for a red-carpet gala. My mother and I, who shared a quiet obsession with the latest issues of *Vogue*, speculated that she must be a fashion model. Turning away from the dining room theater, we ordered white wine and bouillabaisse, broth the color of cinnamon, fragrant with unfamiliar spice, abundant with shellfish and tentacles of octopus.

Over dinner, my mother asked me about a hospital invoice from an emergency room in Aix-en-Provence from the previous September, a month after my arrival in France. She'd been asking me about this bill ever since it had first made its way to New York. There'd been nothing else to do at the time except to hand over the credit card my mother had given me to pay for emergencies. I'd hoped to brush off this medical matter, but my mother persevered in every phone call, undeterred by my attempts to deflect. She looked at me intently over our meal. It was nothing, I said. Just an accident. I'm fine now.

————————

THE FLIGHT ATTENDANT arrived with the drink and snack cart. Liza ordered a Coke. I never stocked soda at home, being a Park Slope Food Coop mama. Liza's headphones were still on. I could hear the muffled refrain of the Band's "The Weight." Could Clark and I at least take some credit for her excellent music taste? Would someone take this load of epic parental fail off me? I sipped a tomato juice, my preferred in-flight drink, wallowing in self-pity.

The flight attendant returned with meals, surprisingly edible, just as my father had promised. We cut and chewed in silence. Later, I watched with envy as Liza dozed off to the drone of the engines and the sway of transatlantic turbulence. I've never been able to sleep in planes. I knew I was doomed to watch at least two terrible movies I would never remember later and arrive in Vienna haggard and unhinged with exhaustion.

In the sparkling Vienna airport, I hovered outside my body, sunlight too bright, all sounds an assault, desperate for a bed in a quiet room. Only the fuel of maternal anxiety kept me on task. Liza and I boarded one of the efficient high-speed trains into the city, emerging onto a street near the apartment I'd rented online. There was no trash anywhere, not even a stray cigarette butt, though plenty of passersby were smoking. The street was quiet, just a few people busy with their everyday doings. As I searched for the number of the house where we would stay—in this city I no longer recognized from my previous time here—I wondered again why I had never been brave enough to suggest a trip with my mother.

Liza and I arrived at the apartment building, and the woman with whom I'd corresponded online was waiting for us. She sent us upstairs with our luggage in a tiny elevator, the same size as the one I remembered from 22 Weimarer Strasse. On our floor she opened the door to a clean, well-appointed studio apartment, very Ikea, the universal décor choice of economy-priced short-term rentals. She asked why we were in Vienna and I briefly explained my research mission.

"I'm not Jewish," she said. "But I married a Jewish man. I converted, and we're raising our children Jewish."

"Really?" I replied, genuinely surprised.

She told me about their Reform synagogue, which sounded welcoming and open-minded.

"And how many Jews are there in Vienna?" I asked.

"About nine thousand," she replied. "Something like that. Some people hid here during the war, but most of the people who could get out never came back. And of course most didn't get out at all."

I'd read that the prewar Jewish population was around two hundred thousand in a city of roughly two million. That ten percent of the population had had an outsized impact on the cultural life in Austria before the war. And now there were so few Jews left. There had been Mr. Weiss all those years ago, and now I'd found another one, a convert no less. As she described the friendly Sabbath services at her synagogue, extending an invitation, I experienced the faintest twinge of guilt that this woman probably knew more about Judaism than I did.

After our host left, Liza and I began to unpack. I was feeling quite smug that the TSA sniffer dogs hadn't found my joint. I shared my smugness with Liza, hoping we might bond over sticking it to the Man. But no.

"I'm still mad at you," she reminded me.

SHE SOFTENED THE next day. Nothing like a table in the sun at the beautifully preserved Café Prückel, plus an endless supply of café mochas piled with clouds of *Schlagsahne* (whipped cream), salads arranged like formal gardens, and decadent sweets served by unhurried waiters to cheer up even the most righteously grumpy teenager. She took charge of our corner table and opened the fat book she'd brought with her—an anthology of five novels by Kurt Vonnegut.

Once we oriented ourselves, I bought Liza a cell phone and then I rushed to my first appointment with a researcher named Elisabeth Klamper at the DÖW—the Documentation Center of Austrian Resistance. The goal of this organization, founded by former members of the Resistance and refugees, was to educate on the history of Nazism in Austria as well as monitor right-wing activities in the present. Alarmingly, in 2012 the rise of right-wing parties in this already conservative country was significant.

Liza was free to wander the area near the Stadtpark for a few hours till dinner. I had the impression when we reconnected that she'd managed to score some weed, which must have taken some doing, as she spoke not a word of German.

One afternoon we went together to the Café Demel, where we ordered coffees, a fruit tart, and a slice of chocolate torte. We watched an older woman consume a full meal, followed by a slab of cake big enough to feed three. She looked like a regular. We agreed that there were worse ways to live than to eat at this café once a week.

At the Leopold Museum in the center of Vienna, Liza and I admired the portraits by Gustav Klimt, where enchanted women peered out through glittering mosaic patterns of gold and jewel colors. We were especially drawn to the more ascetic drawings and paintings of Klimt's follower Egon Schiele, who created his images of women and his own naked body against plain paper or canvas. The colors of the figures were vividly pure, the effect at once tenderly sensual and acidic. Schiele's vigorous, anguished lines told the truth of his fearless personal inquisition in a vocabulary Liza understood immediately, as I had when I first encountered his work as a young woman.

After we left the museum with a shopping bag of postcards and a book on Schiele's paintings, she showed me a silk scarf printed with Gustav Klimt's *The Kiss*, one I hadn't paid for. "It's for you," she said. "For your birthday." Number fifty-three was coming up soon. I chose to be touched, rather than upset that she'd shoplifted. After all, I had my hidden joint; she and I were not so different. Also, the fucking Austrians owed my family more than they had ever repaid or could ever repay. They could buy me a scarf for my birthday.

We traveled by train to the Tiergarten Schönbrunn. After strolling through the meticulous gardenscapes and lush greenhouses, we made our way to the outdoor animal exhibits. Overwhelmed by their adorable faces, Liza nearly tumbled into an exhibit of prairie dogs. I was relieved to see her so engaged and happy.

On another afternoon, warm and faintly humid, we joined the crowd cheering the marchers at the gay pride parade on the Ringstrasse, the wide circular boulevard that surrounded the center of Vienna, lined with former mansions including the Albert Rothschild Palace. After its Jewish owners—members of the far-flung Rothschild banking family—were expelled following the Anschluss in 1938 and its vast art holdings seized, the Nazi Gestapo had taken it over as its headquarters. Adolf Eichmann set up the Central Agency for Jewish

Emigration in the same building. This was where Jews, including my grandfather Julius, lined up day after day to apply for passports and exit permits in return for surrendering their assets.

There was nothing ominous about the mood today on the Ringstrasse. The parade was as gaudy and raucous as NYC Pride back home, with a long stream of marchers and floats bearing costumed men and women dancing and singing along to "I Will Survive" and "We Are the Champions." In such an outwardly staid city, where I always felt Other, I began to find some ease and even delight.

———————————

THE LEO BAECK Institute in New York had arranged for us to tour the old Jewish quarter with an Austrian research colleague. Johann was not Jewish, but had devoted himself to the study of Jewish history in Vienna. A kind of penance, he said, to honor the dead and those who were forced to flee. He promised us a lunch at the end of our tour, the best falafel in town.

"Where did your parents spend the war years?" I asked him.

Johann told me, without hesitation, that his family members had been in the Nazi Party in a small town outside Vienna.

None of the archivists I met during this week was a Jew. I thought back to Mr. Weiss, imagining that the few Jewish returnees would be mostly older people, like him, who would want to live as unburdened by the past as possible. For those who committed themselves to this work of excavation and preservation, there was a continual reckoning and repentance, even as the prevailing culture in Austria tried to move past the time of its full embrace of National Socialism.

Many of Austria's media and politicians still referred to their country as the "first victim" of Hitler's aggressions, though photographic and film evidence as well as witness accounts contradicted this narrative. The Austrofascist government, led by Chancellor Kurt Schuschnigg, capitulated to Hitler's demand for Anschluss, or reunification. Footage from March 12, 1938, showed crowds of Austrians welcoming Hitler across the German border. Women young and old screamed with tears in their eyes, waving flags and handkerchiefs. On March 15, crowds in Vienna raised their arms in Fascist salute to the lines of regimented Nazi soldiers parading on the Heldenplatz, the Square of Heroes. By the time an April 1938 plebiscite ratified the Nazi takeover, Austria had already been negated as a sovereign nation.

Johann represented an important segment of the younger Austrian population motivated by a strong desire to reject the revisionism of the postwar decades, to finally get right with history. As we began our walking tour he pointed out a blockish postwar building. This had once been the location of the grand Hotel Metropole, bombed at the end of the war. After the 1938 Anschluss, Hitler sent Adolf Eichmann to Vienna to manage "The Jewish Problem." Eichmann set up offices at the Metropole because it was close to the *Israelitische Kultusgemeinde*—Jewish Community Center, and known as the IKG— where all the records of Viennese Jews were stored: names, addresses, births, marriages, deaths. Johann pointed out that the only synagogue spared during Kristallnacht (the Night of Broken Glass)—the brutal Nazi-sanctioned pogrom that took place November 9–10, 1938—was the large central synagogue, tucked discreetly on a narrow side street. This temple backed up onto the offices of the IKG. Eichmann wanted the IKG records preserved, to keep track of the Jewish population in exquisite detail, so that he could identify—and ultimately remove— every last one. In 1938, the goal of the Nazi Party was to strip Jews of their money and property and then expel them to any country that would take them. Later, that goal would change, in large part because Jews could not find countries that would accept them. When forced emigration failed, the Nazi strategy shifted to extermination.

Johann took us to Judenplatz, a beautiful square with buildings dating to the medieval period and the Holocaust Memorial and Jewish Museum. Though Jews were at times tolerated, even protected by various rulers, including some of the Habsburgs, they were confined in the central ghetto area. Later assimilation allowed Jews with enough means, like my mother's family, to move into other districts of the city. Frequent and brutal purges of Jews took place throughout the city's history. Johann led us to the center of the square, site of the Holocaust Memorial, and pointed to a plaque mounted on the facade of a narrow white building from centuries earlier, proclaiming that Vienna had been cleansed of Jews. The building with its offensive plaque now housed a gallery on the ground floor that featured artwork on the subject of the Holocaust and other human rights issues. The plaque, the gallery, and the museum—these contrasts spoke to the tension I felt walking through Vienna that I'd also experienced as a young woman on my earlier trip in 1980. I was a small dark-haired Jewess, surrounded everywhere by tall Aryans. Even here, walking in the streets and squares of the former Jewish ghetto, I felt like my people were too small in number to be anything but an unwelcome oddity. My sense of Otherness made me want to howl out loud, with both defiant joy and fury.

LIZA WAS BACK at the Café Prückel, making her way through Vonnegut, as I set off to the offices of the *Israelitische Kultusgemeinde*. Because of its murky history during the war, a cloud of distrust hung over the IKG. Back in New York, researchers had advised me to tread gently as I did my own hunting.

   After the Anschluss in 1938, the IKG leadership staff was purged, its board members deported and killed. Rabbi Benjamin Murmelstein was appointed head of the IKG, but effectively, Adolf Eichmann and his minions ran the organization. Much has been written about Rabbi Murmelstein, most notably in Doron Rabinovici's *Eichmann's Jews*, in which he is described as "a technocrat of the administration of terror." Elsewhere he has been depicted as an outright collaborator or a complicit coward. Under Eichmann's domination, a rabbi was no more than a powerless man in an escape-proof trap. Till his death Murmelstein believed he had saved Jewish lives by cooperating with Eichmann.

The remaining IKG staff took on the task of assisting Jews as they searched for a route out of Vienna. An archivist showed me historical pamphlets describing the necessity of emigration and job retraining, a desperate attempt to present a dire situation in the most optimistic light. Ultimately, after 1941, under Eichmann's orders, it was the staff at the IKG that wrote up the deportation lists that sent people too old, poor, or unlucky to their deaths, first in the ghetto at Theresienstadt and then to death camps farther east. Soon enough the staff members themselves were on those lists. Rabbi Murmelstein was to become the Jewish elder in the ghetto at Theresienstadt, where he survived the war.

I'd come in hopes of finding documentation of my own family's efforts to get out of Vienna, specifically the forms that every head of family had to fill out to begin the emigration process. I'd assumed that Julius would have proceeded like every other Jewish head of family. But the archivist told me that the IKG had no record of my grand-father's efforts from 1938 to 1940, a setback I hadn't expected. As I left, confused and disappointed, I wondered how Julius Singer had managed the family's escape without the assistance of the IKG. I would have to look elsewhere.

———

THOUGH I'D RAISED Liza by choice with no religious observance (I did not consider my love of winter holiday trees and large collection of ornaments to be part of any organized faith), I felt moved to attend Friday evening Sabbath services in the central synagogue around the corner from the IKG, mostly to have a look at the interior.

I suspected that my mother might have included more religion in our lives had she married a man more observant than my father. For all the years of their marriage I listened to him complain about the length of our Passover dinners. He had issues with politics in Israel, settlements in the West Bank, the hawkishness of a series of Israeli prime ministers, feelings I shared. After my mother's death he sent me a heartfelt letter in which he came out of the closet as an atheist. But the truth was that my mother hadn't pressed too hard. Simon and I had next to no religious instruction. She had brought us to the neighborhood synagogue no more than four times during my childhood. She lit candles at Hanukkah and we celebrated one night of Passover. I liked matzo, so a week of unleavened crackers slathered with butter and honey was no hardship. No Hebrew school, no bar mitzvah for my brother or bat mitzvah for me. During a brief flirtation with a more observant Judaism in my early thirties, I attended a few months of Hebrew classes before abandoning the attempt when I understood how much work it would take to master a language that had not won me over. After that, I made peace with my lack of faith. On my Facebook page I described myself as an atheist with Buddhist sympathies. Maybe there was something out there, but whatever it might have been was too infinite for the minds of puny humans. I had raised Liza without any fixed faith, anticipating that if she wanted this in her life, she would choose for herself as an adult. And yet, if anyone asked me about my background, I said that I was a Jew. Hitler had considered Jews a race and my family had nearly perished as a result. Therefore, I was a Jew, part of the Diaspora.

In this spirit, Liza and I put on dresses and walked to the synagogue.

The synagogue entry was almost invisible except for the Hebrew inscription discreetly carved into the archway above the door. The narrow street was dark and confining, and there was tight security that added further tension, but once inside the temple, there was space and light everywhere. The lofty ceiling was painted a glorious cerulean blue with gilded stars. I bristled as we were directed upstairs to the women's section, having forgotten that this was an Orthodox temple where the sexes were separated and women were extraneous to the ceremony. As the cantor began chanting I looked around at the women and girls who sat near us, wondering about their lives. What would it feel like to be part of such a minority in this city, nearly an extinct species?

THERE WERE DISTURBING shadings of the city that its tourism industry did not advertise. I observed groups of unemployed men, many immigrants from North Africa and the Middle East, who loitered on the streets, eyeing Liza and me, perhaps because we, too, were olive-skinned and dark-haired but without head coverings. As in other European cities I'd visited, there was a mutual resentment between the former imperial powers and the people they had once dominated. Something was very wrong here. The tension was palpable, a visible spasm of internal discord. The feeling of unease and fear on both sides reminded me of my time in France as a student, when I'd experienced the same anxiety on the streets at night both in Paris and in the smaller southern city of Aix-en-Provence.

Growing up in New York, I was harassed by men from the time my curves presented themselves. As a defense, I learned to cuss and give the finger to construction workers looking up from a lunchtime sandwich to spit out a *Nice ass*, to ignore guys in open-windowed cars carelessly tossing out a *Hey, baby, I wanna fuck you* like an empty beer bottle. I learned to walk like a take-no-prisoners New Yorker. But now, on the night streets of Vienna, under a furtive but no less menacing male gaze, just like that I was snapped back into a night I had tried so hard to put behind me.

SEPTEMBER 1979. I was in Aix-en-Provence. I'd been in France just a few weeks. In a few days I would begin the academic year in Paris. One afternoon at a café in Aix I ran into Jenny, a friend who attended a college near mine back in Massachusetts. I hung out with

Jenny and her boyfriend, Jas, who were living in a dormitory in Aix for a few months on a different student program. They were both handsome. Jenny was peach complexioned and blond. Jas was from a Sikh family. They made a striking couple.

My host family lived on the outskirts of Aix, a bus ride away from the lively town, and the atmosphere in the house was stifling. Their house smelled of something stomach-turning—rancid cooking oil and musty linens—that depressed me to the point of homesickness. Meeting Jenny was a lifeline and I spent as much time with her as possible. She mentioned that her dorm would empty out for an upcoming holiday and that I could take a vacant room on the hall for a night.

At last I felt like the carefree world traveler I wanted to be. Jenny, Jas, and I wandered around the city square, getting drunk on cheap wine, before returning to their dorm room, where we shared stories till we were too tired to speak words. I'd sensed danger on the streets of the town and I never walked alone at night, but the dorm felt safe, familiarly collegiate. I left my friends and made my way two doors down the quiet hall to the room where I would sleep. The next morning we had plans for coffee and croissants at one of the packed outdoor cafés, another day in the bristling late-summer heat, infused with the scents of rosemary and lavender. It was a beautiful town of ancient stone buildings and gardens, but it wasn't my place, not quite yet. I had gone to a local synagogue for Yom Kippur, only to realize that as the descendant of Ashkenazi Jews I was in a Sephardic temple, Orthodox, where women were separated from men. I clearly didn't belong. Everyone—women and men—stared at me as if I were from another planet. But here, in Jenny and Jas's student dormitory, I felt safe, still pleasantly tipsy. Without locking the door, I pulled off my clothes, flopped naked onto the bed, drew the sheets over me, and drifted off.

When I woke with a start, it was dark, and a hand was touching my side. A strange man, North African, was standing over me. He put a hand over my mouth and then, when I cried out, his hand circled my throat.

Tais-toi, he said to me, using the intimate form of address, as if he knew me. As if I had invited him in. *Be quiet.*

He unzipped and lay down on top of me. I felt his weight on my ribs and lungs, pushing out my breath. I tried to inhale, but I was paralyzed. My body wasn't working as it should have. Except my tear ducts—I was weeping and gasping. *Tais-toi.* I squeezed my eyes tight, his face already imprinted in my memory, a face I knew I would never forget, as he penetrated me and my racing mind told me to just *shut the fuck up*, because there was no way out of this room now and no one would hear me shout, even if I could make my voice work, and so I just needed to live through this terrible thing that was happening. I'd left my door unlocked. I thought I was safe. Now this was my fault. Now I just had to live.

After he was done, he said he wanted to see me again. I was horrified. What had I done to make this man think that I wanted this? He told me his name was Robert. *Tu es mignonne*, he said. *You are sweet.* I was shivering. I wrapped myself in the white sheet and persuaded him to leave by agreeing to meet him again. I locked the door and waited on the bed, unable to form thoughts. I wanted to be clean. I peeked out the door, looking up and down the hallway. I raced for the communal bathroom in the hallway, locked myself in, and took the hottest shower I could tolerate. In my confusion, I'd already decided I wouldn't go to the police. How could I explain what had happened to me in my shitty French? I raced back to the room and locked the door. I lay still on the bed, wrapped in the sheet, trying to remember when I had last had my period. Two weeks ago. Not good.

I lay still on the bed until morning, when I went to Jenny's room, and somehow found words to tell them what had happened. The night before we'd been laughing and joking about the creepy guys loitering in Aix. I had told a story about life in New York, dodging asshole guys, that had them rolling with laughter. Jas said, "Well, if any of us gets raped I hope it's Julie, she'll have the best story to tell later." Now Jas looked ashen, as if he had willed this bad thing to happen. He took me to the hospital emergency room. I struggled to find French vocabulary. I told the doctor on call that I thought I might be *enceinte*, pregnant. He laughed, looking at Jas, assuming he was my boyfriend, that we'd made a mistake. *Non, non*, I protested, suddenly remembering the word I needed, from a French poem I'd read, Verlaine or Rimbaud. *J'étais violée.* Everything sounded softer in French. I was raped. The doctor stopped laughing. He asked me if I'd taken a shower already, and would I be willing to report this to the police. I said yes, I'd taken a shower, and no, no police. I was American, too far from home. I just wanted to get a morning-after pill. He was disappointed, but he gave me the medication. He never tested me for sexually transmitted diseases or referred me to a counselor.

At the hospital discharge desk a woman asked me where to send the emergency room invoice. *Facture*, another new French word for me. She passed me a form. I filled in my parents' address in New York City and handed over the credit card my mother had given me.

Jas took me back to the dormitory. He and I remained writing friends for many years after that, until life took us in different directions. Decades later we found each other again on Facebook. For his simple gift of kindness to me after the most terrifying night of my young life, I think of him as a hero among humans. Some people, the rare ones, are able to step up in a time of crisis.

I spent years in therapy dealing with the aftermath of the rape, wondering why I'd left the door of that dorm room unlocked, why I hadn't gone to the police afterward, why I blamed myself for everything about that night. Like my mother, I hesitated to ask for help from authorities. I didn't trust them. Maybe I was right. And I didn't want to tell my family what had happened: surely they would have insisted on me returning home just a month after my arrival in France. The program administrator and some friends in France and those back on campus thought I should go home. But I wanted to stay, to have the year I'd planned. Later that same year I traveled alone, the way I'd wanted to.

But I was changed, and forever, and I knew it. I'd never get over a certain fear in my guts and bones when I sensed a man walking behind me in the evening, no matter how many other people were around me, whether he was tall or short, large or slight. Girl power wasn't a thing then. It would take me years to shake off the shame of that night, to feel good and even victorious. I'd survived the rape with something of my wits about me, and in a foreign language. I was a survivor.

AFTER THAT SCHOOL year in France, and after my trip to Vienna with Michelle, I took off on my own toward Greece. I took the train to the hot southern port of Brindisi, where I boarded a ferry to Corfu, another ferry to Patras in Greece, another train to Athens, and then a small passenger ferry out to the dry islands north of Crete. I slept on a black-sand beach for a week, before traveling for another week to another small island with Valérie, a French girl I'd met on the ferry. On a secluded beach we met a group of handsome sun-seeking Germans and skinny-dipped in the Aegean Sea. As I admired their tanned Aryan skin and golden hair, I wondered what their parents and grandparents had been up to during the war years.

During that summer I was unreachable, on a series of trains and boats meandering my way through Europe. I was not the most thoughtful daughter then. After my mother died, my father gave me a packet of my letters and postcards they'd saved from that summer and others. I recognized the settings and postal stamps, briefly recapturing the feeling of that time when I traveled mostly solo, in defiance of the terrifying events the previous September.

When I came home from Europe after the summer of 1980, so tanned that my parents didn't recognize me at the airport, my mother asked me again about the bill from the hospital in Aix-en-Provence.

This time I told her what had happened. I kept it brief. I was attacked by a man. I'm okay now. I couldn't say in English what I'd told the doctor at the hospital in France. My mother looked at me and I knew that she'd suspected something terrible all along, but maybe not this. *Oh, you poor child.* It was my mother who found my first therapist. Not an entirely successful match, but it was a start. In these weeks shortly after my homecoming, my mother and I sat with my father, who nodded in understanding about what she had told him. This was the last time she and I would speak about the rape in any explicit way. I had not reached the point of being able to speak openly about what had happened to me. Before long I would discover just how many of my female friends had experienced rape and assault. Though words and feelings hovered below the surface, I was grateful for the brief point of contact with my mother. I knew she was doing her best. Without considering all of her history, I sensed that she could understand how fear and trauma lived in the body even if she couldn't speak the language.

As the years passed and my vivid memories of the rape morphed, surfacing only in dreams or increasingly rare flashbacks, still I knew that I was changed and forever. I often wondered about the nature of different types of trauma: sustained versus the momentary. For an hour of my life as a young woman I thought I would die at the hands of a strange man who had violated the home that was my body. I'd used what mental tools I had to help me survive an act of violence that would continue to live in that body.

The Jews of Vienna, young and old, lived in a continuous state of terror from March 1938 until they escaped, were killed at death camps, or were liberated at war's end. The genocides of the Tutsi people of Rwanda; the Bosnians, Serbs, and Croatians in the Balkans; and the endless suffering in the Middle East made me wonder how a human mind could endure such bludgeoning even if the body survived. Responses might be madness, a deliberate effort to suppress memory, or the discovery of an outlet for expression. The relatively new field of epigenetics posed the idea that trauma endured by one generation could pass on to children and generations beyond. It might take decades to heal a nation torn by war. As Liza and I made our way back to our Vienna apartment I considered how my time in this city was on behalf of my mother, to find a path to belatedly express her unreleased emotions that lived on in me.

———

ONE NIGHT, WHEN Liza and I were back in our apartment after walking home on the dark uneasy streets, I rummaged in my toiletry bag for the foil-wrapped joint. "Let's go sit outside," I said. Liza and I made our way to the rear courtyard of the apartment building, where I lit up with matches from Café Demel. We inhaled, passing the joint back and forth in silence. My mouth pulled up into a smile. I started laughing, an involuntary snortle. Liza looked at me with curiosity. This was a first. And, jeez, this was pretty good for homegrown. The gentle stuff that didn't make you paranoid. I wanted a brownie, big time. Or some of the dense chocolate torte from Demel. I took a quick mental inventory of the extraordinary leftovers in our fridge upstairs.

The night sky was clear ultramarine, the moonlit walls of the courtyard enclosed us, glowing as if phosphorescent. Liza expertly snuffed the played joint with her fingertips. I wondered what we would make of this week in Vienna once we got home. For now I was glad we were together and safe.

———

ON OUR LAST morning in Vienna I traveled to the office of Dr. Hubert Steiner at the Austrian State Archives, located in a sad gray building on the industrial edge of the city. *Dear greetings from springlike Vienna sends you.*

In person, Hubert Steiner, stocky, of vague middle age, had the jittery, sweaty hands and pasty complexion of a man who drank too much coffee and spent little time outdoors. Meager daylight filtered through the dusty slats of his window blinds. There was no overhead light in the cave-like office, just the greenish cast from the fluorescent tubes in the hallway. On his desk a small gooseneck lamp illuminated a landscape of files, a lone family photo (wife, children), and a plain coffee mug rimmed with the remains of that morning's brew. Very J. Alfred Prufrock. *I have measured out my life with coffee spoons.* The room reeked of stale cigarettes, a suffocating, noxious aroma for an ex-smoker like me. I imagined his exhalations infusing these walls, year after year. During our hour-long conversation he lit up one smoke after another, stubbing the butts in his overflowing ashtray. *Then how should I begin / To spit out all the butt-ends of my days and ways?*

He was not Jewish, Hubert told me. He was atoning. Although he had been awarded several medals for service to the nation, he expressed bitterness about the lack of recognition for his work and railed against the Austrian government for its refusal to acknowledge the evils of National Socialism and to properly make amends. To me, the forlorn appearance and location of this building spoke to the ways in which this archive and its work had been marginalized. Surely the government could have situated this important office in a more central part of Vienna, but that would have required a more honest reckoning with the past. This uninviting building on the outskirts of town sent a message that pissed me off mightily.

He told me how important it was to spread word about the work of the Archives. Yes, of course, I replied. He wanted to travel more, to speak to people abroad about his work. He asked me to help him arrange speaking engagements in the United States. I smiled, relieved that this man who had violated protocol on my behalf had a personal agenda he hoped I could move forward in some way. With his awkward English (not everyone would appreciate his e. e. cummings syntax, the same that had appeared in his initial letter to me) and pallor, it was hard to imagine him captivating a crowd at the 92nd Street Y or the Jewish Community Center in New York City. But I said I would try, riffling through my memory banks for helpful people I might know.

I thanked Hubert again for the documents he'd sent me. It was the least he could do, he said. I asked him where I might be able to find the documents that would shed light on how my grandfather arranged passage out of Austria in 1940. "They should be at the IKG," he said. I told him they weren't there. Hubert shrugged and said, "That's where they should be."

———————

LIZA AND I left that afternoon. I closed the door to the Ikea apartment, and we squeezed our bodies and bags into the elevator that creaked and groaned on its way to the lobby. I dropped the key into our host's mailbox and in a few steps we were outside on the bright street, walking to the subway. Liza wanted to be home again. I was also ready to leave Vienna, but I knew I would return.

Soon we were back on the high-speed train, whizzing through the tidy suburbs and industrial exurbs. In our luggage were souvenirs— the filched silk scarf, a box of candied violets from Café Demel, two dresses I'd bought for us at a small boutique on the street of the Ikea apartment. On my iPhone were photos of Liza, in the Stadtpark, at Café Demel, and the zoo.

I had also taken one photo of the gargoyled front doorway of my mother's house at 22 Weimarer Strasse. It was a blinding hot Saturday afternoon when we went there by tram. I got lost, and when I finally found the street, we were both exhausted and parched. Somehow I'd forgotten to buy a bottle of water. The great wooden front door was locked tight. Someone else's name was listed at apartment 5. No Mr. Weiss and daughter, no Manner wafers. I wondered if Mr. Weiss could possibly still be alive somewhere else in the city. I rang some buzzers; no one answered. I hadn't planned this well. I took a photo of the building directory mounted next to the front door. One of the occupants appeared to be a film company.

As we made ourselves comfortable in our Austrian Airlines seats, I made a note to write to the film company for access next time, when I returned. And then I needed to find those missing documents—the ones that should have been at the IKG—though I had no idea where to search. Liza put on her headphones. My mother's city faded away as the plane pierced the clouds.

Interlude

BACK HOME, I arranged time to talk to my uncle Dolfi. Widowed and long retired from a career as a doctor, he was now in his late eighties, frail and recuperating from a fall. Dolfi was not an effusive man. I couldn't fully read my relationship with him, but I'd adored his wife, my warm and affectionate aunt Paula, who had devoted herself to holding the far-flung strands of our war-broken family together. Dolfi was born in 1924, four years before my mother. I hoped that our conversations and emails would reveal more about daily life in the Singer apartment at 22 Weimarer Strasse, as well as a sense of life in Vienna before he and Fritz left for London in the fall of 1938.

My mother had been hurt that her older brothers hadn't come to live in the United States after the war ended in 1945. Had they done so, the family would have been made whole. But by then, the brothers were both in their twenties, and after so much upheaval, settled in London. Fritz was working; Dolfi was still in school, in the early stages of his medical career. Both brothers had relationships with English girlfriends— my aunts Esther and Paula. Eventually Dolfi did move his family to the United States in 1961—years after the deaths of my grandparents—as there had been better financial opportunities for doctors here. The relationship between my mother and Dolfi was always complicated. Some years I didn't see my cousins because of simmering conflicts.

I envied Dolfi and Paula's Christmas tree. Unfortunately, my mother's version of secular Judaism did not extend this far, though my parents both loved other Christmas trappings. Our family Christmas dinner would have made Dickens proud: roast goose and plum pudding, served to the soundtrack of the King's College Choir singing the Nine Lessons and Carols or Handel's *Messiah* (I sang along in my out-of-tune voice). Among friends I called my family the Anglican Jews. I knew what I was: Jewish, a child of refugees, and an American fully entitled to our version of the national winter holiday.

I loved my Singer cousins, and throughout childhood and into adulthood I spent many summer weekends at their rambling house on the south fork of Long Island, where we rode rusty bikes to the beach, and then returned, sunburnt, tracking sand into the house. In the evenings we ate prodigious quantities of grilled hamburgers, swordfish, potato salad, and boiled sweet corn. Despite these quintessentially American summer idylls, Dolfi and Paula retained their English habits. Dolfi's accent was a unique blend of Queen's English with significant traces of Viennese. He wore crisp khaki shorts or trousers and white shirts like a British Foreign Service officer and used a monocle hung around his neck to read the newspaper. In the years since my aunt Paula had died, his dark steel-colored hair had turned white and he'd grown an imposing mustache. Now he looked more and more like my grandfather Julius.

Dolfi remembered the layout of the family's apartment and the complex workings of the coal stove, an innovation of the time, something like the Aga stoves having a moment in fashionable country homes. He remembered my grandmother Anna's Sunday afternoon coffee parties that featured her homemade strudel. He remembered taking his little sister Eva for the short walk to visit their "Tante" Bauer, who wasn't actually an aunt but a family friend. He remembered long Passover dinners—Anna had a separate set of dishes for that holiday—and Hanukkah candles in December, but not much else in the way of Jewish observance. The Singers were Jew-*ish*, though more observant by far than any of my family was now. The Singers were "assimilated," the fully-loaded word used to describe immigrants who dutifully shook off traditional clothing and customs in the interest of blending into the dominant Christian culture of Austria. The Singers were Austrians first, and what loyal Austrians they were.

To my disappointment, however, Dolfi remembered little else about the rest of daily life and the family dynamic. In acknowledging this he said he felt the memory gaps existed because his early life had been uneventful in the best possible way—comfortable and peaceful— without much childhood trauma beyond the crisis when he decided to perform open-chest surgery on my mother's beloved stuffed bear. Dolfi observed that at that time children and parents didn't interact with the same emotional intensity as they do now. I didn't quite buy that, given what I knew about my mother's close relationship with her parents. Dolfi's comment confirmed my sense that it was the two years after Fritz and Dolfi left for England—1938 to 1940—that had changed the emotional life of the family. Eva had spent those two years with her parents under terrifying circumstances that had drawn them closer together.

When I pressed a bit, Dolfi did tell me about the family conflict caused by the behavior of his wilder older brother, Fritz, who habitually stayed out late drinking, chasing young women (not always Jewish), and attending meetings of the Social Democratic Party. I had read about "Red Vienna," the post–World War I period when Social Democrats were in power. Left-wing thinking was very much in vogue in Vienna, especially among Jews. My mother had told me that her father was interested in Socialism and workers' rights as well. But I got the feeling from Dolfi that Fritz had been engaged at a different level, one that had caused his parents great concern, especially as the political climate changed after the Austrian Fascists took power in May 1934 under Engelbert Dollfuss and the Social Democratic Party was outlawed. Julius and Anna had reason to worry that Fritz's activities would bring unwanted attention to the family at a time when Jews were already dealing with rising anti-Semitism.

My uncle Fritz, who had remained in London since he and Dolfi left Vienna in 1938, was near the end of his life. At ninety-one, he had been living for some time in a nursing home for Austrian Jews. He'd had a successful career as a salesperson, and for the years of his marriage, he, my aunt Esther, and my two cousins had lived comfortably in a traditionally Jewish area of north London, where singer Amy Winehouse grew up. Without knowing too many details myself, it was clear that Fritz had endured periods of crisis, both physical and mental. There was no family language for what had ailed him throughout his life since the war—perhaps, at the least, undiagnosed post-traumatic stress, depression, and anxiety. At this point his health and memory were failing.

I hadn't seen Fritz in many decades. On one occasion, I'd passed through London with my husband shortly after our wedding. I'd called Fritz up, but he'd told me brusquely that he was "not well" and didn't want me to see him ill. Now I had only vague memories of him from childhood trips to London with my parents. I recalled a movie-star handsome man with a prickly temper.

For my mother, he had been something more difficult. On random occasions he would call her from London in the middle of our night to rant about the suffering he'd endured during the war years, accusing Julius and Anna of abandoning their sons and my mother of being a disloyal sister. I knew that after years of these phone calls my mother had preferred to have no relationship with her brother Fritz, rather than endure his long-distance abuse. After my mother had been diagnosed with cancer she'd insisted that she didn't want Fritz to know about her illness. Dolfi disregarded her wishes and wrote to Fritz, who then sent a letter from London that must have crushed her spirit: condolences on her imminent death. The letter had caused a rift that lasted until my mother was nearly gone. I regretted all these events, because they'd kept me from having more connection with my English cousins, but I was not surprised that the war had taken its toll in such a lasting way. The arrival of the Nazis in Vienna and the fraught decisions individual parents made to save their children would not have altered the underlying dynamic: rather, it would have exacerbated and frayed any stress points in each family. The Singers were no different.

While I didn't imagine that Fritz had great recall about his childhood in Vienna, I wrote to his daughter to see if she could record any stories he might still be able to tell. She agreed, and I was amazed when she sent some clips recorded at his bedside. Fritz's Viennese accent was stronger than Dolfi's or my mother's. At first he sounded disoriented and I regretted having asked my cousin to disturb him in his last days. But toward the end of the recording he told a lucid, gleeful story about shoplifting art books from a shop in the center of Vienna. His acts of youthful rebellion had remained with him, even decades later, and I had to laugh, recalling my trip to the museum shop in Vienna with Liza, not to mention my own filchings at art supply stores as a teenager. Fritz, a handsome young man of seventeen, had been intelligent, willful, and mercurial, altogether a fatal combination for a Viennese Jew by 1938. No wonder his parents had been so desperate to get him out as swiftly as possible.

My talks with Dolfi continued. In follow-up conversations he shared his memories of one person I was eager to know more about: Herr Mazura, the porter at 22 Weimarer Strasse who also served as the foreman in Julius's paper goods factory. Based on stories my mother had told, I knew that Herr Mazura and his wife, Rosa, had been important to the Singers' survival.

Herr Mazura had been a small sturdy man, Dolfi said, with brilliant white hair, cropped short so that it stood straight up on his head like bristles on a scrub brush. He was always dressed in a bright blue workingman's overall, of the kind still worn in Europe. I was grateful to have this visual—so colorful and descriptive I could have cast a character actor to play him.

Like my mother, he recalled family vacations, summer camp, especially the delights of the last peaceful summer of 1937 spent in Cesenatico, a tourist beach town on the Adriatic coast, south of Venice. By the summer of 1938, everything had changed. Dolfi—a future surgeon—apprenticed with a shoe cobbler. The feeling was that a trade skill, one that would have previously seemed lowly for a middle-class family, was the most practical approach and a way to stay hidden. It was reserved and responsible Dolfi, not the older but more reckless Fritz, who stood on the long lines to secure travel documents for the brothers' passage to England. Once the arrangements with London relatives were made, Fritz and Dolfi left in early September 1938 for London, along with an older cousin, Edith, leaving their parents and Eva behind.

Dolfi recalled the train journey from Vienna to the French coast, where they boarded a ship for England. Once they had arrived safely, they lived with relatives. It wasn't always an easy fit, especially for Fritz. In 1938, the Singer family's hope was to reunite in England, but the severing of the family was to be permanent once Britain declared war against Germany in September 1939.

I wondered again, as I had many times before, why my mother hadn't left with her brothers. Surely this would have been the safer option. Perhaps Anna was reluctant to lose her daughter. Having one child still at home would have maintained some semblance of normalcy in a world gone mad, and a reason to persevere. My guess was that Eva didn't want to leave her parents behind. I'd read accounts of children who refused to leave with older siblings on the *Kindertransport* between 1938 and 1940 that brought unaccompanied Jewish children to Britain, most of whom never saw their parents again. I could imagine that Eva was as stubborn as a child as she was as my mother.

Once, while on the phone with my father, I asked him what he knew about her decision to stay in Vienna. "I remember asking her when we first met, why she stayed behind," my father said. "She just didn't want to go. She felt she could give them some comfort by staying." He paused here, remembering the twenty-year-old he'd met on a blind date in 1947. "She showed real courage and determination doing that. And then everything after that: coming to a new country, learning the language, and a lot of hardship. She was such a rock for her parents. She was a very strong-willed woman."

"I know!" I replied, and then I laughed, spontaneously, before catching myself.

My father acknowledged my laugh with a sigh. Even though he and I were on the phone, I could imagine his face, with his lopsided, knowing smile.

I thought back to all our mother-daughter battles, with a new understanding of her toughness. This had been her essential nature, reinforced by her status as a kid sister with two older brothers, and the ordeal of life under Nazi occupation had made her tougher still. She hadn't known how to reset once the threat was gone, or maybe for her the danger had never felt completely over. During those last two years in Vienna, she had been changed, and forever. I saw a variant of her survivor instinct in myself, and in my daughter. Eva had been ten years old in 1938 when her brothers left, her innocent childhood abruptly over. My childhood had begun twenty-one years later, and I could see now that she had never finished mourning the loss of her family.

Open Door

November 16, 2012
NOVOTNY & NOVOTNY FILMPRODUKTION
Weimarer Strasse 22/4A 1180 Wien

Dear Madams/Sirs:

I am an American author doing research for a book based on my mother's life. She grew up in Vienna and lived in Apartment #5, Weimarer Strasse 22, the building where you now have your offices. I visited the neighborhood this past June while on a trip to several archives in Vienna, but it was a weekend and I was not able to visit inside the building. I hope to make another trip to Vienna in this next year and I hope that it might be possible for me to visit your offices. I am curious to know if the factory building that used to be behind the residential building—and was still there on my previous visit in 1980—is still in use. This building housed a printing factory that my grandfather ran—the factory printed pharmaceutical labels and packaging.

I enjoyed reading your website! Your work looks fascinating.

Very best wishes—

Julie Metz

I T WAS NOW fall 2012. I'd waited months for the bitter flavors of my Vienna visit to pass. I mailed a letter to the unknown tenant of apartment 5, written and addressed by hand. I did not hear back. I wondered if the current tenants imagined that some angry Jewish woman from faraway New York would show up wanting to reclaim their lovely apartment. Chastened by the silence from apartment 5, I labored over an email to Novotny & Novotny, the film company listed on the directory. The tentative search I'd begun after my mother's death in 2006 had become a quiet obsession, but the story of my mother's childhood and her family's last-minute escape from Nazi Vienna in 1940 was still as fragmented as a moth-eaten sweater. So much was missing that I could only imagine writing a novel so that I could fill in the narrative holes.

I received a polite reply from an assistant. Yes, if I returned to Vienna, Herr Novotny would be very happy to welcome me to their offices for a tour. I left the correspondence there, like a placeholder. I was positive that I would return to Vienna within a year, but as other family priorities took over, I let thoughts of Vienna sink underground.

———————————

TWO MORE YEARS passed quickly. As Liza began her last high school years, Clark and I made plans to move away from Brooklyn. He was tired of city life, and even I, a lifelong New Yorker, was feeling worn-out in a neighborhood I'd once loved. We chose a Hudson River town two hours north, where we bought two adjacent commercial buildings with street-level stores and apartments above. Clark handed me a ring full of keys: after decades as a tenant in New York City, I was now a landlady. Then he got to work on renovations, starting in the basement. We had to evict a tenant who stopped paying her rent: a grandma who sold drugs from her apartment and did some moonlighting as a prostitute. Her customers were menacing, stalking the hallways. Some seemed to have keys to our building. Clark told me he had vague thoughts of buying a gun. Other tenants were just garden-variety devious. Landlording turned out to be like parenting three-year-olds, or ornery fifteen-year-olds, except that you couldn't rely on parental love to sustain you through the hard times. Clark and I were apart much of the week. I was worried, wondering what batshit craziness we'd gotten ourselves into.

During the last years in Brooklyn, Clark had been taking banjo lessons. As another year turned, some of his banjo friends persuaded me to join a fiddle class. I agreed. I had taken piano lessons as a child but I'd never attempted a fretless stringed instrument. To the first class I brought an inexpensive fiddle we'd bought online for Liza when she'd expressed interest in lessons, quickly abandoned. Now the fiddle seemed to be mine. During the first lesson our teacher, jazz virtuoso Charlie Burnham, taught us how to tune our instruments and rosin our bows, and then we sawed our way through some scales. We sounded some kind of god-awful, but in a way that made me smile. But by the end of the hour we were playing "Twinkle, Twinkle Little Star," and to my surprise, I was in love. I traded up for a better instrument, which became a travel companion. It was the first time in my life that I'd taken up a pursuit with the full knowledge that I would never master it. And yet, I loved playing. I practiced, took private lessons, and I could hear improvement. Charlie told me that I had a good ear.

The fifteen-year-old teenager I'd taken to Vienna was now almost eighteen. Liza applied to and was accepted at a college on the West Coast. Before I was ready for it, separation was imminent. In August of 2014, we flew to the city that would be Liza's home for her college years along with Eden, her beloved pet white lab rat. The campus was green and glorious in late summer, and as proud parents we strolled through the wooded grounds, wishing we could have a college do-over. The day for parental departure approached too soon. Liza gave us each a hug and walked off to begin her new life, leaving me a blubbering mess all the way to the airport, and for most of the long plane trip back to New York.

We arrived home to begin the job of packing up our Brooklyn apartment, purging belongings I'd held close since childhood. We rented a storage space near our future home for fifty boxes of books I knew would not see daylight for years. That December we moved into the apartment we'd renovated in one of our buildings. In my new office space it took some months to unpack boxes, including the photocopies from the Austrian State Archives. I had given up looking for the documents that should have been at the IKG. I told myself that I'd have more time to look in the spring, which felt a long way off.

Our first winter was brutal, with snow in high drifts until March. But after asking around I met Aldo Lavaggi, a new fiddle teacher, and my lessons continued. My bowing quit squawking; sometimes I startled myself by making pleasing tones. I nurtured a hope that one day I might have enough wrist action to make a vibrato. At last, the hills began to green and the venerable magnolia in our backyard erupted in a canopy of pink-tinged blooms. By summer, we had settled in. After surveying neighboring gardens, I began my own grand plans with the help of Joseph, a local gardener, planting trees and perennials. I planted two hardy roses, familiar from many summers I'd spent on the Maine coast, beginning as a child. I wasn't quite ready for my mother's fancy hybrids. During the spring thaw we met other Brooklyn expats as well as locals, and in short order we found ourselves engrossed in town politics. A gravel company wanted to expand operations on our beautiful waterfront. They had to be stopped.

Summer passed into fall and then into another winter. I learned all about brick pointing and Federal era paint colors as we restored the facades of our buildings. We got savvier at landlording. Liza returned home for winter break in her newest manifestation: her platinum-blond bob was now dark again, her lips stained a deep wine red, and she wore a pink rabbit fur coat. When we went to the city together, tourists stopped her to take photos. At home we had a peaceful holiday. We played with our unabashedly anthropomorphized cats, who took on the roles of children in Liza's absence. During the chilled dark afternoons of late December she snuggled up next to me on the couch and we watched episodes of *Adventure Time*. Another year turned. Liza returned to college out west, another winter ran its course, and then our magnolia unfurled its dusty pink petals and daffodils burst open everywhere.

CHERRY TREES WERE in full flower in April 2016 when I received an out-of-the-blue email from Franz Novotny, the owner of the film company at 22 Weimarer Strasse. He wrote to tell me about a memorial that was to be set into the sidewalk outside the building to honor a man named Dr. Jakob Ehrlich, who had died at the Dachau concentration camp in 1938. Throughout Germany and Austria, *Stolpersteine*, or "stumbling stones," had become a familiar way to honor Nazi victims; each memorial was about the size of a square cobblestone, surfaced with a brass plaque inscribed with the person's name, date of birth, and location and date of death. The announcement of the installation of a memorial for Dr. Ehrlich had somehow jogged Herr Novotny's memory; he recalled my inquiry four years earlier and wondered if I might be related to Dr. Ehrlich.

I'd never heard my mother or uncle mention a Dr. Ehrlich, which seemed odd now, given that he was such a prominent figure at the IKG, as well as a neighbor. Appointed as a high-ranking member of the IKG in 1936, Jakob Ehrlich was described in an obituary as a fierce Zionist who opposed "assimilationist policies." He also spoke loudly against the rise of Fascism in Austria. Ehrlich was arrested in April 1938 and deported to Dachau on one of the earliest so-called "celebrity transports" of prominent Jews. At that time Dachau, located in an exurban town of the same name just outside Munich (where my friend Michelle and I had traveled in the summer of 1980), was set up as a so-called "work" camp. Men young and old were forced into hard labor and subjected to beatings and starvation rations for periods of weeks or months before they were sent back broken to Vienna. Many did not return at all. The cremated remains of Ehrlich's battered body were returned to Vienna some weeks after his arrest, a warning masquerading as a gesture of respect for the dead.

A Jewish-owned building, 22 Weimarer Strasse began to take on the status of an outlier enclave in a mostly Gentile neighborhood. I emailed Franz, explaining that while I was not related to Dr. Ehrlich, my mother's family had lived in apartment 5, and my grandfather Julius had managed a printing factory in the rear courtyard.

Franz wrote back within minutes, telling me that his film company was located in the former factory of Adolf Eisenmann und Sohn.

From thousands of miles away I could hear the heavy wooden door of 22 Weimarer Strasse opening wide. From that first day of contact, our emails bounced back and forth many times a day. I had a thousand questions; so did he. Our initial formality relaxed. Another Austrian business owner might have resented my inquiries as an intrusion into a dark past best forgotten. Franz walked right up to me, shook my hand, and invited me inside.

Franz sent me photos and a short cell phone video tour of 22 Weimarer Strasse. The camera moved through the front door, down a dimly lit corridor to the rear courtyard. An overcast sky illuminated the scene like a studio photographer's bank light, silvering the small-paned casement windows. Through a door, I saw Julius's factory: a large open workspace, daylit under high skylights. The concrete floor was painted bright tomato red. A square pale wood conference table in the center of the room was surrounded by white Eames chairs, fancier versions of the ones around my dining table at home. The walls were hung with Franz's figurative and abstract paintings. Brightly upholstered midcentury modern furniture and lamps completed the décor.

Two long wooden worktables stood center stage in another room, built of thick wood planks held together with sturdy L-shaped metal brackets. Franz explained that these tables had already been in the space when he took occupancy and were so large that they couldn't be moved out the front door. Rather than dismantle them, Franz had kept the tables in place, and now they hosted employee laptops and the office kitchen. From the style of workmanship and hardware, he speculated that these tables might date to the time of Eisenmann und Sohn. I had a sudden image of Julius in his factory as it once was, with his loyal foreman Mazura by his side, inspecting the day's work laid out on the long tables—and then the startling sensation of Julius's warm hand resting on mine, as if he were showing me our family business, not so different from the work life my parents and I had chosen, making packaging out of so much paper.

Franz told me that a member of the family who had acquired the building and the business after the Aryanization in 1938 had lived there until she died. The property had then been passed on to a male relative, who still lived in the building. Franz sent me an image of a page from the Lehmann Vienna street guide of 1938, which listed the city's inhabitants alphabetically by building address. Among the names I saw Fanni Eisenmann (Adolf Eisenmann's widow), Dr. Jakob Ehrlich, S. Mazura, and a woman named Rosa Mazura, perhaps a wife or sister. Mazura was listed as *Arbeiter*, worker. My grandfather J. Singer was listed with his profession *Fabrikant*, manufacturer. The last listing was for L. Steppan, the head of the family that lived across the hall from the Singers, whose son, according to my mother, had threatened my uncles with deportation.

With additional research, Franz discovered that Mazura's first name was Sylvester. I was glad to finally have a name to attach to the image Dolfi painted for me when he described his memories of life at 22 Weimarer Strasse. Sylvester Mazura now stood before me in his blue workingman's coverall, sweeping his hand over his stiff white hair.

Franz directed me to a number of new archives and museums and also did his own sleuthing for documents and images, so useful, as I could not read German except for odd words here and there, and help from Google. When I thanked Franz, he asked me not to. This was his obligation, he said, and he was glad to do this work.

I sent him a photo of handsome young Julius, beautiful young Anna, and another of my mother and her parents from the late 1940s. My mother was in her late teens, wearing a sharply tailored suit and blouse, perhaps sewn at home. As in all their family photos after emigration, my mother stood between Julius and Anna, the trio pressed tightly together.

Franz sent me a video following the *Stolpersteine* commemoration ceremony for Dr. Ehrlich. The now-familiar doorway of number 22 came into focus, filling me with confused emotions, even though I'd only seen this building twice, even though it had never been my home. It was my mother's home, a place she was never able to visit again after she walked out the door with her parents on March 25, 1940. Franz took up a microphone. I noticed that he wore his hair in the same style as Julius, curls swept to the side, with a carefully groomed mustache. He delivered a short speech before representatives of the Jewish community in Vienna. Another man spoke and I could make out enough of his narrative: Dr. Jakob Ehrlich, deported to Dachau, where he was murdered. At the end of the ceremony Franz spoke again, and I was able to understand a reference to myself, and my family's connection to the building. Now Franz and I were connected.

My mother had often described the folded paper packaging for dosages of powdered medicine produced in Julius's factory, but I'd never been able to conjure up a visual. Now Franz searched at a pharmaceutical museum in Austria (who knew there was such a thing?) and at other archives. The once-mythical item was real and it had a name: *Pulverkapseln*, powder capsules or wrappers. Adolf Eisenmann und Sohn had patented a design for *Pulverkapseln* in 1905. In addition to producing labels for soaps and other toiletry items, this packaging had been a huge success. The company had exhibited at pharmaceutical trade expos and cultivated clients in Vienna, greater Austria, and in neighboring countries such as Switzerland, Hungary, and Croatia.

I found an image online of an invoice Adolf Eisenmann und Sohn sent to a pharmacy in Zagreb. The logo was an elaborate engraving of number 22, the courtyard behind, and the factory. Tiny figures carried boxes to and from the factory. Smokestacks behind puffed out plumes, the signifier of commercial progress. The logo included what appeared to be seals of the Habsburg Empire, something like the "By Appointment to Her Majesty" emblazoned on packages of my favorite English biscuits. Franz said that the size of the courtyard was exaggerated, as well as the proportions of the factory itself. And there were no smoke-stacks. And perhaps Adolf Eisenmann hadn't even had a son at all, merely the idea of one that gave the business an aura of history and reliability. Unreliable narrators had been at work creating an origin story and a myth; we would have to be careful as we searched further.

Soon after that, Franz wrote that he had visited the company that still produced *Pulverkapseln* in Austria for homeopathy and compounding pharmacies. He had seen the machine in action and it looked quite old. He described the soothing shushing rhythms of the paper sheets being trimmed and folded. He sent me one of the paper fans, which took pride of place on my desk. My mother had said that the *Pulverkapseln* was important enough to the Nazi war effort that it kept her father alive. I wondered how soon I could get to Vienna to see this factory for myself.

———————————

ON ONE OF my trips to New York City to visit my father, I looked through the Singer family photographs from the old country, as I had so many times before. This time a few small photos spilled out that I had never seen before, as if they'd been waiting for the perfect moment to reveal themselves. I could not understand how I'd missed them.

The photographs showed Julius mountain climbing with small and large groups of hikers, revealing that the trip he took with his friend Jakob Altenberg after the First World War was not the end of his mountaineering days. One photo showed Julius and a friend on a rocky outcropping, captioned with a location—Hohe Wand—and a precise date—May 20, 1928, just a few months before my mother was born. Another photo turned out to be a postcard my uncle Fritz had sent home from a mountaineering trip. In blue ink he had marked the route he had taken to the snowy summit. And out tumbled Anna's 1938 membership card for the Alpenverein Donauland, a Jewish mountaineering club established in 1924 after the main Austrian mountaineering club expelled all its Jewish members. Anna wore a satin evening dress. With three children at home I didn't think she'd had much time for mountain climbing, but perhaps there were annual dinners where members shared stories of their adventures. Whatever the mood of the country then, this family had not felt that they were in danger. In January of 1938, when this card had been stamped for a new year and nine-year-old Eva had posed in her family living room, the Singers had been living their normal lives, making plans for more days in the mountains.

——————————

AFTER WEEKS OF back-and-forth emails and additional research, it was clear to both Franz and me that 22 Weimarer Strasse, a building on a quiet tree-lined street in Vienna, was a microcosm of the terrifying reality for Jews during the Nazi years. Julius was about the same age as Dr. Ehrlich. They would have seen each other as they left for work in the mornings or returned home in the evenings. Each man had very different approaches to Jewish life in Austria: Ehrlich was a Zionist, my grandfather a Socialist and proud Austrian. As a result, their relationship might have been merely cordial, or even cool. However detached their exchanges, surely the sudden arrest and deportation of Dr. Ehrlich must have upended life for Julius and Anna.

But even before Ehrlich's remains were returned from Dachau, Julius would have understood that the threat was real, beginning with their neighbors across the hall—the Steppans. As my mother and my uncle Dolfi told the story, the son of Herr Steppan had never gotten along with Fritz. In our conversations, Dolfi recalled that both boys were quick-tempered and that there had been some unfriendly competition over local girls. Fritz had been dark and handsome, a rebel who'd wasted no opportunity to have a good time. I imagined the Steppan son as a sturdy blond bully. The day after the Anschluss, as the Singer family left their apartment, the door opposite opened and Steppan's son stepped out, proudly wearing a Nazi uniform and armband. The sight of this young man had cast a pall over the Singer family—the danger was all too close.

And then, about a month later, Jakob Ehrlich was arrested. Julius and Anna Singer might never have known exactly what had happened to Ehrlich, except that their neighbor, a man respected in the Jewish community, had been forcibly taken away from his home—their home—and did not return alive. His wife and son left soon after that.

Why hadn't Julius packed up his family right then and headed for London, where there were relatives already settled, or New York City, where Anna's brother Theo lived? For that matter, why hadn't he and Anna seen the signs of what was happening years earlier? Hadn't the threat of anti-Semitism been evident enough after Hitler came to power in Germany in 1933? What warning sign had they been waiting for?

I looked for answers in books and articles. My research expanded as I spoke with academics I met through my readings and attending lectures. I was moved to tears that so much research was devoted to the particular world of Jewish life in prewar Vienna.

One of those academics was Tim Corbett, whom I'd met following a talk he gave at the Leo Baeck Institute. His current area of study concerned Jewish cemeteries and war memorials, the markers a community left behind for posterity both to signify the status of their families and to bring attention to the contribution Jews had made to the nation as a whole through their military service in World War I. Tim and I began a correspondence: he sent me articles to read and I wrote back with questions to which he patiently replied.

———

FRITZ DIED NOT long after my cousin sent the recordings of his childhood memories. Dolfi died a few years later. The three siblings of 22 Weimarer Strasse were gone, but my mother's story hovered around me, still phantomlike, slipping me clues, and pestering me when I lost my way in piles of paper and documents and photographs. *Speak to me*, I asked the piles, *tell me where to look.*

Once again, I knew that I had to return to Vienna. But first I needed to do some time traveling into the past, to visit the part of the story I'd been able to piece together so far, set in that other Vienna, before 1938, when the Singer family still had a good life at number 22.

PART TWO

PART TWO

Based on a True Story

It is spring again. The earth is like a child that knows poems by heart.
—Rainer Maria Rilke, *Sonnets to Orpheus*

— *JULIUS* —

I N A PHOTOGRAPH that does not exist it is a morning in late May 1928. Julius Singer, a modestly built man of fifty-three years with a conspicuous chin, well-groomed mustache, and a thoughtful tailor taps a melody with a spoon on the rim of his coffee cup. He is seated at Café Taube, his second office, where Kurt, the longtime waiter, knows just how he likes his coffee—with a generous dollop of creamy *Schlagobers*. He is here most mornings, after he sets the factory schedule. This hour of his day is a threshold that hovers briefly between his family life and his work life. Here he is alone, while his city swirls around him. The musical score is the rumble of the streetcar, blasting horns, grinding engines of cars and trucks, horseshoes on pavement, snippets of conversation in the Viennese dialect, an orchestration he can enjoy or ignore at will. His memories dip and scurry like traces of wind across a moving river—the Danube, in this case—narrating the story of his life. Today, the weather being fine, Julius is at one of the outside tables. Yesterday's rain clouds have given way to gauzy white brushstrokes across a blue canopy and the scents of fading lilac, a gust of early rose, the vegetal tang of manure dropped by horses pulling delivery wagons, and the exhaust of passing automobiles comingling with his favorite tobacco (just one cigarette in the morning and one after dinner; his doctor says he has a weak heart). This singular decoction of the noxious and intoxicating is the perfume of his Vienna—and he loves it as much as his morning coffee.

"*Guten Tag, Herr Sachs,*" Julius says, recognizing a passerby, one of his clients. A tip of the hat. "*Guten Tag, Herr Singer.*" And it *is* a good day. It is the tenth year since the war's end and he is anticipating the birth of his third child. Perhaps this time it will be a girl.

JULIUS HAD MARRIED late, at forty-five, but at last, to his mother's relief. His determined parents had introduced him to any number of eligible women—all the more urgently after the marriages of his younger siblings—but he had managed to extract himself from entanglements that would have made him as miserable as those young women and had reached the age of twenty-five still a bachelor as the new century began. His mother remained tightly corseted while women of his own generation and younger ones were edging toward a new freedom, clothing loosening its grip on women's bodies. Ruled by the inbred Habsburg family, famous for their jutting lower jaws, his Vienna was still the heart of the empire, a vibrant center of art, music, books, and theater. Julius found work at the stock exchange and like-minded friends in the cafés. And he found women who enjoyed his company, no wedding required, though he had paid for the privilege in theater tickets, dinners at restaurants, and sometimes an even blunter exchange. The city gathered him up into its joy, as if he were just one of so many soluble pigments in water and even a Jew could be part of this painting. He had drifted along through his thirties, still unmarried. His father died, and with his siblings' children to distract her, his mother gave up finding him a wife.

The war brought everything to a halt. Julius was a late conscript in 1916, two decades older than the young men who'd already fought and died for the emperor. He left no particular sweetheart behind, but in between the surges of fighting he made a friend, the kind of which you need only one in life. Jakob Altenberg, another older conscript, was elfin in height, a pointer finger over one and a half meters, but sturdily built, with sandy-brown hair and light eyes. They were the same age, but Jakob already had a wife and children he loved dearly. Jakob's wife, Barbara, was Catholic and Jakob had converted to marry in her church. Religion was a tradition to be respected but it did not rule their lives. The two men bonded quickly in their shared worldview of a Social Democratic future.

The new friends survived the bloodbath, though neither Julius nor Jakob could have imagined the outcome. The empire was lost, carved into pieces by the terms of the armistice. A new republic, Austria, was created from the leftovers, an inland bulbous form on the map, with Vienna no longer the central pivot of a vast territory but still a capital and their home.

In the spring after the war ended, Julius and Jakob traveled by train to Trieste for a monthlong expedition through the Italian Alps and into the Austrian Tyrol. During those weeks, they were mostly alone, with the wind and sky and the trail in front of them. In Italy they managed with Julius's few words of Italian and the welcoming innkeepers' lilting bits of German. After they crossed into the Tyrol, language was no longer an impediment, but they noticed that people in the rural provinces treated them with some suspicion, since they were so obviously city men from faraway Vienna, and also Jews. However, when they engaged the owners of inns in conversation, the unease passed. In one of those villages Julius bought a set of folding eating utensils that he carried with him in a pocket-sized leather pouch like a talisman.

The Vienna they found on their return was a changed city, the vast empire that once orbited around it no more. Many predicted that the new country would collapse amid anger over the harsh terms of surrender, the postwar inflation that followed, and endless political infighting, but Julius and Jakob were doing well for themselves. They were the fortunate ones. As Socialists they talked about a world where religion was no longer the determining factor of identity and the government would support the rights of workers. Some of this was happening under the Social Democrats. People called the city Red Vienna. There was new worker housing, perhaps nothing he would want for his own family, but better than the foul cold-water tenements where some of his own employees used to live.

Jakob returned to running an art and framing gallery in the city center and over time expanded the business. Before the war he took a few paintings on consignment from a destitute and moody young artist who on a number of occasions expressed political ideas that were offensive. He was not a great talent, but the pictures filled out frames well enough. The artist left Vienna for Munich, and good riddance. Now, incredibly, this same Adolf Hitler was a politician on the rise, a leader of the National Socialist German Workers Party. But that was Germany and a very different idea of Socialism. In Vienna, Jakob presided over a profitable business and life was more than comfortable.

Julius looked for work, eventually taking a sales job at Adolf Eisenmann und Sohn, a long-established company that manufactured packaging for the pharmaceutical industry. He was now a full partner.

Old Vienna of his childhood and youth was over, but in this new Vienna, Julius still found opportunity, and whenever he spent time with Jakob the memories of their adventure hovered in the air between them, the unseen energy of their friendship. Jakob was his brother more than his own real brothers, for the two men had found each other in the death fields of the war and were reborn together in the mountains.

Eager to plan more hiking trips, Jakob and Julius joined the Vienna section of the Alpenverein. But then a few years later the mountain-climbing club rules changed. As a convert married to a Catholic, Jakob could have stayed on, but since they wanted to hike together both families joined the new Alpenverein Donauland section and even some Gentiles joined as well. A few years later, after harassment on the trails, the Donauland became a separate mountain-climbing club. Julius could never understand this tension in the mountains, but it was the price of beauty. The mountains were the place he dreamed about. The white foam in his coffee reminded him of their snowy peaks, and nothing would keep him away, not irrational prejudice, not even his weak heart in his aging body.

WHEN I CONTACTED the historian of the Austrian mountain-climbing club, I was relieved to discover how honest the organization was about its anti-Semitic history. I learned that among the prominent members of Alpenverein Donauland was psychologist and future author Viktor Frankl. Originally he was a member of the Naturfreunde (Friends of Nature), the Socialist alpine club that accepted Jewish members. After the Austrian Fascist government shut down the Naturfreunde in 1934, Frankl joined the Donauland. Years later, after surviving life in the Theresienstadt ghetto, a concentration camp, and losing his family, he wrote the memoir *Man's Search for Meaning*. He developed his own approach to psychology in an attempt to grapple with life's purpose in a world that could produce such evil. Another Donauland member was Fred Zinnemann, who left Europe as a young man to become a successful and award-winning director of such quintessentially American films as *High Noon*, *From Here to Eternity*, *Oklahoma!*, *A Man for All Seasons*, and *Julia*, films marked by his commitment to authenticity and realism. His parents remained in Austria and died during the Holocaust.

A PHOTOGRAPH THAT does exist, helpfully dated May 20, 1928, documents such a trip, perhaps just one of many, to the Hohe Wand, a mountainous area not far from Vienna. Two men carrying backpacks are in stages of ascent, dressed in white shirts, knickers, long dark leggings, and sturdy boots. A young woman with a bobbed haircut crouches between them wearing a short-sleeved shirt. Julius is the man in the low foreground, perched on a ladder, carrying a walking stick, his unfailing accessory. The man at the highest point of the rock face appears to be Jakob, based on comparison with the few surviving family photographs his great-granddaughter emailed me. The young woman admires the view. She might be Jakob's daughter, Adela. There is no way to know who took this photograph, or how this feat was managed given the challenges of the location, though there were numerous portable cameras on the market by then. The defined shadows on the rocks and the climbers' faces suggest a sunny day. Julius's right foot is staged to push up from a perilous vertical crag to the relatively safe ledge above, where he would look out over an exhilarating vista, panting, every muscle fiber in his body awake with physical exertion, and his mind clear. Quite a feat for a man with a bad heart.

His wife, Anna, most certainly did not take this photograph, as she was the mother of two young children and seven months pregnant with the baby who would be my mother, the third child Julius awaited as he sat at his favorite café in late May 1928.

IN 1928, JULIUS is a happily married man. One day at the office, a year after the end of the war, he noticed how alluring his young secretary, Fraulein Anna Nichtern, looked in a new blue dress, and when he complimented her on this dress and she flushed, he began to think about her as more than just the capable girl who typed and filed his invoices and correspondence. Apart from her beauty—wide-set eyes, lush lips, coffee-colored curls—and office skills, he knew little else about her. Was she already married?

He discreetly asked Maria, one of the older women at the factory. Fraulein Nichtern lost a fiancé on an Italian battlefield, Maria reported. "He was a poet," she said, and then blurted, "How romantic!"

Julius saw lots of those romantic young men during the war—the ones who thought their youth and vigor would protect them.

So Fraulein Anna Nichtern was unmarried—but whether she would accept a man more than twenty years her senior was uncertain. He wanted to marry her, but he wanted her to agree, not be forced by parents hoping for a good match.

Was he in love with this girl? War erased so many of the tender shadings of life, where deep love could be nurtured. In combat he thought only of survival. Afterward, the mountains were a place to feel a connection to nature, and he had Jakob as his friend, and he had the finely tuned rhythms of his workdays. There were women he wanted and could have, but he missed a different kind of companionship, one that would offer family and fire up his heart.

There was something bright and uplifting about her. Often when he returned to his office from an appointment he heard her humming operetta songs to herself as she worked. She was like an antidote to the ugliness of the war even after he found out about her loss. Somehow she preserved her joy in life. Julius understood that she could not possibly love him at the outset, but he hoped that she would love him in time.

"She has been heartbroken once. She doesn't deserve a life of regret," he said to Jakob, explaining his growing feelings for his secretary, "but she should not die an old maid, like so many of the girls in Vienna." Despite some of the riotousness of his younger years, he knew himself to be a decent and honorable man, ready to be the patriarch of a family, and he was able to provide this girl with a home and children to soften her loss.

"Do you love this young Anna Nichtern?" Jakob asked him

skeptically. "She won't always be young and pretty. And one day she'll have to take care of you, old man. You'll want something more than just sweet good looks."

Julius considered the question. For the first time, after so many years as a single man, the idea of this union felt right. Yes, he wanted her and he loved her.

"And do you think she'll enjoy climbing?" Jakob asked, laughing, but the question was serious. "That's something you should find out first."

Julius was ready for marriage, and unlike so many others in Vienna, he had the means to move forward in good style. During his military service, a doctor told him he had a weak heart (which, given the shortage of men, did not excuse him), but his mind was mathematically sharp for business. A meeting arranged through a former colleague brought him to Adolf Eisenmann, who needed a salesman.

The "son" at Adolf Eisenmann und Sohn existed only as an idea to impress customers who preferred to do business with long-standing firms. Eisenmann was grateful to have a younger man as part of the business and Julius appreciated the interest of the older man, as his own father was long gone. The bond between Adolf and Julius formed early. Adolf took him to meet the clients and taught him the secrets of selling, how to open the briefcase of samples with a bit of authoritative flourish before launching into the fine-tuned sales pitch. Honestly, the products sold themselves, especially the paper fan, the *Pulverkapseln*.

The misery of postwar poverty was everywhere, but years earlier Eisenmann had the money to commission an elegant building in the 18th district. It was called Leopold Strasse then, but now it was Weimarer Strasse, a narrow street conveniently located near the busy Währinger Strasse. Another Jew, an architect named Adolf Oberländer, had designed the apartment building and the factory in the rear courtyard in the *altdeutscher Stil*. Inside the imposing street door, the walls of the long front hallway shimmered in russet tones of faux marble. Arching pilasters decorated with gilded laurel wreaths and goddesses counted the meters toward the courtyard. Abovestairs were flats facing the street. The factory in the rear courtyard was a practical modern structure, daylit with skylights.

Soon after Julius began working at the company, Adolf Eisenmann invited him to become a fifty percent partner and offered him a spacious apartment in the building. "For the future," Adolf said when Julius protested the number of rooms, "when you marry." In this way, soon after his return from war, Julius found himself all at once secure in work and home, ready to think about a gentle family life.

Julius understood the good fortune of his situation. He tried to remain true to his Socialist values by representing workers on the Labor Board, even though he was now financially so far elevated above the status of *Arbeiter*. Or perhaps *elevated* was not the right word. He was not better than they were. The business could not run without his workers. He believed there must be a way to run a business without abusing the people who performed the hardest labor. He wanted to believe that the new republic of Austria could lead the way to a better future, one his children would feel proud to live in.

Though he thought of himself as a good catch, he nevertheless took the precaution of sending one of his brothers as his emissary, so that if Fraulein Anna Nichtern refused his offer, she could continue on as his secretary without embarrassment. Good employment was hard to come by since the end of the war. And a cheerful secretary like Fraulein Nichtern, whose diligence was appreciated by his clients, was also hard to come by. However, Fraulein Nichtern did not refuse him. He lost a secretary but gained a wife.

IN A PHOTOGRAPH from 1928 that does not exist, Julius is watching freshly printed letterheads roll off the press. At the top of each one a detailed engraving shows number 22 Weimarer Strasse and the courtyard and factory behind it (only slightly exaggerated in their proportions). Tiny bustling employees carry boxes of finished work for delivery. This scene is set against the factory smokestacks that do not exist (industrial progress!) and a suggestion of the Vienna skyline, the urban metropolis. Even after the Habsburg Empire was dismembered, Eisenmann insisted on keeping the imperial seals as part of the letterhead, and Julius kept the design after Adolf's death in 1924. The engraving is so detailed that a sharp eye can make out the bay window of apartment number 5, where Julius lives with pregnant Anna and his two sons.

In another nonexistent photograph, Julius is busy on the factory floor, where he will be as soon as he finishes his coffee, supervising the day's work. After the dreary years of war, Eisenmann found the sweet spot guaranteed to open people's wallets by taking the necessary and mundane—the paper wrapped around soap and other toiletries—and elevating it to something finer, as beautiful as perfume bottles or boxed chocolates at Café Demel.

But the company's real moneymaker is paper packaging for the pharmaceutical industry. Some years after establishing the firm, back in 1905, Adolf patented a clever creation called a *Pulverkapsel*. The item is a series of folded pouches made from fine, coated paper, glued together into a piece that when pulled open resembles the fan-shaped bellows of an accordion. Using a type of ball syringe, a pharmacist inflates each pouch with a puff of air and then fills it with powdered medication in precise dosages. In 1905, prescriptions were dosed this way: precisely measured, inserted into the pouches, and hygienically sealed, preventing contamination and ensuring ease of use for a patient. And in 1928, even as pills have come into use, this paper packaging is still in high demand.

And the wonder of it was—Adolf loved retelling this story— the inspiration appeared on a warm spring morning just like the one Julius is enjoying now, sitting at this very café, fiddling with a sheet of cigarette paper. Two young women had sat nearby, their well-coiffed heads bent toward each other in conversation. They were still dressed in evening gowns, no doubt recovering from a ball the previous night. One woman clutched a handkerchief and began dabbing her brow. Her friend pulled a paper fan out of her velvet bag and whipped up a breeze for herself and her friend.

If there was one thing that Adolf Eisenmann loved and understood, it was paper. Adolf was mesmerized by that fan, as if he'd never seen one before, admiring its folds, the way the light and shadow played on the surfaces as the young woman flapped it back and forth. He noticed the depth of the creased valleys, making an unconscious mental note of the precise measurements. As the young women continued to chatter, Adolf watched the fan sway, appreciating how easy it was for a woman with such a petite hand to flick it open and shut. It brought to mind the card players he often saw at this café and others, tricking gullible customers out of their money with brisk sleight of hand, cards sliding into a spread, shifting and trading places faster than the average eye could track. And there were the accordionists who played at the café, sometimes disturbing his morning newspaper reading with saccharine melodies. The pleated bellows of the accordion allowed the player to pump air into the instrument. He returned his gaze to the woman's fan. What would happen if, like the accordion, the folds of a fan were three-dimensional and inflated? Would it be possible to push significantly more air back and forth? The air-filled channels would add sturdiness to the fan, but would the resulting tubes of paper impede movement of the hand?

The empty channels. They could be filled. With something besides air. He considered the channels, their full potential. Strips of paper could be folded and lightly glued together to form such a fan, and each fold could be inflated, filled with medicine, and sealed.

And then, all in a burst of energy, Adolf hunted for a pencil in his satchel and began madly scribbling on the sheet of cigarette paper he'd been fiddling with, and soon the creation emerged fully formed. A package for powdered medicine. *Ein Pulverkapseln.*

It took some time to train his workers to trim, fold, and glue the strips of waxed paper into the fan assembly. Women did this work best, with their smaller hands. But demand was immediate and the patent Adolf secured added quantifiable value to his company. Adolf designed a folding machine to improve production but he still employed workers to glue the pieces.

When Julius took the sales job, he pointed out the inefficiencies of such laborious handwork. He worked with an engineer to develop machinery to streamline the process and along the way made improvements to the *Pulverkapseln*. Now ten workers, supervised by his loyal foreman, Mazura, can do all the work on the factory floor, while others manage the packing and shipping and deliveries.

Till the end of time, fragile human bodies will succumb to illness and injury. Julius sees evidence of this daily in the ruined bodies of veterans of the Great War roaming the streets of Vienna, their empty sleeves and trouser legs hanging in perpetual mourning. People will always need medicine in innovative packaging. Eisenmann himself wisely said that the only business more reliable would be a funeral home.

When Adolf died, too soon, in '24, Julius was ready to carry the company forward. Now there are orders well beyond Austria, from Germany and Switzerland, even Hungary and Croatia. Like a paper fan, the world is expanding.

———————

IN MAY 1928, as Julius sips the last of his coffee and awaits the birth of his third child, he can envision a future when one of his off-spring will take over the business. He wants his children to have equal parts school learning and a life of culture, and thanks to the success of the company, there is money for language tutors, books, art, concert tickets, and music lessons, as well as summer holidays and travel that will give his children an appreciation for nature that has been such an important part of his life.

Now an errant gust lifts Julius's woven hat—he reaches out and catches it before it sails into the street. The pages of his newspapers luff like sails turned into the wind. He has read the Frankfurt and Vienna dailies during this hour of his morning coffee. The news isn't always reassuring. There are signs of distress in the young republic that hint at deeper trouble, which he hopes will pass.

Julius tips his cup forward to see if a last drop of *Schlagobers* remains. Time to return to his factory. Perhaps this evening he will meet Jakob at Neugröschel's, his favorite restaurant in Leopoldstadt. You could miss the place if you didn't know it, as Kleine Stadtgutgasse is just a slip of a street, but of course everyone who knows how to eat well knows Neugröschel's. The schnitzel there is superb, but a transitory pleasure, like the climax of lovemaking, lasting only as long as the heat remains in the fried crust. Inside, the veal is beaten to tenderness. Starchy salted potatoes accented with cucumbers tossed in good vinegar. A meal must be fresh in a restaurant or at home. If there is one thing he cannot abide, it is leftovers. It is true that Neugröschel's desserts will never equal what Anna makes at home, but the atmosphere is always inviting in spite of the owner himself, who prowls through the dining room like a surly king. Herr Neugröschel is famously rude to those unschooled newcomers who dare to ask questions about the menu, and their pitiable attempts to navigate a meal make for amusing dinner theater. Regulars, like Julius and Jakob, know it is best to place your order, accept whatever the waiter presents, smile at Neugröschel, and laugh when his back is turned (but not too loud). Julius is always at home here. Leopoldstadt is still in his blood. He loves to stroll on the broad Praterstrasse, peek into shop windows, and be part of the crowd, though he has other friends who never set foot in the old neighborhood after moving away to more elegant districts like his own Währing.

The men's facilities at the Café Taube are his third office, where he takes a last look at the stock exchange pages and skims the gossip stories that he would not want to be seen reading at his table. Julius's only complaint about the Café Taube and too many other cafés in town is the toilet paper, an item he would consider producing just for his own comfort if he weren't already so busy. How cheap must old Novak be to offer this stuff for his patrons: the stiff sheets appear to be the near relation of butcher paper, a holdover from the impoverished war years. Perhaps Novak bought so much then that he still has reserve. Julius has found that several firm-fisted crumples will break up the paper fibers, creating acceptable absorbency. But still. Such bullshit. He could have managed this so much better. Because if there's one thing Julius understands, it is the beauty of paper sheets, and how to balance strength with a good feel in the hand.

Julius in May 1928 asks my reader to remember this moment in a café toilet. It is not gratuitously scatological, but a bit of foreshadowing here, a trace that will signify later.

Julius returns to his table and pays for his coffee, leaving a generous tip that pleases Kurt. This intermission in his morning is over, his time to connect to the wider world and the workings of his own beautiful city, where he was born, where he hopes to achieve wealth sufficient for a man decidedly Socialist, and where he imagines he will spend all his years. A city where he can live as a respected citizen of Austria, and also remain true to the family traditions he must pass on to his children. As he tells Anna and will tell his children, *When you live in a country that has been good to you, you should not be ostentatious. You should be quiet, but you should show that you are a Jew.*

I HAD BEGUN a journey following a personal family story but found myself digging deeper into the history of Vienna between the two world wars. I had no idea how much excavation and interpretation of this era was still ongoing: the aftermath of the First World War, the complicated politics, and especially the life of the city's Jews. Although they represented ten percent of the population, their impact on culture was outsized.

In her essay "Jewish Memory, Jewish Geography: Vienna Before 1938," Professor Lisa Silverman writes that Jewish sense of identity was intertwined with the city's streets and history. In spite of periods of intense anti-Semitism, middle- and upper-class families like the Singers were often insulated from persecution, especially those who had moved away from traditionally Jewish neighborhoods.

Even before World War I, anti-Semitic outsiders saw Vienna as a "Jewish" city, just as many Americans have chosen to identify New York City as "Jew York." Jewish intelligentsia was an integral part of the vibrancy of Vienna, and in turn Jews aligned themselves with their city, though it was the center of a Catholic empire.

In the aftermath of World War I, the old order was overturned as the victors—Britain, France, and the United States—carved the empire into new nations. In an effort to prevent a war like the one that had ravaged Europe, they intentionally prevented a union of the German-speaking peoples of Germany and the former empire, establishing Austria as a new republic. This forced separation created immediate resentment among the many who wanted a unification of ethnic Germans—not least Adolf Hitler, who had already left Vienna for Munich in 1913.

In Vienna, Hitler had lived poor and his artistic aspirations had been dashed. He hated the Jewish influence on the city's cultural life. As Timothy Snyder writes in his examination of the Holocaust, *Black Earth*:

> The contradictory Austria of the early twentieth century was frozen in the mind of Hitler and many other Europeans throughout the succeeding two decades. Hitler had no sympathy for the Habsburg monarchy, the land of his birth, nor for cosmopolitan Vienna, where he had failed as a painter. He saw the city as an unhealthy mixture of races, held together only by the iniquitous plans of the Jews, who held true power.

Unlike those reluctant new-made Austrians, Jews in the postwar republic wholeheartedly became proud supporters of the new country. Secular Jews in Vienna—and there were many in varying degrees—were especially attached to the physical space of their city, where they felt most accepted and at home. Culturally, they were Viennese.

In his article "The Remembrance of World War One and the Austrian Federation of Jewish War Veterans," historian Gerald Lamprecht describes the *Bund jüdischer Frontsoldaten*, the Austrian Federation of Jewish War Veterans. This group aligned itself with the Austrofascist government that came to power in 1934 in an effort to encourage recognition of Jewish soldiers who had fought for the empire and to stake a claim in the new Austria as anti-Semitism rose during the 1920s and '30s. As a Socialist, Julius would not likely have joined such a conservative population, but as a veteran he might have privately sympathized with the cause. Unfortunately, the membership lists were removed to a military archive in Moscow after 1945, where they still remain, in spite of efforts by the IKG to reclaim them.

Tim Corbett, another historian in the field of Jewish studies, has examined the history of cemeteries and war memorials as records of Jewish life in Vienna during these years. In one article Corbett describes efforts to erect war memorials to commemorate Jewish military service. He cites numerous examples that support the idea that it was Austria's Jews who were its most loyal citizens, including these:

> The earliest such statement I have identified was made by Heinrich Schreiber, a functionary of the Vienna Jewish community organization, who commented in 1918 that "we Jews were without exception and without differentiation [. . .] true and real Austrians." Then in 1936, Max Grunwald, a prolific Viennese rabbi and historian who had witnessed the collapse of the empire first-hand, wrote that "the Jews showed themselves to be the only loyal Austrians."

Until Hitler returned to Austria with his Nazi troops, Julius, Anna, and their three children knew no other home than Vienna and the comfort and security at 22 Weimarer Strasse in a mixed neighborhood increasingly popular with Jewish families of means. Even after the Social Democrats lost power to the Christian Democrats on the national level, this progressive party still had control of the city government of "Red Vienna." Whatever was happening outside the capital, Jews still saw Vienna as their place.

In her moving book-length study of Jewish life in interwar Vienna, *Becoming Austrians: Jews and Culture Between the World Wars*, Professor Silverman also shows that Vienna's Jews were more enthusiastic Austrians than their Gentile fellow citizens, many of whom still mourned the loss of the empire. Many of them blamed Jews for the defeat in 1918 and saw the rise of Jewish culture in "Red Vienna" as a sign of a tainted, amoral world.

Silverman examines Jewish identity through several lenses, spotlighting a series of high-profile trials during the 1920s. The sensational murder of Hugo Bettauer in 1925 was both shocking and a mortification. Bettauer's explicit films and erotica troubled plenty of people who considered themselves liberal-minded, and his left-wing and sexually explicit writing marked him as a target of criticism after the First World War. Though Bettauer had converted from Judaism to evangelical Christianity, he was nevertheless considered part of Jewish Socialist "Red" Vienna. In addition to provocative journalism, he published novels, the most well-known a satire published in 1922 titled *Die Stadt ohne Juden: Ein Roman von übermorgen* (translated in English in 1926 as *The City Without Jews: A Novel of Our Time*). In this prophetic work, Viennese officials expel the city's Jewish population. However, once this purge has been accomplished, the city faces economic and cultural collapse as banks, cafés, restaurants, shops, and theaters close down. Ultimately, the exiled Jews are welcomed back to Vienna. As Professor Silverman points out, the novel is both a savage critique of anti-Semitism and the ignorance that enables it, but also of the willingness of Jews to return to a city that violently rejected them and not for the first time. Sympathizers of National Socialism attacked the "morally corrupt" author of this bestselling book and the successful film that followed, and Bettauer faced legal action and received death threats in the press before a Nazi sympathizer named Otto Rothstock shot him. In court, Rothstock managed to turn everything around, blaming his victim for causing him mental distress, thus literally triggering his crime. Rothstock was acquitted, and he spent only a brief period in a mental institution before being freed.

And then there was the Halsmann trial that Julius would have read about in December 1928. This would have hit close to the bone, because the family was Jewish—and because the murder took place in the Tyrolean mountains he loved.

———————

AT A 2017 Georgia O'Keeffe exhibition at the Brooklyn Museum, I took photos of clothing the artist made for herself, pin-tucked blouses and clever dresses designed without fastenings. I peered into a display of Ferragamo slip-ons similar to ones I'd found in my mother's closet after she died. I vowed to hunt down a vintage pair later (success—in red suede). I noted that Knize, a celebrated Viennese menswear store, was the designer of one of O'Keeffe's favorite suits.

Two familiar photographs of O'Keeffe drew me forward for a closer look. The first, in color, showed the artist posed against a bare adobe wall. Her head was wrapped in a white scarf, the tail draped around her right shoulder. Her black vaquero hat and jacket read as abstract shapes against the textured wall. Sheathed in her stark wrappings, only Georgia's face and the V of her neck and upper chest were bare. Her skin was close in color and tone to the wall behind her. A white cow skull hung above her right side in counterbalance to her body, a reminder that death takes everything in the end, even living legends posing with their still life subjects. In the second image, Georgia was posed in front of Ghost Ranch, her adobe home, beneath a dramatic sky, her famous hands draped over another skull. Stark mountains rose up behind her.

I stepped forward to read the caption. Photographer Philippe Halsman. Spelled differently, but the same Philipp Halsmann convicted at age twenty-two of patricide in two sham trials in 1928 and 1929.

The Halsmanns were a tight-knit family from Riga (in what is now Latvia). They loved hiking together and in September 1928 father and son made a trip to the Tyrol. On that fateful day of his father's death, Philipp and his father were taking photographs of each other along the trail. Then Philipp walked on ahead and thus missed the precise moment his father fell—and a chance to save him.

In *Becoming Austrians*, Lisa Silverman explains that in the conservative Christian communities of the Tyrol, Philipp Halsmann symbolized "Jewish" Vienna—radical, degenerate, and impure. Unfortunately for the accused, the trials were held in the area where the murder took place. Halsmann's citified lawyers from Vienna were not able to convince an already prejudiced court that all evidence pointed to an act of banditry rather than a son pushing his beloved father off a mountain trail to his death.

Halsmann's sister lobbied for his release, recruiting international support to refute the circumstantial evidence. Austrian president Wilhelm Miklas ultimately pardoned Halsmann in 1930, on condition that he expatriate and never return to Austria. He settled briefly in Paris with his sister and mother before fleeing to New York in 1940, where he would later become famous in the 1950s for his series of celebrity "Jumpology" portraits.

Silverman points out that in his "Jump" photographs, Philippe never failed to capture the perfect moment: his subject airborne as his shutter clicked. In his self-portrait with Marilyn Monroe, he looks at her, recording himself in the act of recording a split second of time.

Standing before the Georgia O'Keeffe portraits in the museum I could imagine him waiting for the perfect gaze and body stance before he shot each frame. I was riveted in place. I stepped back at last, wondering if Philippe Halsman had a chance to walk in the mountains during his time at Ghost Ranch.

_____

JULIUS KNEW THOSE Tyrolean villages where the Halsmanns hiked, having explored them with Jakob and other companions in his Jewish climbing club, the Alpenverein Donauland. In the fall and winter of 1928 Julius must have read the news of Halsmann's arrest, trial, and conviction with a chill in his heart, wondering if he would ever be able to return to the Tyrol with a feeling of safety. But this was not the end of Julius's hiking days. My mother had spoken of weekend walks in the Vienna Woods, a wilderness area outside the city, a preamble for more strenuous hikes in the future, when all the children could climb the Hohe Wand. And around 1936, my uncle Fritz had sent that postcard I'd found from a trip he made as a fifteen-year-old to Grossglockner that showed he had acquired considerable skills and perhaps a good deal of his father's passion for the mountains. And in the summer of 1936, the Singer children went to summer camp in the Tyrol. Perhaps as Julius read his newspapers in late May 1928 he imagined that anti-Semitism would fade in time as Austria matured, that the sudden blasts of terrible news were just part of a national rhythm that beat loud only to subside. And as late as January 1938, the date on my grandmother Anna's Alpenverein Donauland membership card, he imagined a future where he and his family could climb the mountains he loved. Given what happened two months later, his optimism broke my heart.

— *ANNA* —

IN A PHOTOGRAPH that does not exist, it is July 1928 and Anna nurses her sweet new baby girl in the front parlor. She has three children now: Siegfried, known as Fritz; Adolf, named after Julius's business partner, who died four years earlier; and now at last, little Eva. The afternoon is warm and groggy. The windows are open to the street to catch a breeze that tinkles the heart-shaped leaves of nearby linden trees. She has love in her life as well as comfort.

Anna has not forgotten her poet. She remembers the intimacy of a single afternoon hour before he was sent to the Italian front as an infantry soldier charged with defending the line near Trieste. She saved the letters he sent and keeps them in a drawer hidden behind her slips and nightgowns. *The sea is shimmering, and the strange wind here, they call it Bora, is like a mighty hand pushing against whatever stands in its way. I will bring you here again when war is over. It cannot last forever.* They were engaged and she worked on her trousseau to keep her hands and mind occupied.

With money tight and marriage still far off, work became a necessity. Her secretarial position at Adolf Eisenmann und Sohn was respectable work and Herr Eisenmann turned out to be that rare employer who paid well, even during hard times.

The ceaseless clatter of the printing presses and folding machines was maddening at first, as were the noxious smells of printing ink, glue, and solvents. But after a time all this became familiar, even soothing. The din of machinery, the phone ringing, the pinging of the typewriter as she tapped out Herr Eisenmann's correspondence—all this quickly became part of the texture of her days. And she made friends among her coworkers, especially Frieda.

She has not forgotten the desperate evening when she learned that her poet was dead. But by then, in private evening hours as she embroidered pillowcases, she already feared that her poet was doomed, a man who belonged in safe, quiet rooms, no match for guns and artillery.

Work was a place to keep busy as she mourned. And a new boss arrived, Herr Singer, a soldier who had survived. A year sped by in this way, at the end of which she found that she could feel proud as an independent woman. The loss of her poet (and also, she was forced to reflect, a life of potential poverty) no longer seared the inside of her chest and throat, but subsided to a dull fluttering ache, like the exhausted wings of the dying fledglings she sometimes saw on the ground in Türkenschanzpark, expelled too soon from the safety of their nests. Some creatures and some people were too fragile to live. She was still in the world and she wanted to live.

One April day Herr Singer complimented her new dress, sewn from cloth her mother bought before the war.

"A sure sign of spring," Herr Singer said, "this color blue."

Anna was pleased with her handwork. Even with her income, she would never buy new when she could make her own.

Over lunch, Frieda said, "Most men never notice the color of a dress—blue, pink, or green—unless they are in love. Mark my words, Anna. A proposal will come soon. And why not you? At least one of us should find a good husband."

Several weeks later Herr Benjamin Singer did pay a Sunday afternoon call with a proposal of marriage on behalf of his brother Julius. Frieda had guessed right. It was true that Herr Singer was older by at least twenty years, but she liked what she saw at the factory. He was calm in the office. He never yelled at workers and neither did his foreman, Herr Mazura. He helped out Josef with a loan when he had to move to a new apartment. He arranged a marriage for Liesl after she ended up in trouble. Sometimes she overheard him telling stories to clients and then there would be a pause and she could hear the laughter of the man on the other end. He loved nature; this was clear from other conversations she had overheard, when he spoke to his friend Herr Altenberg. He had taken trips away from the office to climb, returning tan and fit. She had been to the mountains with her family, but these had been far tamer vacations to *Sommerfrische* resort hotels. Herr Singer was a good-looking man who dressed well. He had soft hands. Perhaps, in time, this man's touch would thrill her like her poet's. It was harder and harder now to recall her poet's lips on her neck and cheek and mouth, and the bristle of his youthful mustache, the hair so sparse and tender that it barely needed trimming.

"Men are scarce enough," Frieda said. "So what if he's older. He's strong and healthy, and I'm sure he can still do what needs to be done."

Frieda's frank words burned Anna's cheeks. Everywhere in Vienna there were lonely women, war widows or the other disappointed young ones like Frieda and Anna who waited without much hope for a man and children. But there were not enough young men to go around, and too many of those who returned from war were destroyed in body and mind. She wondered what her poet would be like if he were still alive. Would she—could she—love a man with a disfigured face, missing limbs, ravaged lungs, a mind wrecked after seeing things she could not imagine? She had not become pregnant from their single afternoon together. She could not imagine being intimate with Herr Singer and was afraid to repeat what had happened with her poet with this man who was still her employer. Anna did want to feel full with a child. Her mother told her that this is what her curvy hips were made for. A baby would heal her. In fact, as Anna quietly said *Yes* to Julius Singer, she was sure of nothing else.

Her father was hesitant at first, worried about the prospect of a son-in-law not so many years younger than he was, but her mother laughed with delight and set out the next morning in search of well-priced material for wedding clothes. No time to lose—the marriage would take place in June.

IN A PHOTOGRAPH that does exist, Anna is preparing for a spring costume ball, one of many she attends. They are all the rage in Vienna. Once, she dressed up as Wolfgang Mozart, in britches, a long coat, and a man's curly white wig.

But today Anna is womanly as Flora, Goddess of Spring. She stands near a tall window through which light is diffused, gentling a bouquet of flowers in a fluted vase on the windowsill, the detailed molding, the folds of her costume, her fresh cheeks and exposed neck. A breeze billows and sways the velvet drapes behind her. But this atmosphere is all an illusion created with studio lighting and a painted backdrop. She wears a long satin gown and cape trimmed with real daisies. She made the costume in haste and the light catches the puckering of the hand-stitched hem. Vibrant shades of leaf and emerald green contrast with her olive skin. Anna's dark hair is covered with a wig of long blond curls, topped with an oversized hat, decorated with roses and peonies. She wears long gloves and holds a walking stick decorated with more flowers.

"Are all those flowers all real?" the photographer asks as he focuses his lens.

"Of course," Anna replies with a tinge of impatience. "And this is why I hope you will hurry. My fiancé is waiting."

"Patience, young lady, all good things take time."

Anna rests her gloved hand over the handle of her flower-trimmed walking stick and tries to imagine herself as a goddess.

"And what about a smile for me?"

Anna tries to conjure a smile worthy of Flora. As the corners of her mouth rise, she can feel the photographer waiting for her gaze to settle and open for his camera. The shutter clicks. What a responsive machine his new camera is, and what a miracle to be able to capture time in a more relaxed way than the usual formal studio portraits. She is excited about her upcoming party, the first time she has felt this way since her poet. She is glad to have preserved this moment. The flowers pinned to her gown will not look so fresh in an hour as they will in the image the photographer has just made.

IN A PHOTOGRAPH that does not exist, taken after the wedding ceremony on Schopenhauer Strasse, Julius and Anna are in a private compartment aboard the night train to Trieste. From there they will travel onward to Cesenatico, an Italian resort town just south of Venice. In the morning they might catch a glimpse of the mountains he loves to climb. Julius tells her that there are coffeehouses just like those in Vienna where the Triestini will speak some German.

It was a hot day in Vienna and the evening is still warm. Julius pushes open the window in their compartment to let in the evening air. He takes off his jacket and places it in the luggage rack and unbuttons his shirt. She wishes she could unbutton her dress with the same casual air. He sits down beside her and looks at her with a playful reverence she cannot quite read. Then he reaches for her, crushing the material of her pale blue dress bought for this trip at a shop on Kärntner Strasse. A nipped waist, belted, with one of the new crinoline skirts.

Everything is new. Anna doesn't work with Frieda anymore. Soon she will be the mistress of 22 Weimarer Strasse, apartment number 5. So spacious, with three bedrooms she hopes to fill with children.

"*Du bist so schön in Blau,*" Julius murmurs, six words that vibrate like notes hammered on a piano. *You are so beautiful in blue.* He presses into the curve of her neck and kisses her cheeks and mouth as he unbuttons the front of her dress. He tastes of the wine they shared in the dining compartment and of the cigarette he enjoyed after the meal. Just one cigarette in the morning and evening, he told her. And she was relieved to know that their future home would not smell of smoke. They kiss until her lips begin to sizzle. She feels his tongue meet hers and dance inside. Down below, somewhere inside, she feels warmth and liquid flowing. She has felt this before, with her poet. He stops his kissing and his hands slide down her legs to her feet. He unbuckles her new shoes one at a time and reaches under the billow of her dress, slowly sliding his hands along her stockings, silk, also new.

"Will you let down your hair?" he asks.

Anna reaches behind to remove the comb securing her curls. His hands have touched other women. Frieda said it must be so and now she is sure. His hands are unhurried, not grasping, as her poet's were in their stolen hour. The hairs of his mustache tingle her neck and her ears, and then her nipples. "Rest," he tells her. "All is well. Anna, I am your Julius. I am so glad we have married."

She wants to rest. Until she remembers all the layers she is still wearing, a silk and cotton fortress of underclothing. A chemise, one of the new long corsets from France to which her stockings are clipped, and a silk slip over everything. Her mother had explained everything to her at home, how to make herself properly ready for her wedding night in the bathroom, not knowing anything about the rushed hour with her poet. He had torn her slip that day.

In her peripheral vision she can see her suitcases on the floor, shivering from the movement of the train. Inside are the carefully packed garments she needs. A cream-colored nightdress and dressing gown, also new. Even a lacy boudoir cap, a gift from Frieda, though something tells her she won't be wearing that tonight or maybe ever. Julius is still kissing her. She wonders if he will be able to tell that this isn't her first time. He lifts up her dress and she helps him by pulling it over her head. Then the skirt. Then her slip. He unclips her stockings and draws them off her legs and feet with care, setting them aside. He unlaces her corset as expertly as the saleslady who helped fit her. The contraption opens and collapses behind her as she takes her first deep breath since morning. He slides it away and places it on her suitcase. Now she is nearly naked, covered only in her chemise—the last layer.

"Isn't this beautiful," he says, caressing the lace and embroidery.

"Thank you, Julius," Anna says. "I did this myself." It still feels strange to address him by his given name, but she has found her voice.

He unties the ribbon at the waist and the night air washes over her damp skin. Now she feels his mouth exploring the hills and valleys of her belly. He moves down to the ridges of her hips. He unbuttons the knickers of her chemise and she feels his hands over the skin of her legs and then his fingers part the curly tangle.

"These hairs remind me of the fluffy seed heads of the pasque-flower. I've seen them in my walks in the mountains." His pointer and middle fingers tickle through the pasqueflowers and her belly heaves with laughter.

"It's important not to crush the flowers when you walk on the trail," he says. "You must step with light feet so that the blooms remain whole and then make their seeds. If not, there will be no flowers to greet you when you visit the next year."

"Will we go to the mountains?"

"Oh, yes, my love, if not this trip then very soon. I do believe you will love it."

"Yes, I think I will."

His fingers tiptoe between the folds of skin where she bleeds each month. He finds the *knopfel*, the knotty button she's discovered on her own, plush and damp, and swirls his thumb over it slowly without stopping. Her ears tingle.

"And this," he says as he slips one of his walking fingers just barely inside her *knish*. "This is like the blue trumpet gentian. And I am like the bee seeking a drink."

She laughs again, encouraged by his playfulness. She looks down at his face and he looks like a boy, almost giddy, as if this is just a game of pretend among children. She is not afraid of whatever will happen next. His finger moves in and out and his thumb circles over the button, around and around without stopping. He is not in a rush. She closes her eyes and drifts in and out, and many minutes pass this way until she feels like she has been caught up in a wind that carries her forward toward an unseen destination, the feeling she has touching herself in bed in the dark. He seems to understand this, that he has caught her. She feels his tickling mustache and mouth on her belly, and then it meanders down and his tongue swirls over the button and around the lips of her *knish*. He begins licking her with the same gestures of his fingers, just a bit faster now, and she can feel the pebbly surface of his tongue. Her button is its own living thing, pulsing each time his tongue swirls around and dips inside her, where some part of her is gripping and pulsing, just on the edge of pain as he licks her and licks her until a flush burns her cheeks and parts her lips and forces out pants of air, and then she sings a high melody above the percussive beats of the train on the rails as an inner spasm grips and surprises her. When she opens her eyes her vision is altered with blind spots pulsing in a sparkling mosaic. This, too, is new.

Julius sighs. "You are the blue gentian." He lies beside her on the narrow bed and she rests in his arms, her breasts vibrating gently to the rhythm of the train. Does he not want more from her, like her poet did? But he seems content to rest. "Julius," she asks, "do you not want more?"

"No, not now," Julius says. "We will wait for the hotel to fully undress for each other. My doctor has asked me to wait, and so I will. I prefer to wait. Do not worry, all is well. I am a patient man and I have learned to enjoy waiting."

He kisses her, and she welcomes his mouth, which tastes faintly of something like salty-sweet pickles. She wonders how the sea waves will feel against her skin and if those waves will taste as briny as her husband's lips do now. The chattering of the wheels lulls them both toward sleep. Julius snores lightly, but when she nudges him, he rolls to his side and his breathing hushes. He wraps one arm around her, and now the compartment feels *gemütlich*, cozy.

In the morning she sees her poet's shimmering sea.

AS A MIDDLE child, Anna grew up in the midst of the noisy battles of her five brothers. At first the quiet of her new apartment at 22 Weimarer Strasse was nearly unbearable. She worried that her work in the factory office had ruined her hearing. The silence didn't last long. Soon enough her own babies came, and then there was no more quiet. Kristina helps with the children and cooking and keeps the new cast-iron stove stoked with coal during the winter. Julius leaves early each morning to meet with Herr Mazura, then goes to the café to read his newspapers, and spends most of the day in his office at the factory, leaving her the mistress of her domestic sphere. She has a generous allowance to pay for all the necessaries of life, and some modest luxuries besides. In winter a fur stole warms her neck and shoulders. She buys good shoes at department stores on Kärntner Strasse. She still sews clothes for herself, but with more expensive cloth. Her poet has become unreal in a way she doesn't have words to describe. His letters live in the darkness of her lingerie drawer. She is glad to live in the real world with Julius and her children. Here she is well-nourished. Her body has become rounder and plumper and so have her *knopfel* and her *knish*.

IN PHOTOGRAPHS THAT do exist, the years unfold before painted backdrops at the Schaller portrait studio on Kärntner Strasse. First it is just Fritz, a handsome boy, dark like his father. He can get wild. Anna gives him a toy to hold to keep him from fidgeting. Dolfi is tender and pudgy and when he is old enough for school, he is calmer and more attentive than his older brother. When Eva arrives she is as sweet-faced as a porcelain doll, an adorable curl on her brow, propped up on a pillow in front of the boys. The next year Evie is a toddler in a white-collared dress hugging her beloved stuffed bear, then a smiling five-year-old in a smocked pinafore meeting the camera with the steady gaze of a confidant child. She wears a beaded necklace, one she made herself. At home she shows a serious side even in her play, trying to keep up with her brothers who are not always as kind as a mother might wish.

Fritz can be moody and impulsive, though he is sure to settle once he finishes school and begins working at the factory with Julius. It will be strange to have a business called Adolf Eisenmann und Sohn run by Julius Singer und Sohn, but the company is so established that no one can imagine ever changing the name, and of course Fanni Eisenmann still lives upstairs. Dolfi might turn out to be the better choice for the factory, as he is a studious boy, good with figures. But at least Fritz should try first. However her sons turn out and whatever paths they choose, little Evalein is her *ketsl*, her kitten, and even at a young age, her companion in a family of men.

———————————

MY FUTURE STERN mother, endless worrier, mistress of lists, keeper of paper shopping bags, is the adorable infant with the forehead curl that looks like an apostrophe. Her baby hand reaches out for her mama as the photographer's shutter clicks, so the photograph feels like a frame from a home movie that does not exist.

— *EVA* —

IN A PHOTOGRAPH that does exist, it is late afternoon in summer. The shadows extend long into a courtyard with a garden to the left. Eva is a well-fed toddler in a sundress and sturdy lace-up boots; the apostrophe curl has grown thick and unruly. She stands in front of a doll carriage—its occupant sound asleep—as elaborately fabricated as one for a human child, and clutches another doll made of cloth. An elderly gentleman with a well-tended white mustache squints at the camera, perhaps a grandfather on the Singer or Nichtern side, or he might be "Onkel" Bauer, whose wife was known as "Tante" Bauer. Dolfi told me that he often walked Eva to the Bauers' to play in the large garden behind their house. Or this might be a city park, or a summer holiday home. Eva smiles at the people behind the camera, probably Julius and Anna, their presence made visible in the shadows at the bottom of the frame. They call to her and she looks up as the shutter clicks. A warm breeze meanders through the trees. This is a moment from a happy childhood.

ANNA AND EVA are baking in the cozy, *gemütlich* kitchen in apartment 5. Anna's Sunday afternoon parties for family and friends are legend, featuring her homemade cakes and strudel. Everyone in the family comes over, Julius's Singers, Anna's Nichterns, and family friends like the Altenbergs. Eva watches her mother's hands stretch strudel dough into a long, almost transparent rectangle until the finished thin veil rests on a clean linen towel. Anna lets Eva brush on melted butter, scatter slices of apples, nuts, raisins, and sugar. Then Anna folds the dough in at the sides and rolls the whole thing up, like a sausage, placing the finished creation on a baking tray. Eva brushes more butter on the top. Once the oven is hot enough, Anna slides the tray into the center. Eva waits with Anna for just the right moment to take it out again. Kristina, the housemaid, brings them cups of warm chamomile tea to sip until the strudel turns golden brown.

IT IS PASSOVER and Papa sits at the head of the table reading from the prayer book. Mama blessed the candles and Eva watches as they burn down slowly. It will be a long time still till they can eat the matzo stacked on a plate and she looks at them hungrily. *Blessed are You, Lord our God, King of the Universe, who distinguishes between the sacred and the mundane, between light and darkness.* Papa hides one piece of matzo somewhere in the salon (last year she found it inside the piano resting above the strings and hammers, the year before it was slipped between two books), but there are many words to read before they can search for it. Papa has set Elijah's Cup out for the Messiah. It is a heavy wineglass, etched and decorated with small blue flowers. She sits between her older cousin Edith and younger cousin Erika. They are the three E's. Dolfi and Fritz say they are too old for hide-and-seek games. *This is the bread of affliction which our forefathers ate in the land of Egypt. Let all those who are hungry come and eat with us! Let all those who are in need come and share our meal. This year we are here. Next year may we all be in the land of Israel. This year we are still slaves. Next year may we all be free.* Her family sent money for a tree in Palestine. Maybe she will see that tree one day. Erika is too little to read, so it is her turn to recite W*hy is this night different from all other nights?* And Papa reads the answer, *We were all slaves to Pharaoh in Egypt. Had the Holy One, blessed be He, not brought our forefathers out of Egypt, then we, our children, and our children's children, would still be slaves to Pharaoh in Egypt.* And there are the four sons: wise, wicked, simple, and the one who doesn't even know how to ask a question. Every year she wonders what is the difference between being simple and not knowing how to ask a question. Which son is stupider, the simple one or the one who doesn't know how to ask a question? *And God said to Abraham: Know that your children and their children will be strangers in a strange land not their own.* It is like a verse in a song. *This is the promise which has sustained our forefathers and ourselves. For it was not one man alone who rose up to destroy us. In every generation they rise up to destroy us. And God, blessed be He, saves us from their hands.* And then there is Laban the Aramaean, who tries to kill Jacob and the Jews. So Jacob and his people go to Egypt with their sheep. And the Jewish people multiply with babies. *I let you multiply like the plants of the field and you have become numerous and grown strong, and you have attained excellence and beauty.* Egypt became jealous of the excellent and beautiful Jews. And then harsh times and suffering came. *We cried to the Lord, the God of our fathers, and the Lord heard our plea and saw our plight, our misery, and our oppression.* Moses asked Pharaoh to let his people go. But Pharaoh refused. *And God pulled us out of Egypt with a mighty hand, and an outstretched arm, with great fear, and with signs and wonders.* Then come the plagues upon the Egyptians. Mama asks everyone to keep their fingers over their wineglasses so that the red drops don't land on the clean white tablecloth. Salt will get out a wine stain. Eva's glass of wine is mostly juice. *Blood, frogs, lice, wild beasts, pestilence, boils, hail, locusts, darkness, the slaying of the* *first-born.* Eva licks the dark red off her finger as the rabbis in the book count and multiply the plagues and discuss their meanings. *Fiery anger, wrath, indignation, trouble, and the messengers of evil.* Eva knows the story. Pharaoh finally allows the Jewish people to leave. They are in such a hurry that the bread doesn't have time to rise, so that's why they eat unleavened bread. Pharaoh changes his mind and comes chasing after the Jews with his soldiers. Moses raises his staff and the Red Sea parts and the Jews rush through on dry land, but then the sea closes up and Pharaoh's soldiers are swallowed up and drowned and dead. Now it is time to sing *dayenu* in all different voices, high and low and mostly out of tune, except for Mama, who sings well. *Had he brought us through the sea on dry land and not drowned our oppressors in the sea, dayenu. It would have sufficed. Had he drowned our oppressors in the sea and not fed us for forty years in the desert, dayenu.* Now Papa explains about the bitter herbs and the matzo. *In every generation, every individual must feel as if he personally had come out of Egypt. As the Bible says: And you shall tell your son on that day—* Her belly whines, like the sound of a winding clock. Edith cracks a smile and squeezes her hand under the table. "Soon, Evie, we will eat soon," Edith whispers. There are two prayers to go. In the second one is a part she likes a lot, also like a song, and it means that dinner will come soon. She shifts in her chair, squeezing her legs together, because now she has to pee. And now the part she likes is here, it is like a story in one of her picture books. *The sea saw them and fled, the Jordan flowed backward. Mountains skipped like rams, and hills like lambs. What frightened you, sea, that you fled, Jordan that you flowed backward, mountains that you skipped like rams, hills like lambs?* And it is the second cup of wine. *Blessed are you Lord, our God, who creates the fruit of the vine,* and then Papa washes his hands and at last blesses the matzo. *Blessed are You, Lord our God, King of the Universe, who brings bread from the earth.* They eat the first bites of dry cracker and she forgets needing to pee. She tries a bite of the horseradish she helped Mama grate earlier, and it is sharp, tingling her nostrils so hard that she squeezes her eyes shut and clamps her hands over her nose as the burn rises up to her cheeks and eyeballs. Papa smiles. "Nice and fresh, eh, Evie?" And then she laughs, even though her eyes are tearing. Mama's haroseth is sweet apples and ground almonds mixed into a paste with wine and this cuts the sharp horseradish. Eva can smell the soup in the kitchen. Mama gets up to check on the roast spring lamb and returns looking pleased. And then Kristina brings out a tray holding steaming bowls of broth with floating carrots and matzo balls and the grown-ups stop talking about the champion ice-skater and the shortage of money and the price of paper and Onkel Theo who has left for America and the latest photographs sent from faraway cousins in Argentina, and everyone clasps hands and Papa says, "Ah, Anna, you have outdone yourself again."

IN A FEW years Eva will spend Passover on a prison island off the coast of Manhattan, while she and her parents wait to find out if they will be allowed to enter the United States or if they will be sent home to a city that no longer wants them. In one of their two trunks are Elijah's Cup and the family's silver Hanukkah candelabra. But as this peaceful family Passover ends, with Anna's legendary chocolate hazelnut torte, this is all in the unimaginable future.

IN A PHOTOGRAPH that does not exist, Eva is in the factory, where she likes to visit after school. Most people say that it is so noisy and that it smells terrible, but Eva loves how the place smells and the feel of paper and all the things into which it can be transformed. She loves the feel of the lithography stones, soft as velvet cloth, but cool to the touch. The glue smells doughy and sweet. She loves watching the rotating wheels of the lithography presses and the folding machines that fabricate the *Pulverkapseln*. She loves the *Pulverkapseln*. The imperfect rejects can be turned into excellent playthings, like paper airplanes, or miniature houses for paper dolls. The possibilities are endless.

Herr Mazura enjoys showing her around, explaining everything once again, even though she already understands how the presses and folding machines work. His eyes are as blue as his canvas coveralls and his short white hair stands up on end like the scrub brushes he uses to clean the lobby of number 22.

"*Der zukünftige Chef, eh, Herr Singer?*" "The future boss?" Herr Mazura says to her papa, winking at Eva. One day she will be grown. Her mother worked in the factory and she will, too. She is good with figures, like Papa, who can add and multiply large numbers in his head, and in this factory she feels at home.

PHOTOGRAPHS THAT DO not exist document summer weeks spent at an informal children's camp away from the city. Every year a professor and his wife choose a new spot, where they rent a house and chaperone a group of Jewish children. Eva is growing up, old enough to join her brothers. When she turns eight, the camp locates in a village in the Tyrolian mountains her father and "Onkel" Altenberg described from their long hike, which has by now taken on the status of family legend. For a few charmed weeks, the children played in a meadow full of wild flowers in the cool air of the mountains.

In the summer of 1937, when Eva turns nine, the professor and his wife escort the children to Cesenatico.

Dolfi told me that the trip to Italy was less than perfectly organized and the older children were perhaps not as supervised as hovering helicopter parents of today would expect. Hardly an effusive man, he lowered his voice, though there were just we two in the room at the time, and described the arrangement for the older children as "fairly lawless." No doubt this was why he retained such vivid and affectionate memories. Whenever my more attentively supervised mother remembered this holiday her face got dreamy, her eyes glassy.

In archival Alinari photographs that do exist, the broad beach of Cesenatico is set against a backdrop of changing cabins and elegant hotels. The town features a canal inset from the sea to create a safe harbor for sailboats. In a colorful poster from the late 1920s these sails are rendered in burnt orange, slicing the blue sky into a cubist composition of hot and cool colors.

If the real town was half as exciting in reality, the week would have offered a visual respite from the more subdued grays and ochres of Vienna's stately architecture. My mother became a graphic designer; surely she appreciated this sensory input as a child. She retained such clear memories of her father's factory and the packaging made there, especially the precise angles and edges of the *Pulverkapseln* she tried so often to describe for me. Her working life was spent designing the folded interior pages of books.

That summer of 1937 Eva was probably not much of a swimmer, having had little opportunity, but she would have been able to manage the gentle waves along this strand. No doubt the professor and his wife placated the children in the heat of a summer afternoon with the cool sweet flavors of Italian gelati and strolls along the canal. According to Dolfi, sixteen-year-old Fritz managed to evade the supervision of the professor and his wife to seek out local girls. At the end of the camp weeks, Julius and Anna joined their children in Italy. While they did not seem to have been overindulgent parents, Cesenatico was a tourist town full of shops with small luxuries a young girl like Eva would have coveted. While no family photographs remain from the weeks in Italy, Fritz, Dolfi, and Eva never forgot this last summer idyll.

THE JEWS OF Vienna adored their city before the First World War and after, even as it teetered from Social Democratic republic to

Catholic authoritarianism under Engelbert Dollfuss, to an outright Austrofascist state under Kurt Schuschnigg. My mother never spoke about politics intruding into the family's life until March 1938. In spite of the chaotic conflict and power battles among political parties in the city center just a few miles from their apartment. In spite of the loss of democratic rights and the rise of fascists in Italy, National Socialists in Germany, and autocrats in Austria. Julius would have read about this while he drank his morning coffee, but he managed to leave it behind at the Café Taube. And the trails Julius created in his city were comfortable and well traveled. Home, work, café, familiar restaurants, homes of friends and relatives, the opera, the theater, the streets where he and Anna shopped, the city parks where their children played.

In my phone conversations with Professor Silverman, she explained the idea of "spatial ethnography," a way of examining how people relate to where they live and how they are emotionally connected to the physical spaces through which they move daily: homes, streets, workplaces, shops, cafés. According to their oral and written testimony, Vienna's layout—a relatively small city organized in concentric boulevards—was uniquely comforting and secure for Jews. As she summed up, "Who you are is often intimately connected to where you are." This made sense to me as a born-and-raised New Yorker. Guided by some internal GPS, I could practically sleepwalk through familiar streets and subway tunnels. It is like muscle memory when you know a place so well.

During fiddle lessons, my teacher Aldo often spoke about muscle memory, a necessity with a fretless instrument. He told me that there was no point marking where the frets would be on the violin neck because once I'd positioned the instrument under my chin the spaces between notes were distorted by the foreshortened angle. The solution, Aldo explained, was to physically experience and then, with repetition, remember how my muscles felt when playing a G natural, for example, and to associate each sound with that physical sensation. He asked me to try practicing with my eyes closed. I found that I played best when I stopped thinking too hard, and just felt the notes in the stretch in my fingertips, hand, wrist, arm, and shoulder. Aldo called it finger yoga. When I was a bit on fire I could feel a melody in my entire body, even though I was still a beginning player and would never be a virtuoso. Yet I had found that repetition created familiarity and a kind of ease and sense of well-being.

Viennese Jews had muscle memory for their city. Julius could play Vienna with his eyes closed. The traces of his life were everywhere, like dots on a map that lived inside him, like musical notes he had learned by heart. He knew where he was, and he knew who he was. So did Anna and Fritz and Dolfi. And so did Eva, even at the age of nine in January of 1938. For this family, at least, it was a good life of family and work and mountain climbing and books and music and good food and as much of Jewish tradition as they chose to celebrate. It was a full life and a good life. Until it wasn't.

A Third Visit to the Old Country

It was sweet to live here, in this atmosphere of spiritual conciliation,
and subconsciously every citizen became supranational, cosmopolitan,
a citizen of the world.

—Stefan Zweig, *The World of Yesterday*

SEVEN YEARS HAD passed since I'd last seen Vienna in the summer of 2012, but now I was back, in March 2019, on my own. Woozy from my flight—I watched movies I'd missed at the theaters and slept not a wink—I unpacked my bag at a studio apartment on Lerchenfelder Strasse and made my way to the Leopold Museum. The imperial buildings along the Ringstrasse were magnificently gilded in the afternoon light. When I emerged from the galleries into the open courtyard it was dusk. Viennese birds warbled an unfamiliar *Spring!-spring!-spring! is coming soon!* melody that echoed in the open square. Being back in my mother's city filled me with confusing emotions, and in the blue gloaming a wash of melancholy stung like pins and needles. As a distraction, I wandered through the Imperial Palace grounds of the Hofburg and then onward into the touristy glitz of the Kohlmarkt, almost noonday-lit by the lights beaming from luxury-brand store windows. My grandmother must have brought my mother here for special shopping trips, followed by a visit to Café Demel, just nearby.

On the walk home I found a hotel with English signage and a restaurant in the straight-outta-Brooklyn lobby, where I grabbed one of the hotel's promotional newpapers to read as I ate soup with thick crusty bread. According to the UK *Independent*, Vienna had been voted most livable city for the tenth year in a row, in part because of its progressive housing policies. A little bit of 1920s-era Social Democratic "Red" Vienna had returned, it seemed, in spite of the conservative federal government currently in office.

I had a lot to do in a week. Just one full day on my own to be a tourist and then I'd be meeting Franz Novotny in person for the first time. I would see my grandfather's printing factory and the machine that still produced the *Pulverkapseln*. I had meetings planned with historians Tim Corbett and Johann Kirchknopf, who had given Liza and me a tour of the Jewish quarter in 2012. I had an opera ticket. And without doubt I was going to eat a lot of desserts.

After my meal I walked back to the apartment, trying to acclimate my ears to the new language, heard in musical snippets of passing conversation. The streets were as immaculate as I remembered from my previous trip: no flattened pastel wads of chewing gum, no trash, no cigarette butts. Unlike in New York, people waited for red lights to turn to green even when no cars were in sight. A trolley clattered by with Viennese on their way to the center city, for this Saturday night was still young. Shoe stores, cafés, hair salons, a promising-looking vintage clothing store, and a CBD shop lined the street. I passed by a chapter of the Austrian mountain-climbing club—the Alpenverein—that had once rejected Jewish members like my grandfather. Back at my studio apartment I descended into a leaden sleep.

———————

IT WAS MIDMORNING, predawn back in New York, as I walked to the Belvedere Museum, and the sunshine tasted like a vitamin infusion. Below the palace formal curlicues of hedge cloaked in early-spring green swirled in an ocean of pea gravel. The stark contrast of green against tan and the absence of blooming flowers gave me an appreciation for the detail of the geometry and soothed me. I was ready to look at art. In the lower Belvedere I walked through an exhibit of early twentieth-century women artists whose lives and work had been mostly forgotten: Nazis opposed what they saw as the decadent influences of modern art as well as the idea of women having lives outside strictly defined ideals of motherhood and home. Some of these women artists were Jewish and had died in concentration camps. Some had survived National Socialism, but their work had been neglected in the aftermath of the war.

Now I was prepared for one of the Vienna bucket list tourist experiences—Gustav Klimt's *The Kiss*—and I tried to gird myself for what I knew would be an onslaught of iPhone-snapping tourists as absurd as the crowds surrounding the *Mona Lisa* in Paris. Liza and I had run this gauntlet on our trip together when she was young. I hurried up the marble stairs, ahead of a busload of foreign tourists, who moved like a school of fish circling their tour guide, hoping to beat them to my destination. Once in the gallery I found the portrait of the embracing couple and took a spot where I could study the layering of pigments that created the rich flesh tones and the intricate mosaic of jewel colors and gold leaf.

The clump of tourists arrived, filling the room with the burbles of their language. They surrounded me in an arc and their leader began to explain the painting with words and gestures. They began to press in for a closer look and pulled out their phones. A few took positions on either side of me to snap selfies. A snobby rage ignited and seethed. *Goddamn fucking phones.* One man tapped me on the shoulder and gestured for me to move so that he, too, could take a selfie. And that was it. I could have blamed jet lag, but really it was all me, my inner New Yorker, the caretaker who navigated crowds on Fifth Avenue and crowded subways and spent years shutting down catcalling guys with a sneer.

"No," I said, knowing full well the man couldn't understand a word I was saying. "I'm not moving." I was feeling suddenly quite protective, even proprietary about *The Kiss*. "I came a long way to see this painting and I am going to stay here until I am finished looking at the painting." The tour guide, who could understand me, stopped explicating the glories of Vienna 1900 and tried to calm her school of fish. Like a snotty teenager I thought to myself, *I'm gonna stay here as long as I goddamn please*. But after five petulant minutes I moved on. The fish swarmed in toward the bait and I raced off into quieter galleries. Later I rewarded myself with a plate of apple strudel swimming in a pool of crème anglaise.

In the gift shop everything was *The Kiss*. How expertly Austria had monetized this painting, an effort that must have accelerated after the equally legendary *Woman in Gold*, whose Jewish face once adorned the nation's postage stamps, was returned to its rightful owner in the United States. I had visited her many times at the Neue Galerie in Manhattan. She felt like family.

I WAS A few minutes late the following morning to the Café Hawelka to meet Franz, who stood up to greet me. "And here you are," he said, beaming, "finally in person." After all our correspondence and Skype calls, our meeting felt as natural for me as if we worked together in Vienna every day. He ordered me a *kleiner Brauner* (espresso with a splash of foamy milk) and then ducked out for a quick smoke, an urgent necessity, though he was nursing a cold. When he returned, I told him I'd seen a portrait at the Belvedere Museum the day before of an art critic named Novotny, was he related? "No," he said. "*Novotny* means 'Newman' in Czech, so there are pages and pages of us in the phone book." However common his name, he was a singular and stylish dresser, with swagger. He was color-blind, he told me, so he chose bold colors and patterns he could see clearly.

Franz had arranged a tour of the Jewish Museum, just up the street from the Hawelka. After a walk through the exhibitions, our guide brought us upstairs to view additional collections, including walking sticks topped with crude anti-Semitic caricatures of long-nosed faces—appalling—even more so when she told us that one could still find these relics in antique stores. Some buyers still found them humorous. The museum also housed a collection of religious objects from synagogues destroyed during Kristallnacht in November of 1938, including candelabras and eternal lamps blackened and warped in the fire that gutted the temple in Währing, where my mother attended services as a child. The objects had not been repaired or cleaned but were instead a ghastly visual reminder of the terrifying pogrom. The sound of smashing glass at the Währing Temple would have carried throughout the neighborhood, empowering to many Viennese who had welcomed the Anschluss, terrifying for families like the Singers whose lives were already in turmoil, especially for a young child.

WIND WHIPPED THE bare tree branches as I made my way to the State Opera for a performance of Mozart's *The Marriage of Figaro*. Often described as one of those comedies where it's best not to dwell too much on the logic of the plot, my reading of a detailed synopsis suggested that the story of the servant Susanna, who evades forced sex with her superior, Count Almaviva, and exposes his lechery felt freshly relevant. I took my seat way up high in the balcony and waited for the performance to begin.

Before I left New York my father had reminded me that when he and my mother visited Vienna in 1956, her first trip home since fleeing in 1940, they had seen this same opera. At that time, the city was still in tatters following heavy Allied bombing and the opera house was still being rebuilt, so that night's performance was held in one of the spaces of the Hofburg, an opulent setting that required no stage sets.

After the performance—breathtaking even in the cheap seats—I crossed the street for a late supper at the hushed Café Sacher, home of the celebrated eponymous chocolate cake. With the opera's melodies still ringing in my ear, I imagined how extraordinary that long-ago evening must have been for my mother: a performance of light comedy in a city that was struggling to re-create its former elegance and chase away the ghosts of the recent past. It was nearly midnight when I rushed across the nearly empty square to a taxi stand, the wind still blowing hard.

I MET TIM Corbett for lunch at the Bräunerhof café, which was charming and packed with customers. It was impossible to avoid politics, so we got that out of the way.

While Vienna had done much to shake off its musty fur coat, Austria at large had tilted to the right along with other European nations. In the aftermath of the 2017 election, with no party winning a majority, the center right People's Party (ÖVP) had formed a coalition government with the far right Freedom Party (FPÖ) founded by former Nazis in the 1950s. Sebastian Kurz of the ÖVP became prime minister and Herbert Kickl of the FPÖ became interior minister, espousing a populist anti-immigrant platform. In just one of many shocker statements since joining Kurz's government, Kickl said he wanted to "concentrate" immigrants in one place, using the German word *konzentriert*, a startling reference to the prison camps of the Holocaust. After much criticism, Kickl tried to walk back his statement, but his position remained powerful in that the interior ministry controlled issues related to immigration. There had been calls for his resignation, but during my week in Vienna he was still very much in office.

When I mentioned to Tim that the government appeared to be in the process of revising its citizenship laws to permit Jewish descendants of Holocaust victims and refugees to apply, Tim commented that the government might be motivated by a circular anti-immigration idea: *We will amend the citizenship laws; Jews can apply; but Muslims hate Jews, so let's allow Jews (Europeans) to return and keep out the Muslims.* In my desire to reclaim my mother's birthright, I hadn't thought about this.

A few weeks earlier Tim had sent me several articles by Klaus Hödl, a historian little known outside the German-speaking world, as most of his writing has not been translated into English. In some of his work Hödl looked at the idea of Jewish "difference" and "similarity" as social constructs. He has considered prewar Jewish life in Vienna from this point of view, focusing on "similarity" rather than "difference," by noting how much daily and casual interplay there was between Jews and Gentiles. This interaction included everything from work to love. The overlapping was pervasive enough that even during the rise of Austrian fascism and finally the incursion of the Nazi Party, a man like my grandfather could continue to genuinely self-identify as Viennese, Austrian, and Jewish, in that order, without self-delusion about his family's safety.

Assimilated was the word traditionally used to describe my family's life as Jews in Vienna, an adjective that Tim and other Jewish historians disliked.

"'Assimilate' to what?" Tim said. "Austrian-ness? What exactly was 'Austrian'?" Jews like the Singers had been in Vienna for several generations. They spoke German, or more correctly, the Viennese dialect. They didn't speak Yiddish at home. The Singers wore the same clothes as their Gentile neighbors, ate the same food except during Jewish holidays (however traditionally those were observed), and enjoyed the same culture, both high and low, Mozart and light opera.

Tim pointed out that Vienna had been a migration hub for centuries. A huge population of Czech immigrants arrived in Vienna during the nineteenth century, for example, but no one used the word *assimilation* to describe their cultural integration into the larger whole of the Austrian Empire. In fact, Tim remarked, most people didn't realize how much natural and everyday flow there had been between Jews and Gentiles in work and social environments. Even the dialect bore evidence of this exchange: there were many Czech words and, unknown to most Viennese, many words derived from Hebrew and Yiddish.

I asked for examples. Tim offered *Tohuwabohu*, or "chaos," from the line in Genesis, "without form and void." Another was *beisl*, Yiddish for "cozy eatery," like the one where we were sitting. I had already seen this word posted in signage for cafés, restaurants, and inns.

"Cultural encounters are not one-way," Tim said. "There is give-and-take with language, ideas, and culture. All Europeans went through processes of secularization, modernization, urbanization, nationalization, et cetera, that led to sweeping changes in language, culture, practice, social structures, and so forth. And Judaism itself isn't a homogenous or static religion or culture."

I could certainly understand this. The range of "Jewishness" I'd observed at home included Hasidism (a nineteenth-century fundamentalist emergence), Orthodox, Conservative, and Reform communities, as well as secular Jews like myself who identified with the culture but not the practice of faith.

Tim continued. "The crucial point is that Jewish Austrians in the early twentieth century didn't 'imagine' or 'kid themselves' that they *were* Austrians; they simply were Austrians."

Just like I was an American, whatever that was. Just like my mother, Eva, who had become an American Eve.

"Simultaneously," Tim said, "the society around them wasn't exclusively anti-Semitic. The very cultural fruitfulness of the fin de siècle, for example, is a prime example of the complex interplay between Jews and non-Jews. And this despite the fact that Vienna had an anti-Semitic mayor— Karl Lueger, who considered himself an opportunistic anti-Semite— who counted a number of Jews in his circle of friends and advisors."

Interplay seemed like a word to try out as a replacement for *assimilation*. People and communities changed, evolved, and at their best they interplayed, like children bouncing a ball back and forth.

"With language," Tim said, "what's important is the word, who says the word, and in what context. I hope we will see some paradigm-shifting in how we see the Jews of Vienna, not so much how they were different, but to focus on similarity."

I liked this idea. It was more complicated, but comforting to think that my grandfather Julius, whom I considered to be a world-savvy man, had not been delusional in loving his city and feeling at home here. As I forked up my first dessert of the day—a sweet apricot cake, specialty of the house—I wondered how often Julius had eaten lunch at the Bräunerhof alongside the great variety of his Viennese neighbors.

Franz, Vienna native, descendant of Czech immigrants, arrived as we finished our desserts, and drank a *kleiner Brauner*. And then we were off.

FRANZ DROVE TOWARD a small factory on the outskirts of Vienna, where we would see the machine, the one that made the paper fan, the *Pulverkapseln*. We parked in a grassy driveway. I could smell spring in the air, and something else, potent, pleasantly toxic, and familiar.

In a cramped front office, Franz introduced me to a man about my age who to my relief spoke in English. My hands were jittery. I could barely endure my over-caffeinated anticipation. Still, one had to do and say the polite things. Here I was, an American, barging into their factory with a story from the past. I had learned to be patient, to give people time to understand that I wasn't here to reclaim anything from them, in spite of what had happened to my family decades earlier. A woman who looked to be in her seventies came forward as well. She and her son—this was a family business—smiled and we all shook hands. "*Danke*," I said nervously, like a kid on the first day at a new school. "Thank you for your time." The son pushed open the door into the pressroom and we followed.

The scent I'd caught a whiff of in the parking lot—the bittersweet perfume of ink and solvent—and the not-quite-deafening metallic cacophony of a live printing press smacked me hard: the sensory memory of my parents' working lives and mine. I was the third generation in the ink and paper business.

Scenes rushed back: a long-ago trip during my childhood to a typesetter in New England where I'd watched a man busy at the Linotype machine keyboard, the metal slugs of typed lines in reverse clanking down one by one until paragraphs and pages formed. He typed out my name and my brother's onto individual slugs and I hung on to that piece of metal for years until it was lost in a house move. Then years later, my first solo trip to a printer for a press check on behalf of the art director at my first publishing job: it had been an honor to be trusted with this task (the cover for a memoir by a famous author and a soon-to-be bestseller!) and I belabored it, my ears ringing as I watched sheet after sheet of paper spit out of the press, each with subtle variations of color tone and ink density, wanting to be surer than sure that I'd done my best. So much paper.

And then, my eyes and throat already smarting with emotion, I turned and saw it: something at least a century old, not so large, about four feet high and eight feet long, a much-tinkered-with one-off, made of hundreds of hand-fabricated metal pieces. I stopped, stupefied, and clapped a hand over my O-shaped mouth so that I wouldn't lose it completely. Franz caught my eye and smiled. I wiped the damp from my eyes and tried to focus. It was a miracle. Maybe Franz had really found it: the machine so complicated that the Nazis had kept Julius alive to run it.

The son began to explain how the machine operated. Two fat coils of paper about two and a half inches wide were mounted on posts on two levels. The paper fed through a piece of curved metal about the size of a man's palm, which gently folded the piece in half, and then on that strip went, down the line, and the fold was made precise and crisp, and then narrower sections were folded in, and then the thrice-folded strip was cut into sections about one inch wide and four inches long, which were then glued one to another. At the end there were fifty of these folded sheets joined into a finished piece that resembled the pages of a closed book in the days when you still had to slit each page to read it. This was one fan. When I unfurled it to reveal the hidden pouches formed from the folded and glued sections, the effect was even more magical than when I'd opened the first one Franz had mailed me a year earlier, because now I understood the mechanics of it all and I had seen this machine.

Could there be more than one of this strange contraption? As I peered at the machine closely I could see that the individual components had been custom fabricated and then later repaired, right down to nuts and bolts. Could this be my grandfather's machine? Translating for his mother, the son told me that his father had purchased this machine in 1951 or 1952. She couldn't recall the details, he said, but they could look into that.

My mother had told me that after the war her father had tried to locate his factory machinery but he'd been told that the equipment had all been sold to a company in Germany. That had always sounded like a political dodge to me. I could understand how attached Julius would have been to the machine, his mechanical baby. What if instead of being shipped to Germany, the machine had instead left 22 Weimarer Strasse for another family-owned factory in Vienna? That made more sense to me.

The son pointed to a horizontal box mounted on the wall with a series of small drawers in a row, each with a white china knob.

"This came with the machine," he said.

He pulled out one of the drawers. Inside was a copper die stamped in traditional blackletter Gothic type with the name of a pharmacy: Hans Sachs Apotheke. The address was listed as Wien 18, Wahringer Strasse 84. I looked up the address on my phone, and the pharmacy was still operating in the same location, about four streets away from 22 Weimarer Strasse.

I studied the machine again, the whole length of it. I touched a small section of pitted metal that looked like it had been rewelded some time long ago and it warmed under my skin. I felt a zingy sensation, like there was some friendly presence near me, my imagination's Julius, asking me to look closer, to understand that he had touched this machine every day of his working life and that he and Herr Mazura had made those repairs. This had to be it. In that moment I could feel it as sure as I knew anything in this world. This was it. Not just a similar machine, but The Machine.

I stood there in a trance state, imagining the day when I would be able to connect all the dots with absolute certainty, but Franz tapped me on the shoulder, reminding me that we had two more stops on our afternoon itinerary.

THREE OR FOUR stops, actually, because with Franz there was always a good reason to drink another coffee and maybe eat something. He pulled up in front of an impressive old stone structure, telling me that this had once been the site of a business that fabricated funerary monuments—which made sense, as we were now just across the street from the Jewish Central Cemetery. We each ordered a *kleiner Brauner*. Franz ordered chocolate torte and suggested something for me, in German, and I agreed without understanding what would arrive. It turned out to be two generous pieces of apple-and-cheese-filled strudel floating in another frothy pool of crème anglaise. I got through half and then set my fork down, defeated. "Do you mind if I have some?" Franz asked. Apparently, the man was bottomless. "There are small deer in the cemetery," he said as he ate my leftovers. "We call them Capricorns. It's quite a wild place, you'll see."

It had rained lightly while we were inside, but now the afternoon was clearing, sun-washed with racing clouds. Dodging afternoon traffic, we crossed the busy road and made our way through the iron gates into an enchanted city of monuments overhung with reawakening tall trees and vines, a vision from *The Sleeping Beauty*. Leaves were swelling on the understory shrubs. Snowdrops were peeking out of the leaf cover and clotted grasses. The concrete paths were lined in damp moss. Sunlight broke through the canopy in shafts that reminded me of the mystical and romantic landscapes of the German painter Caspar David Friedrich, who in his later years spent time in cemeteries, sketching mausoleums and even creating funerary art. The farther we walked in, the more remote the city felt. I heard the same unfamiliar birdsong from my previous days in the city and squirrels cackled in the rustling branches. Otherwise it was quiet. Franz pointed down a long pathway toward a sunny clearing and, sure enough, a small deer stood rigid as a statue, alert to our presence, before it leapt into the woodland.

Now I could look at the monuments. Some were grand mausoleums designed with neoclassical nods to Greek and Roman styles, evidence of the same nineteenth- and early twentieth-century pastiche of styles I saw at home. The typography on the mausoleums and headstones was also varied—from classical lapidary Romans to more florid cursives, familiar to me as a graphic designer. I found a Singer family, and for a moment I was hopeful, but I didn't recognize the first names, and Singer was a common-enough Jewish surname. We made our way along the paths, admiring columns of polished veined marble that must have come from Italy, and ornately carved birds and animals, both realistic and fantastical. I noticed fancier "neighborhoods," where wealthy families had spent lavishly to leave a trace of their lineage and impress the competition, alongside clusters of more modest memorials. Here in the city of the dead, class distinctions were preserved just like in the living city.

We continued along the avenues. Some stones were pitted, toppled, or broken in pieces. Franz said this was from the heavy bombing at the end of the war. One long stone was tipping precariously on just one corner, held in place by a tree branch that would eventually give way, that afternoon or the following week or twenty years from now. In my mind I could hear the sound of the branch cracking and the stone slowly toppling and shattering as it hit the neighboring monument. I wondered who would witness and be startled by that event, perhaps just the Capricorns and squirrels and birds. Then I rewound the scene, imagining how it all might unfold without the forest sounds: branch breaking, stone toppling, Capricorns and squirrels fleeing, birds rushing upward accompanied by a lamentation of strings composed by Max Richter. I could hear it. Right then I wanted everything, all the feels, as Liza liked to say, and a good cry later.

For a moment I wondered why no family members had come to repair the damaged stones. Then I remembered how few Jewish families from that era were left in Vienna. Those small numbers who returned—people like Mr. Weiss—might not have wanted to visit such a vivid reminder of their eviscerated culture.

———

BACK IN FRANZ'S car we made our way back into the city. It was rush hour, so as traffic jerked forward I had a chance to admire buildings and squares, pleased that I now had some familiarity with the inner-city landmarks. The last clouds had broken up and a sparkling, late-afternoon sun filled windows as if with flames. We wound our way through the center city, and soon we were heading out toward the Gürtel, the "belt," or outer ring, of Vienna.

"Another coffee," Franz announced as he parked near Türken-schanzpark. We walked to the café near the small pond where Liza and I had fed ducks in 2012.

"Are you ready to see your grandfather's factory?" Franz asked as we drank a *kleiner Brauner*. It had been an emotional afternoon, but I would have time to myself later to sift through everything I'd seen in one day. I was ready.

A short drive away Franz parked again, and there we were, at number 22 Weimarer Strasse, with its imposing door and gargoyle. Franz unlocked the door and we went inside, my first time since that summer of 1980.

I was completely disoriented. This was all wrong. There was no white-marble lobby, no grand winding staircase or cage elevator. Instead we walked down a long stone-cobbled hallway. The walls were decorated in amber-toned faux marble, accented with pilasters topped with gilded sculptures of goddesses. It all looked original. Where the hell was I?

I followed Franz down the hall to a door leading out to the rear courtyard, and there, to my relief, I could see the factory building I recalled from my earlier trip with Michelle. To my left was a short flight of stairs leading to a locked gate through which I could see a landing, apartment doors, a flight of stairs, and a narrow elevator shaft. Is this where the painters had been in 1980? I was so attached to that memory, and now I could see that my memory was faulty. I was an unreliable narrator of my own story.

I told Franz that I needed to walk back to the front door and start over. I paced the hallway again, touching the wall surface, inspecting the goddess heads. I joined Franz and looked up at the flight of stairs, still bewildered.

"Are you all right?" Franz asked.

"I don't understand. I remember this hallway so differently. I just need a moment to collect myself." I walked to the stairs and rested my hand on the burnished wooden banister and it was as smooth as I imagined it would be and somehow familiar.

"This wooden railing, your grandfather's hand touched it, and your mother and the rest of your family."

And then, in a flash, I remembered a lunch hour after I'd been hired as an assistant at a small design studio a few streets away from the Waldorf grade school I'd attended for several years as a young child. That day, in the grip of nostalgia for kindergarten, I had decided to visit my former school, located in a fine old limestone townhouse on East Seventy-Ninth Street. The lobby was large, especially for a young child, with a marble floor and a sweeping staircase and a wooden banister that my small hand glided over every morning and afternoon. For the most part, these were sweet years that included the magical thrill of learning how to read and draw and to play Beethoven's "Ode to Joy" on a wooden recorder. In fact, as I'd walked up the stairs, I could hear a roomful of children hooting away, as if no time had passed at all. My yearning for lost childhood temporarily sated, I'd walked back down, my hand sliding along the banister—

—And now I dropped back into myself in front of the stairs in the lobby of number 22, my hand still resting on the wooden banister.

"Oh, I understand now," I said to Franz. It made sense as a kind of emotional transference. I'd conflated two childhood experiences, my own and my imagining of my mother's here in Vienna. I tried to reorganize my memory banks so that I could replace my recollection of the white school lobby with this image before me now. Had the painters been standing on ladders in the amber hallway? What had they been painting? Everything else about the story I'd held on to so hard still felt intact: Mr. Weiss, the Manner wafers, the piano shawl, and the bay window.

"Come, let's go in," said Franz. "We'll have a coffee." This would be my fifth for the day. He led me into the factory, and this space felt known to me from the photos he had sent me when we first connected by email. Here was the red concrete floor and the two heavy wooden tables, where a young woman sat now, finishing up her day's work. Farther on was an ornate desk where Franz worked. There were the metal racks packed with project files. Down a short flight of stairs was the daylit room with the large square conference table surrounded by white Eames chairs. The skylights overhead cast a cool light. Franz went into a side room and soon I could hear the espresso machine. He set a glass before me with a perfect shot.

"This must be where the machines were, don't you think?" I asked Franz.

He agreed. "Yes, the machines down here and then the big tables up above for packing everything, and right out the door would have been a truck waiting to deliver."

"Do you think clients ever came here?"

"No, I don't think so," he said, and then downed his espresso swiftly. "More likely Julius started out as a salesperson, with a sample book, going around to all the pharmacies. This kind of factory was mostly a Jewish business and most of the *Apotheken* as well."

"Julius was a handsome man," I said. "I'm sure he did very well as a salesman." And soon enough he was a partner and then Adolf Eisenmann died, leaving Julius to run the firm.

I sipped the last of my coffee, vowing to decaffeinate as soon as I got home. I asked Franz where he was planning to spend the summer and we spoke about our plans for the upcoming months.

Franz asked, "Did your mother ever tell you about the family *Sommerfrische?*

"*Sommerfrische?*"

"Summer holidays. Do you know where they went?"

I told Franz about the informal Jewish summer camp my mother and her brothers had attended.

"There were these big resort hotels that were popular with Jewish families," Franz said. On his laptop he showed me photographs of the grand Südbahn Hotel in Semmering, a sprawling building nestled like a castle in the mountains, its vast open terrace offering a vista like something out of *The Sound of Music*. "This hotel was very popular with Viennese Jews. Some hotels even in the twenties didn't welcome Jewish guests."

"My mother never mentioned anything like this. Nothing this grand."

I wondered if maybe the Singers had gone to one of these hotels when the children were younger. It seemed like Julius enjoyed being in real wilderness. Perhaps it was Anna who lobbied to join the children at the beach in Cesenatico during that last summer in 1937. The photograph of the hotel made me smile. I could understand why Jewish émigrés would later flock to resort hotels in the Catskill Mountains, which didn't approach the grandeur of the Austrian Alps but were still beautiful with just a taste of something rustic.

—————

FRANZ DROVE ME through his childhood neighborhood, then onto the street where his family had lived called Lange Gasse. The name was so familiar to me for no reason I could think of until I recalled that Michelle and I had stayed here back in 1980. How strangely circular everything had turned out to be. Franz pointed out two small hotels as we navigated the narrow street.

"Do you remember the name of where you stayed?" Franz asked.

"No, but it would have been whichever was cheapest. We were on a tight budget." I remembered Michelle and me jumping up and down on the eiderdown quilts.

"Back then it was cheap to live here."

I saw an appealing small side street and decided to walk back to my apartment from there. Franz's car darted off and I headed down the quieter street, stopping to look in the window of a violin shop. There was one instrument hanging up on the wall that looked like mine. Inside, a woman was trying out violins, playing musical phrases I recognized. A man dropped by who just happened to be the concertmaster for the Vienna Philharmonic. He played, too. The proprietors, a husband and wife, didn't seem to mind that I was hanging around for the impromptu concert. The wife told me she would be glad to identify my humble instrument if I sent her a photo of the label inside. Later that evening I did that. The following morning she wrote that my violin had been made in a town that was once called Schönbach, part of Prussia, now part of the Czech Republic. She said practically everyone in that town was involved in some aspect of making violins. My violin was now connected to a particular place in the old country.

SHORTLY AFTER FRANZ and I connected in 2016, he suggested that I contact a law firm in Vienna to explore regaining Austrian citizenship. The lawyer who replied to my inquiry told me that he was disappointed to confirm what I already knew—that the Austrian government had changed the laws in the mid-1980s so that children of refugees could only apply for citizenship if their fathers had been Austrian. He said that his firm had tried and failed in previous attempts to petition against the unfairness of this law and that he regretted having to send me this news because he was, in fact, the same young man who'd interviewed my mother in 2004 for the Leo Baeck Institute.

I wasn't surprised by the coincidence—it was just another charged moment of synchronicity in my research. I was also not surprised that Austria had placed this legal obstacle in the paths of so many children of Jewish refugees at a time when my generation had been navigating early adulthood, more focused on finishing college and getting a job than in reclaiming history. The injustice of this law stung me whenever I dwelt on it.

After the Austrian coalition government formed in 2017, Israel protested the FPÖ's history of anti-Semitism. In response, Chancellor Kurz promised to restore citizenship rights to the children of Holocaust survivors like my brother and me, intending to win over Jews both in Israel and the Diaspora while maintaining Austria's anti-immigrant policies. After my talks with Tim Corbett, I understood the dark pragmatism of this gesture, but I still thought to myself that this was something I could reclaim for my mother, and I relished the idea that I might be able to gain EU citizenship for myself and pass it on to Liza.

And so, on my last morning in Vienna I went to the law firm to meet with one of the principals who worked on citizenship and restitution cases. I expected him to tell me that the Kurz government was dragging out the process as long as possible, but to my surprise he explained that the law had passed the previous autumn and that an amendment was now being drafted to allow for dual citizenship, so that American Jews who weren't ready to give up on their country could still apply. "It could be ready soon," he said. "As soon as August." I was ready to move forward.

After this hopeful meeting I met Franz, his daughter, and her boyfriend for lunch at a nearby restaurant. After we finished our main courses, Franz insisted I order *Lekvártascherl*. My last Viennese dessert—crispy light pockets of potato dough bursting with thick plum jam—filled me to overflowing. How did Franz do it? I wondered as he ate what I left behind. Franz drove us back to number 22 for one last visit to Julius's factory. As we drank a last coffee together, I marveled again at my tangled memories, relieved that I now had the correct image of the building imprinted where the previous one had lodged for so long. Franz drove me back to my apartment, we did the double-cheek kissing, and then he sped away. I climbed the stairs to my apartment and began to pack.

PART THREE

PART THREE

Two Years

"Overnight! This was all overnight." Years later, Erika M. still could
not hide her astonishment at the collapse of Austria, at the end of her
country, on the night of the eleventh of March, in the pivotal year of 1938.
                                    —Timothy Snyder, *Black Earth*

*There, on the balcony of Sissi's palace, speaking in a voice that
was terribly strange, lyrical, and disturbing, ending with a hoarse,
unpleasant cry, was Hitler.*
                                    —Éric Vuillard, *The Order of the Day*

— ANSCHLUSS —

THE ANSCHLUSS, THE German annexation of Austria,
began on the night of March 11, 1938. Hitler and his soldiers
had already crossed the border into Austria and were making their way, town by town, toward Vienna. They were greeted by
throngs of cheering Austrians who had wanted to be joined with their
fellow German-speakers since the end of the First World War. While
progress was slower than Hitler had hoped, it was all happening now,
like a coalescence of two water droplets drawing toward each other.

The lead-up to this day had been years in the making. The once-impoverished artist in Vienna who had consigned several mediocre paintings with Jakob Altenberg had become chancellor of Germany in 1933. As part of an overarching vision of establishing Aryan dominance, fueled by his rabid anti-Semitism, he wanted his German empire to absorb all the German-speaking people of Austria and the Sudetenland before he launched his grander schemes for European domination. As Tim Snyder describes in *Black Earth*, Hitler's goals were expansionist and exclusionary from the outset: more territory for Aryan people meant the removal of those he considered pollutants—Jews, other minorities, all dissenters who resisted his goals. This was a zero-sum game.

The Austrofascist government in Austria, led by Chancellor Kurt Schuschnigg since the assassination of Engelbert Dollfuss in 1934, was determined to maintain its independence in keeping with the Austro-German Agreement of 1936. Schuschnigg was himself very much a dictator, of the Catholic variety, but Austria was still a republic on paper. Julius Singer had done well enough under this rule. Many Jews in the IKG—Jakob Ehrlich, for example—and in other organizations were at least tacitly supportive of the authoritarian regime, as it maintained the independence of Austria and a status quo in which anti-Semitism was kept at bay.

But in early 1938, an impatient Hitler issued a series of threats; he summoned Schuschnigg to a meeting in Germany on February 12, 1938, and the ultimatums began. Hitler wanted the Nazi Party to be allowed to operate in Austria, for all jailed Nazis in Austria to be released, and for the Austrian government to reinstate Nazis who had lost their jobs in the civil service and military. He insisted that Arthur Seyss-Inquart, a Nazi, be named as Minister of the Interior, a position that held power over the police. (Seyss-Inquart was an enthusiastic mountaineer, at one time head of the German-Austrian alpine club that had evicted its Jewish members years earlier.) Hitler also wanted influence over the all-important propaganda efforts in Austria. He gave the Austrians three days to accede to these demands. Fearful for his own fate, Schuschnigg ultimately surrendered.

It wasn't quite that easy to dissolve a republic, even one governed by Fascists who were not exactly bound by the will of the people, and even under threat of imminent invasion. But it wouldn't take long for independence to unravel.

Once back in Vienna, Schuschnigg dutifully appointed Seyss-Inquart as Minister of the Interior. But then, even after the process of Austria's absorption into the German Reich had already begun, Schuschnigg had second thoughts. He announced that Austria would remain independent after all. Austrian Nazis demonstrated against this decision, but Schuschnigg, in a last gasp, ordered a plebiscite to determine the public's desire for an independent country.

Hitler, who thought he'd made his position perfectly clear, was furious. His response to Schuschnigg's act of defiance was to close the border at Salzburg and stop railway service between the countries.

By the morning of March 11, German troops were massing close to the border. Hitler sent his latest ultimatum: Schuschnigg must cancel the plebiscite or Germany would invade. Schuschnigg paused for a few hours, then canceled the plebiscite. But now Hitler insisted that Schuschnigg be immediately replaced by Seyss-Inquart. Nazis stormed the Austrian chancellery; Schuschnigg resigned. President Miklas, in a futile act of defiance, at first refused to accept the resignation, or to appoint Seyss-Inquart in his place, to Hitler's further fury. But by the end of that day, Schuschnigg was out, and Miklas had duly installed Seyss-Inquart. Nazis were on the move from Germany to Austria. Like a long-penned dog that has been trained to attack, the monster of anti-Semitism was about to be unleashed in Vienna.

ON MARCH 11, many people went about their usual business unaware of the high-stakes ultimatums from Berlin. It was a Friday. Children went to school. People went to their jobs. Women at home took care of young children and shopped for the weekend. Religious Jewish families prepared for the Sabbath.

What could even a worldly Jewish man like Julius have known about Adolf Hitler's belligerent pursuit of his homeland? Julius may have gone to his usual café, where he may have been able to read through the lines of the newspaper stories and sensed that the republic of Austria was facing a grave danger. Perhaps he left his café troubled, but still put in hours at his factory, and then returned home to apartment 5. On the night of March 11, people attended the opera in the center of Vienna as if it were just another evening in late winter. It is possible that Julius heard reports on the radio of German troop movements or perhaps Julius spoke to Jakob, whose centrally located gallery may have given him a better sense of the brewing unrest.

———————

FOR ITS VICTIMS, the violence that began in Vienna on the evening of March 11 appeared to be random and unplanned, but a ground game had been organized in advance. For Hitler and his many Nazi supporters, even Vienna under Austrofascist Schuschnigg (who had banned the Austrian Nazi Party) was still "Red Vienna" and a Jewish city. Hitler's aim was to undermine everything that had made Vienna unique as a cultural center, to bring it to heel, to render it into a backwater of his larger Reich. This meant taking over the city with an iron fist and implementing a plan to identify Vienna's two hundred thousand Jews, extract their wealth, and remove them by force. This had always been the plan.

In Gregor von Rezzori's 1969 novel, *Memoirs of an Anti-Semite*, there is a chilling description of the morning of March 12. The narrator of the five stories that make up the novel is not an evil man. He is not a Nazi. In fact, he doesn't care about politics as long as world events do not affect his own pursuits and desires. He cares about his own comforts, without regard for the consequences of his casual acts of prejudice and cruelty. Born in a remote eastern region of Rumania—then still part of the vast Habsburg Empire—he has a sense of self-regard based on his aristocratic heritage and a strong connection to Vienna, where he was educated. As a narrator, he is eloquent, self-deprecating, ironic, and sometimes, to my own discomfort, hilarious. From his child-hood onward, he is fascinated and repelled by Jewishness. In one story he is a young man with few prospects, in the employ of a cosmetics company. His demeaning job requires him to approach shop owners for permission to clean and redecorate their display windows featuring his company's products. (As I read this story I imagined that some of these fictional stores carried soaps and other bath items with labels printed by Adolf Eisenmann und Sohn.) The narrator begins an affair with the Jewish widow who owns one of the shops, his desire fueled in equal parts by his attraction to the physicality of her Jewish Otherness, and his frank disgust for her less-than-highbrow style. In another story, he befriends a young Jewish woman in the boardinghouse where he is liv-ing, only to callously betray her trust, with devastating consequences.

In the story "Troth," the narrator arrives in Vienna on March 11 to meet his lover. On March 12, as they wake, the world has changed.

> Next morning, we stood at the windows and looked down at the Opernring, now empty, where all the night through there had been ecstasy—a sudden ecstasy that had its source in the silent marching blocks, and that drew people out of their houses and made them run toward the marchers, shouting, roaring, embracing one another, swinging flags with swasti-kas, throwing their arms to heaven, jumping and dancing in delirium. It was an icy-cold yet gloriously sunny day, quite unusual for the middle of March. . . . Over the radio we had learned that Austria was about to unite with the German Reich, and the Germans were expected to come here triumphantly, as our brethren, in a huge parade, under a rain of flowers.

There were Austrians who lamented the end of their sovereign nation. My uncle Dolfi recalled that on March 12 a radio station played Schubert's *Unfinished Symphony* over and over, from its dark opening, to the plaintive woodwind melody, broken at intervals by full orchestral explosions. Dolfi remembered this radio broadcast as a wordless plea for listeners to remember what they were losing on that fateful day.

The Singers must have felt somewhat insulated from the unfolding madness as they woke up on Saturday, March 12. Their apartment building in the neighborhood of Währing was beyond the Ringstrasse, the wide circular boulevard that separated the center city from the outskirts, a world away from the old Jewish quarter of Leopoldstadt in the 2nd district. While the percentage of Jews was statistically below ten percent, it was increasingly a neighborhood where upper-middle-class Jews chose to live. By 1938 Julius had been settled in the district for at least fifteen years. The familiar streets of Währing included his home, his business, and the synagogue where he'd married Anna and where my uncles had celebrated their bar mitzvahs.

Radio news must have sounded the first warning with reports of crowds in the center of the city and on the larger streets in Währing. Hitler had ordered his troops to take the same route into the city's center as emperors and dignitaries had in the past: along the Praterstrasse in Leopoldstrasse, which must have been terrifying for that Jewish neighborhood and just a hint of what was to come. But for a brief moment, in spite of news reports, the family might have continued with plans as if this were any other Saturday in March.

Whatever those plans might have been, when they opened the apartment door, the sight of young Matthias Steppan leaving his apartment across the hall in his Nazi uniform was the first visible sign that the news on the radio was real. For Julius and Anna, the world must have felt suddenly insane, an upending that should not stand in a republic. On the morning of March 12, Julius still believed that he was a citizen of Austria, with civil liberties.

Hitler's masters of propaganda understood that most people need time to adjust to a new reality and form a new plan of action. The Nazis wanted to make sure that for most Jews there would be no time to process and adapt.

My mother shared recollections of that day with her Austrian interviewer in 2004. *I remember right after the Anschluss that my father went downtown, I guess because he wanted to know what was going on, and he saw the troops coming in, and he saw people cheering. . . .* Her voice trailed off here before she continued. The sight of marching soldiers, shouting crowds of people with arms raised in salute to the arriving German soldiers must have been a chilling sight. *My father told all the people in the factory that they should join the party because it would be better for them. I think he was right.* Without understanding what would unfold in the next months, Julius was already trying to adapt.

By the time Hitler appeared in Vienna on March 15, before a crowd of several hundred thousand people assembled at the Heldenplatz— Heroes' Square—Austria as a sovereign republic was already erased. The election that followed was a mere formality. Austria was absorbed into the expanding fascist empire, renamed *Österreich*, after *östliches Reich*, or "eastern realm."

"The same blood belongs in a combined Reich!" proclaimed a banner above the entrance to the modernist building known as the Looshaus on Michaelerplatz in central Vienna. There was no room for Jewish blood in this pure Aryan land.

As Hitler and his supporters took over Vienna, Austria's always-simmering anti-Semitism fully exploded, quickly creating a state of fear in a Jewish community that had grown accustomed to a measure of acceptance. In welcoming the German Fascists, the Austrians had been officially granted permission to express their grievances with violence.

ONE SUMMER, LIZA and I were in Maine hiking on a cliff trail when an eerie storm cloud appeared seemingly out of nowhere. I had been walking straight on the path and the sky was bright blue ahead. I was vaguely aware of a chill and whine in the air and glad that we would be back at our inn soon. "Mom," Liza called out. "Look what's behind us!" The cloud hung down like a frigid inky hand that reached toward us with malice, as if prepared to seize hold of us. "It looks like a Dementor," Liza said, and I agreed, taking her hand tightly. A flash of lightning illuminated the cloud, followed by a low rumble and then a clap of thunder that set my ears ringing. Liza looked scared, and I was, too. We had been reading the Harry Potter novels as they were published, aware of the growing menace in that magical world, the gathering forces of darkness and evil that had already taken the lives of beloved characters. The soul-sucking Dementors were terrifying for me, the faceless manifestation of mind control and authoritarianism. Dreamland was not always a safe place for me. I had carried childhood nightmares all the way into adulthood, and now there was something right out of a nightmare coming right for me and my child. As the monster hand gathered up force, it shape-shifted, whipping up gusts from the open Atlantic. We sprinted on the uneven dirt path, trying to outpace the cloud, but it dumped its load of cold rain upon us as we ran for cover. How did we not see this thing coming? The sky was still blue in front of us and we just didn't see the approaching darkness, until it was on top of us.

For the Jews of Austria, changes blew in from Germany like that storm cloud. Decrees were issued curtailing Jewish civil liberties. Synagogues were desecrated. Shop windows were marked with anti-Semitic graffiti. The vibrant life of the Jewish intelligentsia came to a halt. Random street attacks of Jews became commonplace, the victims surrounded and forced to scrub the sidewalks on their knees. Jews were summarily kicked out of their apartments and homes, and their belongings were smashed or stolen. The climate of sudden despair was so catastrophic that hundreds of Jews, including entire families, committed suicide in March 1938 alone.

Steve Hochstadt's *Exodus to Shanghai* includes personal accounts of Jews who fled to Shanghai, a city that became an unlikely Jewish outpost. Eric Reisman, two years older than my mother, described the sudden change for young Jews in Vienna, one my mother must have experienced as well. The Anschluss immediately disrupted that beautiful muscle memory the Singers and other Jews had for their city.

The friends that we used to play football with, tag, hide-and-
seek, whatever young people played, they didn't want to know
you anymore. Suddenly you were an outcast.

Some normalcy continued, briefly. Those still employed went to
their jobs and ran their businesses. Work at Adolf Eisenmann und
Sohn continued, perhaps because most of the employees were Gentile.
If business for fancy soaps dropped off somewhat, there were still
plenty of orders for *Pulverkapseln.*

A month later, in April, Jakob Ehrlich was arrested.

A month after that he was dead.

Soon, Jewish children were forced to leave their neighborhood
schools and were herded into Jewish schools, taught by teachers
forced to leave previous posts. But this didn't happen overnight in
all cases. Fritz was still attending school with Matthias Steppan when
the neighbor boy failed—for the second time—his final high school
exams. Fritz, a year or so his junior, passed. Humiliated by his failure but emboldened by the status his new uniform gave him, Matthias
began making threats in the lobby of 22 Weimarer Strasse to anyone
who would listen. He would see to it that both of the Singer boys were
arrested and deported to Dachau.

Sylvester Mazura heard Matthias's threats and took them seriously,
the fate of Dr. Ehrlich all too present. As building porter, Mazura was
often invisible and Matthias may have had no idea that the man in the
blue uniform with the short white hair who swept the hallways and
polished the brass was also Julius's loyal factory foreman. Alarmed by
Steppan's threats, Mazura told Herr Singer that there was no time to
lose. Fritz especially was a marked young man. Relatives in London
agreed to take Fritz and Dolfi. It was possible to secure a visa to
England for a student attending boarding school and Julius still had
enough money to pay for this necessary fraud.

THE INITIAL WAVE of anti-Semitic attacks following the Anschluss calmed somewhat once Adolf Eichmann arrived in Vienna, set up his offices at the Hotel Metropole, speedily established the bureaucracy of "Aryanization," and officially opened the *Zentralstelle für jüdische Auswanderung*, the Central Office for Jewish Emigration. This office was located around the corner from the IKG, near the old Jewish quarter. Order had to be restored, for the sake of the Reich and international appearances. The IKG, minus its former director and board, including Jakob Ehrlich, was reopened, and new procedures for emigration were put into place. A wave of forced emigration began for those lucky enough to leave. In 1938, Eichmann's aim was to strip Jews of property and money, with an air of legitimacy, and force them to emigrate empty-handed.

The wealthy banking family Rothschild was evicted from their palace on the Ringstrasse—their home became Gestapo headquarters—as were other wealthy Jewish families like the Ephrussi, whose losses are movingly recorded in Edmund de Waal's *The Hare with Amber Eyes*.

This process of financial extraction moved forward with brutal efficiency. By July 1938, Julius was forced to sign away his fifty percent ownership of Adolf Eisenmann und Sohn. The hundreds of photocopies Hubert Steiner at the Austrian State Archives sent me in 2012 validated this "Aryanization" as a legal sale.

The new owner of Adolf Eisenmann und Sohn was a man named Ferdinand Zakovsky. Franz Novotny researched a few revealing details of his life. Born in 1896, he was forty-two years old in 1938 when he acquired this highly profitable business at a fraction of its real value. Julius was twenty years older than Zakovsky. Perhaps the younger man owned a rival packaging business and eagerly snapped up his competition, along with its machinery, workers, and the patent for the *Pulverkapseln*. Zakovsky must have been a Nazi party member with Aryan credentials.

But Adolf Eisenmann und Sohn wasn't just about the patent, the hardware, or even the loyal workforce. Julius's years of expertise were integral to the value of the company. According to my mother, the new owner understood nothing about the day-to-day operations of the factory, not to mention the workings of the machine that made the *Pulverkapseln*. He kept Julius in charge, and the Singer family remained in apartment 5. This was a victory for Zakovsky and some kind of humiliation for Julius, who had all at once lost the work and investment of many years without recourse, for he was no longer a citizen with rights to claim. At least his family still had a home. So many others were homeless, and a few of those unfortunate Jews, evicted from their coveted apartments, would ultimately move into Fritz's and Dolfi's bedrooms in apartment 5 after the brothers left Vienna in early September 1938. Whatever money Julius had left would have to sustain the family for however long it took for the terror to pass—Julius still had that hope in the summer of 1938—or to secure safe passage to England.

During those summer months, Dolfi apprenticed with a shoemaker and kept out of view. Fritz was not cautious, causing the family more anxiety. Dolfi's reserve and discipline were foremost in Julius's and Anna's minds when they asked him, rather than Fritz, to make the necessary visits to Gestapo headquarters and the British consulate to secure the paperwork that would get the two boys to safety. They knew that Dolfi, not quite fourteen, unlike his older brother, would manage the terrifying Nazi bureaucracy without calling attention to himself or his family. At last all was arranged. On September 1, 1938, Fritz and Dolfi left Vienna with their older cousin Edith.

It was illegal for Jews to leave the country with currency or items of value. Julius worked around the restrictions by giving each son a secret gift of a gold signet ring he'd ordered from a jeweler, to be sold for its metal value if needed once the boys arrived safely in England. Fritz and Dolfi held on to their rings, despite the significant financial strain of the war years and all the years after that. Dolfi lost his ring decades later when his Long Island house was robbed.

Eva stayed behind. When Eva made up her mind, there was no changing it. All right, then. All right. Evalein would stay. And maybe it was a good thing after all. The three of them would join the boys in

England as soon as they could secure visas and passage. Eva's momentous decision would prove to be the engine of Julius and Anna's efforts for the next two years. Perhaps they would have given up and accepted an unknown fate for themselves. But for their young daughter they had to do more.

—— ARREST ——

MID-SEPTEMBER 1938 BROUGHT another international event that layered yet another dark cloud over all the Jews who still remained in Vienna. On September 12, Hitler demanded a return of the Sudetenland in Czechoslovakia. In an attempt to make peace with Hitler, and eager to avoid a war for which there was little popular support, Neville Chamberlain of Britain and French president Édouard Daladier agreed to meet with Benito Mussolini and Hitler to negotiate terms. The Munich Pact of September 29-30 handed over the Sudetenland to Germany. Chamberlain and Daladier returned home, temporarily satisfied that they had avoided another war with Germany. By agreement the Sudetenland handover was to be completed by October 10. Emboldened by his success, Adolf Hitler planned more aggressive expansion.

————————————

SOME WEEKS AFTER Fritz and Dolfi left Vienna, the Nazis raided a number of Jewish businesses, including the jeweler who had made the signet rings. The Gestapo inspected his customer list and made arrests. These included Julius. Perhaps Steppan's son played a part here, directing the police up the stairs to the door across the hall, eager to wreak revenge on the father even if the true objects of his rage had slipped away to safety.

WHEN MY MOTHER would tell us the next part of the story, it always sounded far-fetched. It was the stuff of family legend, one of the narratives internalized like lines of a play. The story of Julius's arrest and the aftermath was one of the few stories my mother ever told us about her childhood. She told it often and the same way every time to us kids, and I heard her tell it the same way to guests at her dinner parties.

She told the story the same way to my friend Stefan, a German exchange student at UMass during my Smith College years, whom I'd met through friends. One year he came home with me for Thanksgiving dinner. I already knew by then that his grandfather had been a famous general during the Third Reich, stationed in Trieste and Venice. I didn't dare mention this to my mother, fearing that she would reject Stefan as a guest, but she probably did the math herself and calculated that his family had been involved in some way on the dark side of history. I hoped she would restrain herself during this most American holiday and not tell the story again, just this once. What was I ashamed of? Everything, at that age. And with Stefan I wanted to set aside the burden of being Jewish and the history of persecution and suffering in a friendship that so far felt so good and easy. On Thanksgiving, I hoped we could just be an American family welcoming a foreigner with roast turkey and stuffing and pumpkin pie.

But of course, my mother did tell the story. Before the meal, even, while we were sipping sherry and nibbling Wensleydale cheese on crackers. The Anglican Jews. And then, to my astonishment, Stefan said something to her in German and then my mother began speaking in German, and soon she and Stefan were laughing and joking about who knows what. I hadn't heard her speak her first language in years. Stefan told me later that he loved her soft Viennese accent. Of course, I couldn't tell the difference in their German, but I loved that this was even a thing to notice, that her Viennese had its own special charm among German speakers.

Stefan and I remained friends. He translated the dates, signatures, and official stampings on my grandparents' Third Reich passports, creating a side-by-side diagram that allowed me to fully piece together a clear timeline, and he translated many other documents for me. He said it was part of his national penance.

My mother told the story of her father's arrest the same way to the young Austrian man who interviewed her for the Leo Baeck Institute in 2004. Minus some of the colorful language and overt outrage she'd have added for an audience of friends or family. The young Austrian interviewer was also performing a kind of national penance. She went easy on him, but in a few instances I could tell she just couldn't restrain herself entirely. Either the young Austrian didn't catch her dark sarcasm, or he'd been well coached in advance not to let the long-simmering bitterness of Jewish refugees unsettle him. At seventy-six years old, she looked like her mother, who had not made it past sixty-six. She had always suffered from winter bronchitis and allergies, but looking back, the still undiagnosed lung cancer had already weakened her lungs. She got tired easily. But her memories—what she chose to share—were as sharp as ever. This story was so vivid and unlikely that I accepted it as the truth of a ten-year-old girl, terrified, but with her eyes wide open.

How can I put this politely? The authorities came. They took away our passports and everything else they could get their hands on. This was two weeks after Fritz and Dolfi left. They had arrested the jeweler who made the gold rings.

In a separate paper questionnaire from the Leo Baeck Institute, my mother added handwritten details about this house raid. The police accused Julius of deliberately smuggling money out of the country, a crime against the newly expanded Reich. As they searched for valuables in their Biedermeier dressers and armoires, they smashed up dining chairs and perhaps some china, a gratuitous demonstration of their power. I imagined a terrified Eva watching the scene with Anna. I imagined the aftermath, when the police were gone at last: Eva helping her mother gather up pieces of broken furniture and dishes, restoring some illusion of order to the apartment, while Julius sat at his desk, head in hands, wondering how he would get the three of them to England without their passports. A few days passed, enough for the family to hope that the worst had passed. Perhaps during this brief lull Julius wondered again about the disappearance of Dr. Ehrlich just a few months earlier. If Ehrlich's fate was any indication of his own future, the madness was just beginning.

Then police came to our apartment and took my father away. It was late September 1938. My mother and I were petrified.

Here my mother paused in the story as if reliving the event. She dropped the thread of her narrative, unable or unwilling to unpack the full emotional impact of that day. Her Austrian interviewer waited patiently. She continued. *What they made at the factory* [the Pulverkapseln] *was considered important. They* [the Nazis] *had installed a manager at the factory* [she wouldn't have known the name of the new Aryan owner, Zakovsky], *who was a member of the party, but he didn't know anything about printing.*

Mazura must have understood that after just a few months of ownership Zakovsky still knew little about the day-to-day operations of the factory and saw an opportunity to advocate for Julius. *So the next day* [after the arrest], *the foreman* [Herr Mazura] *said to the manager, "We don't know what to do here. Every day Herr Singer comes down, and he tells us what we should do, and what is more important, and what would take longer, and so without him we can't do it." And this was true. My father would go there every day before breakfast. My father was very fortunate, and I think it was because he had always had good relationships with the working people. Anyhow, the police had taken my father down to the train station.*

In the paper questionnaire my mother mentioned that the Nazi-appointed manager was actually "good to them" after Julius's arrest. Given Julius's value to his newly acquired asset, it was in Zakovsky's interest to do whatever would maintain normal factory operations, even if it meant supporting a Jew he disained. The *Pulverkapseln* would be vital to the war mobilization already in progress. Soldiers would be wounded. They would need medicine. There was money to be made. And apparently, only Julius understood how to manage the workflow and those finicky folding and printing machines.

Then, according to my mother, after some days, Zakovsky and Anna were summoned to the train station.

In the novella *Chess Story* by the Jewish writer and onetime Viennese celebrity Stefan Zweig—the last he completed before he and his wife committed suicide in exile in Brazil—a man describes his incarceration for some period of months in a room at the Hotel Metropole, where Eichmann had his headquarters. During the course of his imprisonment the man is periodically summoned for questioning, and during one of these sessions he manages to secure a chess handbook someone has left on a desk. The man learns how to play chess against the only opponent he has available during long days of desperate solitude—himself. This doesn't end well. The story reads as a metaphor for the madness that can overtake anyone who is forced to spend too much time confined in circumstances where their fate is wholly unknown, and speaks to Zweig's despair as a roving exile who had no idea when, if ever, he might be able to return to his home.

Michael Simonson, my research contact at Leo Baeck, considered it likely that Julius may have been held in this same hotel for at least a few days.

What would the Gestapo have wanted from him? He couldn't easily transfer the knowledge he had acquired over so many years to anyone except a devoted apprentice. Even Mazura couldn't run the factory without supervision. At some point a decision was made to send Julius to Dachau with the latest shipment of Jewish businessmen and political enemies. But by the time Anna and Zakovsky went to the train station, they had changed their minds.

When I spoke to Elisabeth Klamper, an archivist at the DÖW (the Documentation Center of Austrian Resistance) in 2012, she thought it unlikely that Julius would have been at the train station when Zakovsky and Anna were summoned. She thought that he would have still been in police custody.

But that's not how my mother told this story. *You know how organized the Austrians are? They knew exactly what train car he was in. They called him out. My father thought they were going to shoot him. And they told him to go back and run the factory.*

During every retelling my mother always smiled and paused here for the full effect of the story to sink in. Her father was spared because he'd been a good Socialist who'd looked after his workers, and because the *Pulverkapseln* had value for the Third Reich. Julius was temporarily as safe as any Jewish man could be in Vienna. He must have understood that he and his family were living on borrowed time while he had something to offer the Reich. Once his knowledge had been passed on to the new owner, he would be doomed to the same fate as Jakob Ehrlich and the jeweler who had made the gold rings for his sons.

Julius's task now was to take inventory of his knowledge and dispense it in measured doses, sufficient to not appear obstructionist, but never enough for a full command of the company operations. I cannot imagine that Zakovsky ever came to care about Julius as a human, but they had enough shared interests to form an unlikely alliance. Zakovsky needed Julius alive, at least for a while. And Julius needed time to understand and work the bewildering process of restoring his and Anna's passports and securing visas for England.

Julius's predicament upon returning home to 22 Weimarer Strasse, miraculously spared, recalls the legend of Scheherazade, the heroine of *One Thousand and One Nights*. A king discovers that his wife has been unfaithful. To avoid being betrayed in the future, he decides to marry a new virgin each day and behead her predecessor. So it goes until he meets clever Scheherazade, who agrees to marry the king on condition that she be allowed to say farewell to her sister Dunyazade, who then requests one of her sister's famous stories to pass the night hours. As dawn is breaking, Scheherazade stops in the middle. The king, eager to hear the end of the tale, spares her life for a day. This goes on for 1,001 nights, by which time the king has fallen in love with Scheherazade. Whatever power the king wielded in the political sphere, Scheherazade ruled with the power of her storytelling.

Julius had to create a story of his own, and draw it out as long as possible. He did not have the luxury of 1,001 nights.

— *THE WAY OUT* —

MOST VIENNESE JEWS looked for emigration assistance at the *Israelitische Kultusgemeinde*. But the IKG focused most of its effort helping younger people, the next generation of Jews, who could more easily join the workforce in whatever country they landed. As I saw during my visit in 2012, the IKG, in an attempt to normalize the desperate situation, offered retraining programs, and published brochures about the options for emigration, including countries like China that did not require a visa. However practical and optimistic the brochures were, the reality was that the IKG now operated under the authority of Adolf Eichmann.

Though experienced as a businessman, Julius was no longer young. With his weak heart he would not be able to do any physical labor. His wife hadn't worked since their marriage. His daughter was still a child. Julius was a private and self-sufficient man by nature and, perhaps, after Jakob Ehrlich's arrest and disappearance, he no longer trusted the IKG. This might explain why the IKG had no record of my grandfather when I visited in 2012.

Every day, would-be emigrants petitioned for passports at the Rothschild Palace—now transformed into Nazi headquarters. In photographs of the lines, so long that they wrapped around the entire city block, men and women are bundled against the cold—frigid winter had blown in—waiting their turn to plead their case. And this was just the first part of a long opaque process. If you were lucky enough to be issued a passport you then had to visit individual embassies to request a visa. Only then could you apply for an exit permit, which, after paying various "atonement" taxes and exit fees, would allow you to leave the country, with nothing left in your pocket. Julius joined those lines, waiting and waiting for a turn to fill out forms. The Nazis loved their paperwork—it gave legitimacy to their policies—and Adolf Eichmann wasn't interested in making Jewish emigration easy.

ON NOVEMBER 7, 1938, a young Polish Jew named Herschel Grynszpan hiding out in Paris shot a German diplomat named Ernst vom Rath, an act of retaliation after his parents were expelled from Poland. Vom Rath had actually expressed opposition to the Nazis treatment of Jews, but Grynszpan would not have known this. Following vom Rath's death from his injuries on November 9, a Nazi-sanctioned pogrom erupted in Germany and Austria, known as Kristallnacht, the Night of Broken Glass. Any remaining Jewish businesses were destroyed. Synagogues were desecrated and set on fire, with the exception of the central synagogue located near the IKG, the one I visited in 2012. As our tour guide, Johann, explained, Eichmann secured the central synagogue to avoid losing the important records stored around the corner at the IKG. After Kristallnacht, full-on anti-Semitic terror took hold in Vienna, worse even than the period right after the Anschluss in March.

From the collection of first-hand accounts at the Wiener Library in London, I read stories of those arrested in the days of the pogrom. After being arrested with hundreds of others and detained in a packed room without food or water, one man wrote,

> There is no compassion, no mercy, it is a brutish Volk [people] enraptured by the most intense sadism. . . . Those who did not prostrate themselves immediately when confronted by the police were punched or hit—it was awful to see and then have to hear the cries of pain. How many are dying or have perished already—there is no information. I was there and my report only covers part of what happened.

The man was released, having been found too weak for a labor camp, and hid out at home with his wife and child. The authorities told him that he would lose his home at the turn of the year, and this desperate father had no idea where his family would go once rendered homeless. In this next excerpt it is clear that he had given up hope for his own survival, worrying only about his wife and child.

> My child—despite being highly intelligent—is forced to wither away on account of not being able to go outside. Perhaps my wife will manage, as a more robust person, to move on in England where the child might also be able to get out.

In another account from the library's archive, I read about the fate of a famous Jewish restaurateur whose establishment was targeted from the Anschluss, onward:

> Among the atrocities of 10th November, the death of the well-known Viennese Jewish restaurateur Herr Schwartz, Vienna II, Rotesterngasse, caused in the most horrible way, has attracted considerable attention. The poor man, who came from a well-known Viennese restaurateur's family, and whose business, taken over from his father, occupied the rank of the highly renowned Viennese Jewish restaurants á la Neugröschl and Tonelle, was severely distressed from the first day of the turmoil. Immediately after the turmoil the restaurant was plundered by the SA, so that its refurbishment caused great financial sacrifice. Then it was announced that all Jewish restaurants in Vienna would have to close on 1st August, and Schwarz attempted suicide from sorrow at this news and was saved at the last minute. Now on 10th November he was trapped in his own refrigerator and died an agonizing death.

THE SINGERS STILL had their home, at least for the time being. My mother's interview continued. *And then, from '38 to '40, they wouldn't give him back the passport. He had some money. He had some mortgages. They wanted all of it. My father said, "Take it, go ahead, take it." The only thing he wanted to save was—when each of us children was born he bought an insurance policy, in American dollars, so that when we were twenty-one, we would get money. And he didn't want to give that up. But in the end he gave it up. Because, because. You know.* Here she caught her breath. If she'd hoped for an apology from her young interviewer, she was disappointed. He encouraged her to continue. *The offices where the Gestapo did some of their wonderful work were at the Rothschild Palace in the center of town. Well, my father spent days and days and days there. He had a very good personality and—I wouldn't say he made friends with some of them—but they treated him like a human being. Which was unusual. And they finally agreed for him to leave.*

Julius worked the one bit of leverage he had in his favor—the factory—with the persuasive skill he had learned in his years as a salesman and businessman. He was a reserved man, but evidently he knew how to charm when it suited his purpose. Having lost control of his livelihood, saving his family became the sole purpose of his days. I tried to conjure the scenes of him making his case, assuring the Gestapo that if they would let his family leave, he would make sure that his foreman learned how to keep the machinery running smoothly. And as I thought about my grandfather, I kept asking myself why the work of this factory was important enough that the Gestapo even engaged in a bargaining game with him at all.

Norman Ohler's controversial book *Blitzed* tells the story of the heavy use of methamphetamines by the Nazi leadership, soldiers, and even general citizens during the Third Reich. One drug of choice was marketed under the brand name Pervitin. I began to consider the *Pulverkapseln* in a new way, as an item that might have played a part in this medication of the public. I wrote to Franz, and he made the connection immediately, telling me that German soldiers marched sixty kilometers a day, without sufficient food, sleep, or warm clothing. Everyone used Pervitin, even housewives, to have sufficient stamina to work for the new Reich. Pervitin was even an ingredient in some peppy chocolates. It was distributed to soldiers in pill form in small metal tubes. But Franz pointed out that by 1939 metal was being saved for military use and an item like the *Pulverkapseln* would have been used instead, at least one reason to keep the Adolf Eisenmann und Sohn factory running at peak efficiency. It was no wonder my mother remembered the paper fans so vividly; they had been vital in saving the family.

— PASSPORTS —

JULIUS'S AND ANNA'S precious passports were dated July 21, 1939, three days before my mother's twelfth birthday. Eva was listed as a dependent. That birthday must have brought some lightness, in spite of the terrible changes in Vienna. At least on that summer day, escape seemed possible.

Julius's passport shows haste—or was it exhaustion—in his signature. He raced through his first name, the required "Israel" as a middle name indicating that he was Jewish, and then flubbed up the end of his last name, the terminating "r" rolling twice before rising up in a final surge.

In his photo he appears in three-quarter view, well-dressed as ever in a suit, pressed white shirt, and a narrow striped tie. Anna kept his hair neatly trimmed. He has deep bags under his tired eyes. His left brow is raised, the way my right one does when I am stressed. His gaze is steady.

In her passport, Anna looks off to the side as well, her eyes glistening in the flare of the camera flash. Her hair is carefully waved and pinned in the style of the late 1930s. I wondered how she managed to maintain such careful grooming and look after their clothing, given the privations of their daily life. I concluded that for her, maintaining these standards was a quiet act of defiance, even survival. She wears a perfectly pressed striped blouse with long pointed collars, square buttons, and slightly puffed sleeves, perhaps an item she made herself. Her full lips are my mother's. Her left brow is also raised, hinting at the anxiety of the prior months. One important hurdle had been overcome.

My mother continued. *In the meanwhile I was going to the Jew school, where we were taught by professors from the university who weren't allowed to teach there anymore, so they taught us little children. I worked hard and I did well. My brothers were gone and I'd lost my friends, so I was very lonely. It was a very cold winter and we weren't allowed to go on the trolley cars. So I walked. But I survived.*

She would never have used such a derogatory expression—"Jew School"—with family or friends. It was as if in retelling this story to the young Austrian interviewer, she re-created the atmosphere of anti-Semitism as she experienced it then, using the same painful language she heard as she walked on the streets.

Before the Anschluss, my mother would have had various educational options: a *Gymnasium* would have led her toward a university degree, whereas at a *Hauptschule* she would have learned a trade. Without options, she attended a Jewish girls' school called *Öffentliche Hauptschule für Mädchen in Wien* at 8 Albertgasse in the 8th district, about a mile from her home in the 18th district.

She saved her final report card for the first half of the 1939/40 school year. It looked as official as any school document. You wouldn't think anything was out of the ordinary except that it is stamped: *Schule für jüdische Kinder* (School for Jewish children). Eva did well in German language, geography, history, arithmetic and geometry, natural history, writing, and handwork. Four excused absences. Four unexcused absences. She must have loved going to school. At least there in the company of other students and teachers she found some relief from loneliness. Both 1938 and 1939 were especially cold winters, with serious food shortages, little if any coal for heating, and terror on every street corner of that walk to and from Albertgasse. And yet with all these hardships, Eva's attendance record was better than my daughter's at the same age, who lived an easy five minutes walk away from her school in Park Slope, Brooklyn.

Mathematics would remain one of my mother's strong subjects.

For all the years of her marriage she managed the family accounts, paid bills, prepared tax materials for the accountant. Like Julius, she easily calculated three-digit figures in her head. When she worked out complex computations on paper I heard her muttering numbers in German. She taught me multiplication and long division when I switched schools in the middle of fourth grade. I know I exasperated her with my slow grasp of concepts and methods she found as easy as play. She haggled in German over the prices of choice meat cuts with her butcher, Harry. She loved numbers. During her thirty-four years at Simon & Schuster as an interior book designer and then art director, she calculated page counts, paper purchases, and department budgets. She loved the smell of ink and appreciated the poetry of elegant typography. She never forgot the *Pulverkapseln*, the useful beauty of those folded paper fans. Though being a female company manager would have been unusual for the times, had history turned out differently, she could easily have taken over Julius's printing factory.

Her teachers appreciated her effort at school, perhaps especially because the conditions were so difficult. Professor Paula Fuchs, who did not survive the Holocaust, wrote this inscription in Eva's *Poesiealbum* in June of 1939, a year after daily life for Jews had been reduced to privation, humiliation, and begging:

> "Through this world everyone has been able to march easily, who knew well to be grateful and knew well to beg." (Ebner-Eschenbach) To my dear pupil in friendly memory!

The girls whose inscriptions appear in Eva's *Poesiealbum* must have been classmates at the "Jew School." Renate's drawing of the Big Bad Wolf was dated January 12, 1939. As I read through their entries again and again, I could only hope that some of these children made it out in time.

ONCE JULIUS AND Anna had passports in July 1939, they would have applied for a visa to Britain with the goal of reuniting the family. Wherever they were in this process by the late summer of that year, world events intervened. England and France declared war against Germany on September 3, 1939. Hope of joining Fritz and Dolfi in England was lost, and the search for a way out grew even more desperate.

Daily life went on under harsh conditions. *And . . . life was very difficult, but you know how that was. We had this big apartment, so we kept having more and more people living with us. You know, Jews who were without places to live. And we ate. What you could get. Food was very scarce, I'm sure you've heard that. And we survived. You couldn't go anywhere. You couldn't do anything. There was no synagogue, because the synagogue, which was in Währing, was destroyed in Kristallnacht.*

In the winter of 1939, my dark-haired, olive-skinned grandparents and their dark-haired daughter were easily identified as Jews. If they were brave enough to leave the apartment at all, they would have been able to buy the meager foodstuffs available at the few shops that still sold to Jews during restricted hours. Mazura must have helped here, bringing supplies to the family. All around there were signs of cruelty and terror. *I saw people on the street, old people, being hit. I saw people scrubbing the sidewalk with a toothbrush. Yes, I did see all of that. Right across the street. But it was the same for anybody there, which is why we hardly ever left the house. I went to school and I came home. And that was it. And my father went downtown to the Rothschild Palace and he came home. We did nothing. We had books at home, so I read. My mother loved music. I think she had a few records and she played them for us.*

After years of comfort, days were now full of danger and privation. Till the end of her life, my mother remained a homebody and a saver of food bits. Inside our fridge you might have found a wee piece of cheese, mostly rind, wrapped up in plastic. My mother could make magic with cabbage and potatoes, staples of Viennese home cooking. Nothing was wasted.

The Singers still had one occasional visitor, Jakob Altenberg, Julius's best friend. Though he had married a Christian woman and converted, I knew from the box of photocopies Hubert Steiner sent me from the Austrian State Archives that Altenberg's business was also Aryanized in 1938. *So, once or twice Jakob Altenberg would come and stay with us and have dinner and sleep, and we would hope nobody would come.* Without the documenting photographs, their blissful mountain expeditions from earlier years must have seemed like a dream.

— *VISAS* —

JULIUS AND ANNA were now focused on getting American visas—no easy matter, given the strict quotas in place.

A Nichtern brother in Detroit agreed to provide the required affidavits for an American visa. Another relative stepped forward to provide financial assistance. His name was Theodore Mann, or Teddy, as he was known in the family. My uncle Dolfi remembered his name but had no further details. My father recalled only that he was a wealthy executive who lived in New York City. His home address, typed on Singer immigration documents, was an elegant apartment building just off Central Park West in the Seventies, one I've walked by many times, musing about the hidden lives of the one percent. By this point, Julius had little money left and the United States insisted on seeing some guarantee of support. My father recalled that Anna spoke reverently about Teddy Mann—"a hero, the man who saved the family."

THE REAL IMPEDIMENT to salvation was the American immigration quota as enforced by the Johnson-Reed Act of 1924. "America must be kept American," President Calvin Coolidge declared in December 1923. True Americans were white, Anglo-Saxon, and preferably Protestant. Though by 1923, previously persecuted Irish Catholics were considered acceptably American.

The Johnson-Reed Act was the culmination of decades of anti-immigrant America First fervor, exacerbated by the fear of Communism after the revolution in Russia in 1917 and worker strikes throughout the United States. It was supported by an unholy alliance of Boston Brahmins, a revitalized Ku Klux Klan, as well as previous waves of now-established immigrants eager to reinforce their one hundred percent American status by refusing entry to newcomers. The law placed strict limits on immigration from Southern, Central, and Eastern Europe, and banned immigrants from Asia and Africa. No Italians. Definitely no Jews. Even as the threat of Nazism grew and Hitler made his genocidal ambitions clear, the political forces aligned against immigration and engagement in foreign wars resisted any relaxation of the quotas that would have made rescue efforts possible. Although it is difficult to get accurate information about precise quotas from Germany and the former Austria during the years after 1938, they never exceeded forty thousand. The odds against getting an American visa were as remote as the lottery. At one point Julius and Anna considered sending Eva to safety in Argentina, where relatives had already settled. Like many other Jews, they may have considered Shanghai as an option, as a visa was not required. But in the end, they set their hopes on the United States, hoping that the affidavits they had would be persuasive and that they could win the life-and-death lottery.

———————

WHO KNOWS HOW many trips Julius made to the American consulate during the summer, fall, and winter of 1939, once Mr. Nichtern's affidavit letter was in hand. The consulate was located on a street now called Jaurésgasse, currently the site of the Iranian embassy. At that time the street was called Richthofengasse. Franz estimated that this was roughly five kilometers from 22 Weimarer Strasse, on the other side of the city. As public transport had been forbidden to Jews since the Anschluss, Julius would have made this journey on foot, more arduous after the winter cold set in. At the American consulate the lines of hopeful emigrants were as long as at the Rothschild Palace. Franz described a process that was yet another test of endurance, especially for a man with a weak heart. People waited and were given a red ticket if they weren't called on the first day. Three red tickets were required before being admitted to the consulate to apply for a visa. If you were fortunate, you would at last be granted an appointment for an interview with one of the consular staff. Friends or colleagues helped arrange these interviews, especially if they knew of a potentially sympathetic official. Then, as now, getting an interview was all about who you knew, reducing the degrees of separation between petitioner and an all-powerful representative of the American government who issued visas.

EVA FINISHED HER school term in December 1939. It was bitterly cold and snowy, with little or no fuel for the coal stove that had offered such comforting warmth in easier times. The Singer's apartment now housed several Jewish families all hoping to leave, living out their days as quietly and as invisibly as possible. If the Steppans across the landing were fully aware of the number of dislocated Jewish families packed in apartment 5, they would surely have been outraged.

The year turned. Eva did not return to school after the winter holiday. At this point it was too dangerous and too cold for her to leave the house alone for the long walk. Women were being harassed and assaulted on the street. An eleven-year-old girl would not have been spared. January passed indoors, cut off from the few remaining friends she had at the "Jew School."

In spite of the cold and the danger, Julius made his trips to the American consulate. A month can pass like an eternity when each day is an ordeal against time and nature. But the days rolled by, the last of a cruel winter. A rare sunny morning in January may have given Julius hope as he set out again on his mission, leaving Anna and Eva in the apartment.

———————

FEBRUARY 1940 BROUGHT good news at last. Donald W. Brown, the American vice-consul stationed in Vienna, stamped and signed Julius's and Anna's passports with the longed-for visas and American immigration quota numbers on February 17, 1940.

From the time I had first examined the Singers' passports before my mother's death in 2006, I'd read Donald W. Brown's name and wondered about that brief meeting. The Singers were not ideal immigrants, even with the guarantee that Mr. Nichtern offered, even with Teddy Mann's money. Julius was now sixty-five, and looking worn. Anna was a housewife who hadn't worked since 1920 or so. Eva was still too young to work. How did Julius make the case that he and his family would become productive Americans, especially in a time when there was so much antipathy toward immigrants?

In November 2016, after a bitter election season concluded with the election of an isolationist America First president, also named Donald, I was outraged and gloomy. Liza was still far away on the West Coast, and as winter rolled in and fierce partisanship took hold, I wondered how bad things would get. While Portland, Oregon, was a liberal city, Liza reported that there were growing numbers of white nationalists. Almost as a distraction, I decided to hunt down this mysterious Donald W. Brown. I emailed the Office of the Historian at the State Department. I imagined Brown as a longtime Foreign Service officer, stiff and formal, doing his best to maintain order in a city gone quite mad. Aiyaz Husain, from the Office of the Historian, wrote back promptly:

> I believe the consular employee you are referring to was a junior officer named Donald Winchester Brown. According to the Register of the Department of State, Brown was born in New York City

in May 1910. He attended school in Switzerland before returning to the States and earning an A.B. [Bachelor's] from Harvard
(1933) and an L.B.B. [law degree] from Columbia (1936). He
practiced law in New York from 1936–1938, and entered the
Foreign Service, before being posted to Vienna on March 2,
1939. He appears to have served there until 1940, after which
Brown served as Third Secretary in Bogota and posts in both
the Department of Justice and the US Army before returning to
the Department's Division of European Affairs in the mid 1940s.

BORN IN NEW York City, with such a Waspy-sounding name,
an expensive boarding school education in Switzerland, followed by
degrees at two of America's most prestigious universities, Donald
Brown sounded like one of the preppy boys I met during my college
years. In contrast to the older man I'd pictured in my mind, he was
a young man of twenty-nine when he arrived in Vienna a year after
the Anschluss of March 1938, and not yet thirty when he issued my
grandparents' life-saving visas. Had lawyering disappointed him so
soon after graduation that he'd looked for another line of work where
he might use his skills? Was he feeling burdened by the expectations of
his wealthy family? Did his years in Switzerland influence his decision
to join the Foreign Service? Was there anything especially important
to him about this part of the world, so many thousands of miles away
from his hometown? If he had wanted to put some distance between
himself and his family in New York City, he had succeeded.

Whatever Donald Brown had thought he was signing on for when he
arrived at his post in Vienna, the actual experience of life in Nazi Austria
must have been a rude awakening. My grandparents were just two of tens
of thousands hoping to get out of Vienna. If he had been a caring man, he
could not have helped feeling burdened by decisions he was now forced
to make each day. The quotas were the quotas, as immovable as the walls
our new president wanted to erect along our southern border.

I thought about what my mother had said in her interview, that

Julius had a "good personality." Given the circumstances, being an agreeable man would have had limits. I wondered what might have tipped the balance during their brief exchange.

The following morning, while sipping from a cup of Clark's fortifying espresso topped with velvety frothed milk, I searched online for "Donald Winchester Brown."

The only hit was an obituary, from 1952, in a journal of the American Alpine Club. I nearly fell off my kitchen stool. What now? Mr. Brown, scion of a New York society family, surprised me from the outset.

DONALD WINCHESTER BROWN, 1910–1952

Donald Brown died on 21 December 1952 in a tragic automobile accident near Poughkeepsie, New York. Thus ended a career into which a love of mountains and travel were inextricably woven.

Donald was drawn to the mountains, as are many others, through the good fortune of attending a preparatory school in Switzerland. As early as 1921 he rambled among the trailed summits of the Vaudoise Alps and, as his experience and enthusiasm grew, he tasted the delights of the Bernese Oberland, Pennine, and Mont Blanc ranges.

In 1929 he entered Harvard College and, during his residence there, his love of the mountains found a sympathetic response among the young mountaineers who have since blazed such distinguished trails across the high ranges. Thus it was that he joined college companions in summer excursions to the Alps in 1930 and 1932. Upon graduation in 1933 he passed several weeks in the Coast range of British Columbia, where poor weather and bad luck restricted his climbing activities.

The high peaks alone could not lay full claim to Donald's enthusiasm for the out-of-doors. He was as content to wander across the lake-dotted tundra of Finnish and Swedish Lapland, or through the sub-Arctic reaches of Norway, the Outer Hebrides, or Iceland, as he was to seek the granite of the Chamonix Aiguilles or the snows of the Combin. And during the greater part of these excursions he traveled alone, living with isolated groups and studying their customs.

Undeveloped country held a particular fascination for Donald, and in 1937 and 1946 he accompanied Wiessner on reconnaissance trips to the Stikine Ice Field of British Columbia and Alaska, during which special attention was given to the approaches to Kate's Needle.

In World War II he served with the Army Ground Forces, and, rising from a private soldier at the Mountain Training Center, he was relieved of active duty with the War Department General Staff, having attained the rank of Major.

During the post-war years Donald's law practice permitted fewer opportunities to climb, yet he was able to visit the Tetons in 1947, and in the following year he paid a final visit to the Alps, during which he traveled on foot from Klosters to Zermatt via Pontresina. This trip, a noteworthy accomplishment in itself, included many noble ascents along the way and in the vicinity of Zermatt.

A strong and enthusiastic climber, Donald sought the mountains not alone for the satisfaction of physical accomplishment, but especially through an intense desire to understand and appreciate the fullest expression of nature. That he succeeded in such large measure and in so short a life is a tribute to his boundless energy and determination, qualities that he brought not only to his avocation but to his professional life as well. His sense of humor, dynamic companionship, and loyalty to his friends are assets that mountaineering can ill afford to lose, but they stand as bright monuments that will long be remembered and respected.

—Walter A. Wood

Walter Wood must have been a close friend with firsthand experience of Donald's good spirits. The man he described was a nature lover, who was probably happiest out of doors in the wilderness, perhaps not a man cut out for office life.

That tingling sensation returned again. Julius also loved the mountains. Again I recalled my mother describing the trip Julius and Jakob Altenberg made after the First World War. The family photos from the 1920s attested to that continuing passion, especially the fact that these images made it to America. The one from the Hohe Wand in 1928 moved me in ways I could not describe—the drama of the setting, the challenge for a man of fifty-three who had a weak heart. I ran upstairs to our bedroom and took out the leather pouch from my jewelry box to admire the excellent folding bone-handled fork and spoon that also made the journey from Vienna to New York.

The prickling hairs on the back of my neck told me that this shared passion for mountaineering was important. While everyone in Austria seemed to love hiking in the mountains—the Alps and surroundings were the singular feature of the Austrian landscape—mountaineering in the United States had always been a more rarified pursuit. As I read the obituary I had never set foot in the Rocky Mountains, and had only glimpsed these wonders from the windows of airplanes. I knew I was not alone. America's vastness meant that most people rarely left the familiar area of their birth. I could feel it: the mountains were the link here, the connection to connections.

My grandfather, who had managed to navigate the many rounds of paperwork to get as far as the American Consulate, would have searched for any connection to one of the consular employees, through friends or former work colleagues. Julius's closest friends and possibly his clients were also alpinists and not all of them were necessarily Jews. Perhaps one of them cared enough about Julius Singer that he made a phone call or wrote a letter to help out an old friend.

I contacted the American Alpine Club. The librarian sent me links to two first-person accounts of climbing expeditions that mentioned Donald Brown. In one, a friend described a trip into the Italian Alps full of mishaps, bad weather, visa irregularities, but also good times. After evading the Italian border police, the group finally washed off the grime of their trek in a mountain lake. In another account from the Alpine Club, a fellow climber described an awe-inspiring trip in the western United States. Finally, I read Donald Brown's own account of his solo expedition through the Swedish Lapland. Whatever professional success this man had achieved as a lawyer and in the Foreign Service, mountaineering and a connection to nature had clearly been his most genuine passions.

The night in Singistugan I had to myself, both spirit and body being happier thereby. . . . Being alone, I could spread out at my ease; and gaze contentedly over the surrounding country. The flat valley bottom is green with meadows, filled last year with herds of reindeer. On all sides rise abruptly bleak and rocky mountains, in early July likely to be well covered with snow. In the midst of such a scene, the world seems unreal in the eerie light of a white summer night. The sun rests in the north, and there is a long, lingering afterglow. Then the atmosphere is permeated gradually by a light similar to neither dawn, nor dusk, nor daylight; but unique unto itself. Familiar scenes become strange, and the world changes.

As I read his remembrances of a solitary morning in a landscape I could only dream of, I felt like a witness to the interior struggles of a man trying to fathom the liminal space between night and day and the eternal cycles in nature. His morning is magic and his eyes are open as *familiar scenes become strange, and the world changes.* This introspective, meditative Donald became my personal antidote for the thoughtless, careless Donald occupying the White House, whose idea of nature was limited to the manicured lawns of his golf course at Mar-a-Lago.

I could not find a photo of Donald Brown, but an image was forming in my imagination of a different sort of man than the ones I'd met at beery fraternity parties years ago. I recalled a Somebody-or-other the Third, fondly dubbed Trip, rumpled and tousled, who'd lived in the coed "hippie" former frat house where a woman I'd befriended also had a room. Sometimes I'd see him in the shabby living room on a snowy afternoon, pretending to read an assigned text, looking like he'd rather be outside, tossing a Frisbie. I had a fierce, unrequited crush on that guy. Donald Winchester Brown had been a joyful man when he was dirty and windblown with friends, but the quiet beauty Brown described in the Swedish Lapland also suggested a man who valued solitude. This man could not have been spiritually fulfilled confined in a suit and tie, sitting behind a desk, stamping forms.

With further searching, I discovered that my Donald Winchester Brown had been the son of another Donald Winchester Brown. The family lived for a time in a Beaux-Arts mansion at 40 East Thirty-Eighth Street, though young Donald spent most of those years at a prestigious boarding school in Switzerland, where he had first started mountain climbing.

Still searching for a photo of Donald, I discovered that his sister Charlotte had been a high society debutante in 1928 and had married the son of Condé Nast at her family home.

In her formal wedding portrait, featured in *Vogue*, she poses like a sculpted goddess in front of a gilded side table topped with vases of showy white blooms, her lacy train sweeping around her feet. She holds her arms stiffly in front, grasping what looks like a prayer book. The bottom half of a painted portrait is visible behind her, perhaps of her mother. Charlotte does not look like a happy bride. Her mouth is a joyless flat line. That marriage ended in 1933.

I studied her elegant features and figure, trying to imagine a more masculine version of this face, replacing the long white gown and veil with a mountain climber's anorak, boots, and gear. I contacted the Harvard Mountaineering Club, the Harvard Library, and Columbia Law School's Alumni Association. Where are you, Donald Winchester Brown? I asked myself. He was starting to feel like a long-lost friend. Or another ghost, who had something important to tell me.

AT LAST, HARVARD'S Pusey Library sent me a photo from Donald Brown's Class of 1933 yearbook. And when I looked at it I smiled, because this part of the story didn't surprise me. Donald looked very like his sister, a handsome, fresh-faced young man, with light eyes and sandy hair. Cheeks so tender he probably shaved once a week. He was beautiful. In his tightly knotted tie and stiff white shirt, he looked as serious as his sister in her wedding photo. His home address was listed as the Guaranty Trust Company. A trust fund kid. He spoke French. He was a member of the Harvard Mountaineering Club. He had joined several of Harvard's exclusive "finals" clubs. He was a member of the Hasty Pudding, famous for its theatricals featuring men in drag. I imagined Donald performing in one of these shows: he must have been a natural, given his reputation for humor and adventure, not to mention his refined features that would have taken easily to makeup, wigs, and gowns. Donald had also joined and served as president of the Signet Society, where professors and students mingled to discuss art and culture, and the equally exclusive club called the Spee. I noted that Donald had concentrated in anthropology—rather than government, economics, or political science—choosing a true passion, rather than a field more obviously geared toward a career as a lawyer. He had managed to compress his undergraduate studies into three and a half years. Perhaps his boarding school classwork had given him extra credits toward his Harvard degree, or perhaps he had a trip planned that encouraged him to pack his college course load.

Wealthy New York families I'd encountered in literature and real life often stuck to their home turf. For one thing, they had wonderful town houses or apartments to pass on to their descendants. And trust funds, like Donald Brown. I wondered if there was another Donald Winchester Brown still in New York City. Some exploring revealed that there was indeed someone else with the same name who went by Win and worked in real estate. When I sent him an email, Win Brown replied promptly. Yes, he wrote, my Donald Winchester Brown had been his grandfather.

One afternoon a few weeks before Christmas, I called Win while walking in the city, peering into the glittering shop windows, mindful that this was the time of year when my Donald Brown had died. Win Brown told me that his mother was the keeper of the family genealogy and that there wasn't much information about his grandfather. Win's father, Stephen, was the eldest child from Donald Brown's first marriage. Unfortunately, Donald Brown's second wife had inherited the mother lode of memorabilia after his early death. Win confirmed that Donald was still married to his first wife, Prudence, during his Vienna posting at the American Consulate and that she had given birth to Stephen in the early months of 1940, in the United States. Perhaps she had returned home to her family for the Christmas holidays, in her last months of pregnancy, and stayed home after that. Donald seemed to have left Vienna not long after he granted Julius's and Anna's visas. The American Consulate closed in July 1941.

"Did you know that your grandfather was a mountain climber?" I asked.

Win said yes.

I asked if there were any photos of Donald. My fantasy image—something like the one I had of Julius climbing the Hohe Wand—didn't exist, at least not that Win knew about.

Win told me that after leaving his post at the American Consulate in Vienna, Donald Brown had served in the military, reaching a high rank of major in the ski patrol. I wondered whether he'd worked in intelligence, given his fluency in German. Win told me that at the end of his life, Donald Brown had practiced as a lawyer in Cooperstown, New York, a town on Lake Otsego, west of Albany, known as the location of the Baseball Hall of Fame. Donald's mother had owned a grand home there, now an inn. Situated between the Catskills and the Adirondacks, Cooperstown would have offered opportunities to climb in the mountains. Not the Alps or the Rockies to be sure, but a spectacular wilderness far from the city. Here Donald had set up a private law practice and lived with his second wife before dying so young in a car crash.

I pressed Win for an interview with his mother, but I sensed some caution and accepted that this might be as much as his family wished to share with me. We exchanged a few more emails. He mentioned that his aunt knew more family stories and might have some photographs. Our correspondence was an ebb and flow, but as the year rounded the corner into a slushy postelection January, there was silence. I sent a few more emails into the void. Maybe the family did not share my fondness for Donald Brown, given the divorce and its bitter aftertaste. Donald Brown had been a passionate mountaineer, and, I suspected, a quiet hero in my family's drama, a principled man during wartime, but evidently not an ideal husband or father.

I POSTED A notice on Facebook, searching for anyone who might have information about Donald Winchester Brown. Several months passed during which I thought about him often, wondering how such a complicated life could be so forgotten, before remembering that so much of my mother's life remained a mystery.

SPRING STIRRED MY garden, and the birch trees we'd planted burst into chartreuse, and coiled ferns unfurled and the first flowers popped up. I was already counting down the weeks till Liza returned from college in May.

One morning a message appeared on Facebook from a woman named Elizabeth Heichler. A former journalist, she was also looking for information about Donald Winchester Brown. In her family, this man was a legend.

Elizabeth's father, Lucian Heichler, was born in 1925 in Vienna. In later life he joined the Foreign Service and in 2000 he gave a lengthy interview to the Foreign Affairs Oral History Project of the Association for Diplomatic Studies and Training. Lucian's father had been a physician and he described a "relatively normal" life in Vienna until the Anschluss of 1938. Elizabeth said that her father was known as a great storyteller in the family, and the narrative of the family's escape in 1940, like the ones my mother told, were established family lore. He was a few years older than my mother, with the perspective of an adolescent, rather than that of a young child. Here is Lucian, describing the aftermath of the Anschluss, when he was thirteen:

> After a few weeks I was no longer allowed to attend school. My family tried at first to teach me at home, but that experiment didn't last very long because everybody was too nervous, too anxious, too busy. I ended up spending most of my time reading, daydreaming, keeping a diary. Our principal concern was leaving the country, and young as I was, I quickly became an expert on most of the world's immigration laws. Our first intent was to go to America. My father had been to America several times in the late '20s and early '30s and liked it and thought if we wanted to settle anywhere at all it would be in the United States. Now this is a little funny; it's almost miraculous. Under the American immigration law, my father, having been born in Czernowitz (which before World War I was part of Austria-Hungary, but then became part of Rumania) was placed on the Rumanian immigration quota and my mother and I, even though [I was] born in Austria, along with him. Given the small size of pre-war Rumania, the quota was tiny, only about 295 people. And my father went down to the American Consulate to register. A few weeks after the Anschluss he was told that it would be at least ten years before his number came up and he might as well forget it. So we started casting around for other places to go, and then he remembered that in the early '30s, probably about 1931, he had toyed seriously with the idea of going to live in America and had been to the Consulate to register. . . . [H]e had registered for a quota number. Miracu-

lously, the consulate found his application, even though it was by that time seven or eight years old—something that would never happen today. They found it, and they told him that he was now practically at the head of the quota.

Elizabeth told me that it had been Donald Brown who had searched through old boxes of records in the consulate basement, where he'd finally found that previous application. His extraordinary effort had saved the Heichler family.

It took two years for Lucian's mother to locate a distant cousin in Chicago who would agree to send the required affidavit on condition that the Heichlers not contact him ever after. And so, with the quota number and the affidavit, the Heichlers were able to secure American visas in January or February of 1940, around the same time as the Singers. Here Lucian describes the final days in Vienna:

> Then came the problem of how to pay for passage to America, at an unbelievable inflated rate of exchange. The Deutschmark was worth practically nothing at this time—something like 30 marks to the dollar—however we had to pay at the official rate, which was 2.5 marks to the dollar, with the proceeds going to Vienna's Jewish Community Center [the IKG], which used the money for such purposes as trying to save members of the Jewish community in Vienna by "buying" them free from the Nazis. Buying the three steamship tickets took about all the money that my parents had, but apparently it sufficed. We packed up. We sold most of our goods at auction but were allowed to send a lift van to America. We were allowed to take the official equivalent of 10 Reichsmark a person out of the country with us—$4.00 . . . and a very limited number of goods, like no more than 100 books, no clothing less than two years old, no jewelry, no medical instruments. . . . And we booked passage on one of the last—perhaps the last—

Holland-America Line ships to leave Rotterdam for New York,
the S.S. *Volendam*, scheduled to sail on March 28, 1940.

This fantastical coincidence inspired me to email Win and his sister again, but I did not receive a reply. My cell phone rang on a Saturday morning about a week later. It was Penelope Brown W., another of Donald Brown's three children from his first marriage and Win Brown's aunt. On the phone, Penelope had a cheerful and musical voice. She didn't know very much about her father's life, just that his first marriage to Prudence ended in divorce in the early 1940s. An affair was rumored to be the cause of the breakup. Donald had been something of a womanizer, Penelope said, her voice trailing off. Prudence had blamed the divorce on the upheaval caused by the war. The couple had been apart for some of the time after Prudence had returned to New York to deliver their first child, Stephen. Then Donald had joined the army. The war years must have been a terrifying but exhilarating adventure for him, and family life back in America must have felt abstract and distant. Prudence was living near her family in New Jersey, caring for baby Stephen and then his siblings.

Donald was a restless man who wanted to be in motion, doing things, not in a Manhattan apartment or a suburban house in New Jersey without a mountain in sight.

After the war and the divorce he did more roaming. He taught for a year at the University of Chicago, but evidently academia didn't suit him. He returned east, where he met and married Margaret, his second wife.

I asked Penelope if she had any photographs of Donald in outdoor settings and she said she would send me the few she had. When her snail mail envelope arrived, I tore it open while standing in front of my mailbox. In three photos, I saw this man's life unfold like movie stills.

On the first photo Penelope had written: "I think this is the earliest—maybe even still in college?—based on his face looking younger than in the other two pictures—and from the amount of hair he has. ☺"

What a beautiful young man, was my first thought.

Shorter than his friend, whose biceps and chest filled out his shirt, Donald stood in contrapposto, close by his companion in the clearing of a campsite. Was there a third friend who dashed off on a sudden errand, leaving an empty space in the photograph, or was that third person the photographer? The two men wore nearly identical knickers, loose in the thighs, with fitted hems, not so different from those that Julius wore, and comfortable shirts with flap pockets. Donald wore high socks and low shoes. His friend wore tall lace-up boots. Donald's boots must have been the same, still in the tent when the photograph was taken. So, a uniform of some sort, in sturdy olive drab or brown, mountaineering wear circa 1930 to 1932. A breeze billowed the friend's trousers, but the weather appeared to be mild, as neither man wore a jacket. A tent was just visible behind a stand of slender trees, a flap sheltering an overturned washbasin. On the far right, cut and stacked wood suggested a cooking area nearby.

A moment later Donald pulled his boots on, and the young men were ready to hit the trail. Where exactly were they? The trees looked like whitebark pines, found in mountainous parts of Canada and the western United States.

In the second photo, some years had passed. Donald's thinning hair, filled-out torso, and the style of his pleated trousers suggested that we were now in the 1940s. On a snowy day, he stood at the base of the stairs to a simple cabin, perhaps in the Catskills or the Adirondacks or somewhere in New England, judging from the clapboard siding, small paned window, paneled door, and plain stair railing. This man was not put off by cold weather: his boots were caked with snow, and he wore no jacket, scarf, gloves, or hat. He must have worked up a sweat clearing snow off the stairs with the shovel propped to the left of the door. His Henley sweater looked eminently American, an item you could still order today from an L.L.Bean or REI catalog. A faint smile, a steady gaze. A friend, or perhaps Margaret, his second wife, took this photograph. When he issued the visas for Julius, Anna, and Lucian Heichler's family, he would have looked something like this.

Penelope had scribbled this on the back of the third photograph: "I'm sure this is the latest. The boy is my brother who was born February 1940 and don't you think he looks about ten?"

This was in 1950 or 1951, not long before his death. Donald looked out with the same steady gaze, just a hint of a smile. The years had begun to weather his handsome face. Three ploughed lines crossed his broader forehead, his face narrowed, his brows more prominent with shadows below his eyes. But he had kept fit outdoors, doing as much of what he loved as his life allowed. It felt like late summer or early fall. Donald still loved a uniform. He wore a rugged shirt and loose khakis of some army-green drab or brown and had a full backpack strapped over his shoulders. He carried something, perhaps a map, in his left hand. His son Stephen was a skinny shy kid in rumpled T-shirt and too-loose jeans cinched up high with a belt. He'd worked up a sweat and trailed his jacket on the ground. He carried a small pack and held something in one hand, a tool of some sort or perhaps a cool object he had picked up on their hike. Donald rested his right hand on his son's shoulder, in a gesture affectionate but not effusive.

Where were they in this photo? By then Donald had already moved to Cooperstown. Stephen might have seen little of his father except for rare summer adventures like this one. The landscape was a flat mown field dotted with firs and a distant soft gray tree line.

Here, even with his son, there were no posed "Say cheese" smiles. The photographer had let the camera capture an authentic moment in the life of an introvert. Perhaps Margaret had also taken this one and sent a copy to Stephen's family to record the day.

From Donald's obituary published by the Century Association, his New York City–based club: "In 1951 he and his wife came to live in Cooperstown, with which Brown was familiar from his childhood. He was fascinated by the idea of practicing law in a small community, and he opened an office over the local dry-goods shop on Main Street. He got off to an excellent start, and in a year had almost more to do than he could handle. All this was cut short by his sudden death in an automobile accident while he was driving from New York to Cooperstown."

It happened on the Taconic Parkway, Penelope told me, a venerable New York State highway with narrow curving lanes, notoriously treacherous in bad weather. Donald was returning home from his nephew's wedding in New York City. Charlotte, once the *Vogue* debutante, was the mother of the groom. The date was listed in the obituary as December 21, a few days before Christmas, though Penelope remembered it as Thanksgiving. I could easily imagine how the holidays conflated into a season of grieving. I knew what it was like to mother a child who had lost a parent. Three children lost their mostly absent father that day.

The obituary closed: "Brown was only forty-two, and it is tragic that he died so young. He was becoming important in the community activities in Cooperstown and would have been a most useful citizen. He had a love for skiing and mountain climbing and was full of life and energy and enterprise. He was true to his own ideals and undeterred by pressures to be ordinary."

I reached out again to Win and this time he put me in touch with his mother, Lisa. She described a family and a man with a strong sense of honor for whom the Foreign Service had been a natural choice. I asked her what she knew about Donald's personality and character.

"A bit of a cold fish," she said. "A distant father, complicated, definitely a loner." And then, as if to change the subject, she added, "Did you know that Donald Brown was a professional-level pianist?" She described a man I could see clearly now: solitary, uncomfortable in large social gatherings, a man who showed up to a family dinner and wandered off to a corner of the living room, where he communed with the piano. There Donald was content to play Beethoven sonatas and Chopin preludes until guests made their way to the dining room. He continued to play until the hosts ordered some young cousin to go tell Uncle Donald that dinner was served. His hands lingered on the keys, and the young cousin retreated. Reinforcement was sent in, perhaps his sister Charlotte, whom Lisa described as forceful, perennially unhappy, "a real piece of work." Reluctantly, Donald stilled his fingers and closed the instrument. In the dining room, everyone else was already seated and the food was getting cold.

————————

AS IF THROUGH a thaw in a frosted window, thirty-year-old Donald appears, dressed in a well-cut suit, seated behind a heavy wooden desk in his dark, paneled office at the consulate. A circle of incandescent light from a brass desk lamp casts a glowing circle over a stack of files. On a bookshelf nearby, a clock ticks, measuring the seconds, minutes, and hours of this workday. In other offices, phones ring, secretaries answer callers in singsong rehearsed greetings, typewriters pound out letters and documents in jazzy syncopation, accompanied by the swing-time tap and shuffle of men's shoes and women's high heels in the hallways.

Every day, he must decide who will be able to leave. The task has only grown more difficult because in addition to a strong anti-immigration sentiment, the anxiety of wartime has generated further resistance to European Jews. Despite all evidence to the contrary, there are those who feel that the Nazis are sending spies into the United States, in the guise of refugees. The very people who most need to escape are themselves suspect, especially those coming from German-speaking areas.

The quota for German and Austrian immigrants is available to Jewish refugees, but that number does not come close to the desperate need. The number of visas granted is already above twenty thousand, and it's only February. In accordance with the 1924 law, the combined German-Austrian immigration quota for last year was 27,370. Donald selects and opens a folder, the next case on the morning's roster. Someone referred these people to him for an interview, but he can't seem to recall who that was. There are so many. Someone from the mountain club.

Singer is the surname. Julius and Anna. One child, Eva, not yet twelve. Three more in the endless flow.

A wintry Vienna sky hangs like a heavy velvet drape beyond his office window. He spends too much time indoors these days. Fearful cold and the coal shortage have made life unpleasant even for the Foreign Service. He prefers to be in this office rather than his cold flat, where he is now living as a bachelor. Prudence endured the last months of her difficult pregnancy, unhappy and ill, often swathed in blankets on the divan, drinking endless cups of weak chamomile tea with other consular wives. She went home for the holidays and stayed behind, having decided to deliver their first baby near her family. It is a boy, named Stephen. The chain of Donalds has been interrupted. He hopes Prudence will send a photograph soon, but the mail service is less reliable with every passing day.

Not much to see out the window today. Flat cloud cover, afternoon fog rolling in from the Danube. Over a foot of snow on the ground. Building roofs trimmed in white. Some mornings he has worn his hiking boots to the consulate, as there are not enough workers to clear all the streets. He wears a scarf even in his office, except during meetings.

Donald allows himself a quick glance at the single, framed photograph on his desk. Walter took it. Donald and a few other Harvard friends on a climb in the Italian Alps, grainy, the focus shaky. Walt was standing at the edge of a cliff when the shutter clicked. What a crazy guy. He'll do anything for a good picture. Those were great days. He smiles, remembering how they managed to elude the Italian *carabinieri*, a good thing, as their passports were all in disarray, without the required travel visas. The rain was relentless on that trip. At the end of it all, the sun came out at last, and they washed up in that glorious lake in the clouds. And then made their way to the nearest town, where they ate enough for twenty men, platefuls of pasta washed down with good red wine.

He misses Walt—in California, last he heard, lucky devil. What Donald wouldn't give to get him, or any of those fellows, on the horn right now to plan the next expedition.

He misses the trail, and the solitude. There's no solitude here at the consulate, even when he closes his office door. Machines clacking, phones ringing, and then the evening events that persist even as war begins to envelop Europe.

Mostly he misses the euphoria of physical exertion, the thrill at the top of the world, or on an expanse of open plain. He misses silence that clears the mind. Even when he's on treks with friends, real climbers understand the beauty, the necessity of quiet. How else can you hear the reassuring clench of boots on a trail or crag, or the wind gusting up a valley, or the call of a bird in the trees far below? Walt would tell him not to feel so low, but there have been days here when he can barely suppress the urge to make a run for a peaceful trail somewhere far from this city.

Perhaps everyone here will be stateside soon, from the looks of things.

His pretty secretary raps gently on his office door, kept slightly ajar because the intercom has stopped working and there's no one to repair it these days. "Mr. Singer and his wife are here."

"Thank you, Miss Taylor. Send them in."

He wonders if he'll have a chance to climb this spring. Not likely, given the situation. He sighs and swivels Walter's photograph, as has become his habit, so he won't be distracted by memories of beautiful Alpine days.

This couple is no different from others this week. Maybe better dressed than some, or even most.

"Good morning," Donald says with practiced professional stiffness, waving them toward two chairs in front of his desk. His German is good, but it's always useful to understand from the beginning how much English these people have.

"*Guten Morgen*," Mr. Singer replies, helping his wife with her coat. He looks tired and old. She, less so.

According to the file, Singer owned a printing factory until '38, but those days are over. The woman, his wife, she must be younger by fifteen, twenty years. Quite beautiful still, in spite of everything.

He watches as she peels off her gloves, wondering how this mismatched couple met, before it dawns on him that this might be the old story of employer and secretary. Happens all the time in this consulate, just like anywhere else. Henderson married his secretary, and now she reigns from their expansive flat near Kärntner Strasse.

Mrs. Singer's blouse and jacket are well-tailored. She must be a skilled seamstress. She's managed to wave her hair impeccably. She has style, he'll grant her that. If she weren't a Jewess, this Anna Singer wouldn't look so out of place at one of his mother's stuffy afternoon tea parties. Donald watches as husband and wife sit before him. He, at thirty, could be this old man's son. A surge of boyish insecurity envelops him. Mr. Donald Winchester Brown must set the tone with the usual formalities.

Passports are in order. They have a letter of affidavit from Mrs. Singer's cousin—or is it a brother?—in Detroit. And another relative in New York, well off, apparently, as he's agreed to pay for travel expenses. And there's another brother in Brooklyn, who will take them in. Donald has never dwelled much on those wretched and cramped apartments in the unknown borough of Brooklyn, where all these people seem to end up, even ones as well-dressed as this couple. Not that he's ever seen one, but they are, no doubt, a far cry from the Brown home on East Thirty-Eighth. But even if they have somewhere to live, what will this old man be good for in New York? The wife, at least, can sew for a living. The daughter is still too young to work, for a few years anyway.

Donald looks up from the file. Singer is distracted by something on the desk. Now he's leaning forward for a closer look. Donald resents the man's wavering attention. What could be more important than the matter at hand?

It is Walter's photograph. Donald realizes, with embarrassment, that he turned it around so far that it is facing the couple.

Singer leans back in the chair, and as his mouth curves upward, ten years fall away from his face, like layers of gray scrim cascading onto a stage.

"You are a mountain climber, yes?" Singer asks.

"Yes," Donald replies awkwardly. "I am."

Singer looks over at his wife tenderly. Something tugs inside Donald's chest, an unseen hand grasping the beating muscles of his heart, and he knows in that moment that what he feels has a name. His internal engine quickens again and he inhales deeply. Despite the terrible circumstances of this couple sitting across from him, he acknowledges that he feels something like envy.

"When I was younger man," Singer begins slowly, mixing German into fragments of English. "After the war, with my good friend." Singer looks over at his wife again, as if for moral support. "We walked. We took train to Italy and walked through the mountains. So wonderful. Some best days of my life. Then, *natürlich*, I meet my wife. And when children were young, I still go up mountains, near to Vienna. Have you never been to the Hohe Wand? Or Rax? Until two years ago, it was possible to go."

Donald catches Mrs. Singer reaching for her husband's hand, discreetly, no doubt worrying that he is talking too much.

"I have been to both those places," Donald says stiffly. Part of him would love nothing more than to compare notes with this man, but the other part is repelled by the weakening of his formal professional shield. He moves some papers around on his desk, hoping to reset the conversation.

"You know," the old man continues brightly, "I carry these with me, always, just in case." From his coat pocket Singer withdraws a membership card that he opens proudly. Donald recognizes it immediately—the Jewish mountaineering club, Alpenverein Donauland. And then Singer takes out a small leather case, snaps it open, and removes two bone-handled folding utensils. A fork and a spoon. A corkscrew on the side of the spoon. "You never know when you might need," Singer says. He laughs as he slips the utensils back into their case, the case and card into his coat pocket, which he pats affectionately. The coat shows some wear, but his wife has mended it carefully. Good wool, and a fine curve to the lapels.

Donald's mouth relaxes from its professional rictus. Back at the apartment he has his own set of folding utensils, similar to Singer's. They've been trusted companions on all his climbs. Amazing they haven't been lost.

Now Donald remembers the gentleman who referred this couple.

A paper manufacturer who climbed with him a few times. Said Singer was a reputable man and a good businessman before '38, made some kind of packaging in the medical field.

Donald fixes his gaze on Singer, and more years peel away from the tired, lined face, revealing a younger man, in an energetic body, as healthy as his own, sturdy enough to carry a rucksack along an Alpine trail. Mrs. Singer looks at her husband, then down at her folded hands. Donald no longer wonders how Julius Singer won the heart of this woman. He notices the pleasing taper of her soft fingers. She has not done rough work, but that might change soon.

"Do you sew, Mrs. Singer?"

"Yes, I make clothes." She has a warm, musical voice. As if she might burst into song right there.

"Good, that's good."

Mrs. Singer nods.

Donald has no more questions. He looks over the forms again, looking for—he doesn't know what. A reason to say no, or yes. A hush envelops the room, as thick as the fog drifting in from the Danube. He feels calm, soothed, his heart and lungs full, as if he were breathing clean mountain air. The silence stretches out like a perfect afternoon, not too warm, a light breeze.

Donald reaches for his visa stamp and ink pad. He opens Mr. Singer's passport, riffles through the pages to the last empty one. He pounds the stamp onto the ink pad—Mrs. Singer startles at the noise—and presses it onto the empty page. He opens Mrs. Singer's passport and does the same.

Mr. Singer, realizing what is happening, leans forward. "Thank you, Herr Brown, *danke schön*," Mr. Singer says.

"We wish you can meet our wonderful little Evie," Mrs. Singer adds. "She will also be thanking you."

Donald searches for his fountain pen, rummaging under files. "Don't forget to take those tools with you, Mr. Singer," he says, not looking up from his desk. He finds the pen and begins filling in the immigration quota numbers: 20146 for Julius Singer, 20147 for Anna,

20148 for the daughter, Eva. And it's only February. He signs his name to both passports, waves the booklets like paper fans to dry the ink, and passes them across the desk toward Mr. Singer.

"Good luck to you both," Donald says. "Perhaps you will have time to do some hiking when you get to America. The Catskills are just a train ride from New York City. Nothing at all like the Alps here, of course. But beautiful all the same."

THERE WAS STILL that piece of the puzzle I did not find in Vienna in 2012, the IKG forms. Even though Julius had managed the entire ordeal of passports, visas, and exit permits on his own, he would still have had to fill out an emigration questionnaire at the IKG, and, as required by Eichmann's regulations, someone from the IKG would have visited the Singer apartment to conduct a house visit. When no record for my family appeared in the IKG database in 2012, I'd given up, assuming the documents had been lost, though this seemed odd given the meticulousness of Nazi record keeping.

Now I decided to search again after a colleague referred me to Anatol Steck, an archivist and researcher at the United States Holocaust Memorial Museum in Washington, DC.

THEY GOT OUT very late, Anatol Steck remarked in an early email. He began by detailing the role of the IKG and the importance of the documents I hoped to find.

> Following the so-called Anschluss, on March 12, 1938, Nazi officials shut down the Jewish community offices (IKG) and deported its president and board members to the Dachau concentration camp.

I knew that one of those IKG members was Dr. Jakob Ehrlich, a resident of 22 Weimarer Strasse.

Beginning on May 2, 1938, when the IKG reopened, it had been transformed into a de-facto welfare organization, one of whose most pressing priorities was to facilitate emigration. Jewish individuals and families seeking to flee Nazi persecution began to register for financial and logistical assistance with the community's emigration department. Each head of household (or single individual, including wives whose husbands had been arrested by the Gestapo, the secret state police) had to fill out a detailed questionnaire, which included: the applicant's name, address, birth date, birth place, marital status, nationality, residency status in Vienna and whether and how long the applicant had resided someplace else, information about the applicant's profession and last-held position, any newly learned profession, languages spoken, financial circumstances and monthly income, as well as comprehensive emigration-related information.

The emigration-related information includes specifics about the ability to obtain the necessary documents, the destination, financial resources for emigration, relatives and friends living abroad (including names, addresses, and relationship to the applicant), the applicant's personal references, and passport information. In addition, the questionnaire also lists the dependents, including names, birth places, birth dates, and professions. In some cases the questionnaires also supply information about the applicant's parents.

These Emigration Questionnaires ("Auswanderungsfragebögen") are one of the most extensive, self-contained sources of personal data of Jews from the Holocaust period. The questionnaires are often supplemented with additional documents, such as letters, affidavits, official papers, internal IKG forms and correspondence, etc., as well as stamps and

handwritten notes in the margins through which one can follow the processing of each case.

As individual applications were processed, the forms
were placed into an alphabetically arranged order for ease of
retrieval. Several card indexes to the questionnaires—a numerical one, an alphabetical one, one by profession, another one
by nationality, and a card index arranged by birth date—were
created at some point during processing. Three of these,
the numerical one, the alphabetical one, and the card index
arranged by profession, have survived (although all three have
gaps). The original card indexes are held at the premises of
the IKG in Vienna where the [United States Holocaust Memo-
rial] Museum microfilmed them. The original emigration questionnaires to which the card indexes correspond (and without
which the questionnaires are only partially accessible) are held
by the Central Archives for the History of the Jewish People,
located in Jerusalem, where the Museum microfilmed them.

The IKG, and all these meticulous records Anatol described, ultimately became an essential part of Eichmann's hideous machinery. By
1941, the Nazis determined that they couldn't expel their Jews because
not enough other countries would take them in. At this point, the Final
Solution was implemented. It was the staff of the IKG that would draw
up the deportation lists for the camps. At first they tried to save young
people and able-bodied adults who could be employed in other countries. Older people and families with small children were not so lucky.
Soon no one was safe. According to IKG reports, by late 1939 there
were only 53,403 Jews left in Vienna from the community that had
once numbered around 200,000.

Anatol searched his database for me, hoping to find the missing
documents, without success. He said the last place to look was in Jerusalem, where the original documents had been sent after the end of the
war. It might be in the microfilm records there, he suggested, but he

wasn't optimistic. He'd never seen a case yet where the originals still existed without some record of the family members in the digital database. I prepared myself for disappointment.

Anatol emailed me a few days later:

> I am pleased to report to you that we were able to locate your grandfather's emigration file on microfilm (even though there was no entry in the database). As I mentioned before, I did not expect that there would be an emigration file. In over ten years of working with the Vienna materials, this is the first case I have encountered where there is no reference in the database for any of the family members listed on the emigration questionnaire but the emigration file exists on microfilm. This proves that when it comes to archival research, it pays to leave no stone (or in this case, page) unturned.

I couldn't wait to see the questionnaire, but Anatol wrote that I would have to sign a release before he could send me a copy of the document. I'll explain why later, he wrote. Since I didn't read German, we arranged a phone call to go over the material.

The first thing Anatol noted was the date on the questionnaire—February 15, 1940, two days before the American embassy granted the Singer visas. Perhaps Julius had hurried home on the fourteenth, with temperatures hovering around ten degrees and snow on the ground, having finally secured an interview at the American consulate, one that had given him hope that the waiting would soon be over. The next morning he'd walked to the IKG office to hastily fill out the required questionnaire and arrange for the house visit. He and Anna had returned to the American consulate for their interview and had received the visas on February 17. The "*Hausrecherche*" house visit was dated the nineteenth. A lot of walking in a dangerous Vienna for an exhausted man with a weak heart, during a frigid winter month.

Anatol confirmed that unlike most emigrants Julius wasn't asking for help. He'd done all the work himself and the questionnaire was merely a necessary formality.

In hasty script, Julius recorded his profession as "paper goods manufacturer," but left blank the lines where others would have listed retraining classes undertaken to learn a new trade. Julius wrote (optimistically, perhaps) that in addition to German he spoke English and some French. Most valuable for the IKG, which by then had precious little financial assistance to offer, he wrote that he had been able to finance the entire emigration process on his own. In a chart that asked for relatives and friends overseas who could provide assistance, he included the names of Anna's relatives in Detroit. The Nichterns had provided the required affidavits and Teddy Mann had guaranteed funds.

Farther down the questionnaire, there was another chart to list relatives in his immediate family. Julius filled in the names of Anna and Eva. Below the chart was a line that translated as such: "Above relatives to emigrate now or later?" Julius wrote, *Alles mit mir*. All with me.

Anatol explained that it was this particular written answer that necessitated the release form I'd signed. The responses to this question had caused pain and family conflict for many survivors who discovered that they were either not included in a list of relatives or were deliberately left behind, for financial reasons or because of preexisting ill will. When I looked at images of Holocaust-era Jews—waiting in lines, humiliated in the streets, concentration camp survivors—it was easy to forget that before the Nazi persecution began they had all been individuals from families with the usual complications, some plagued by bitterness that ruined holiday dinners, marriages, and childhoods. For the three Singers, the crisis had strengthened their bond, as if the long and anxious wait had been a spider spinning an unbreakable web.

The house visit form was completed on February 19 by an IKG interviewer in a fluid but rushed script. According to the form, the three Singers were living in "two rooms, two hallways, and one bathroom." The other rooms in the large apartment were given over to Viennese Jews who had been evicted from their homes. The form indicated that the Singer furniture had already been sold except for two beds, though my father told me that at least some of the family furniture was shipped to New York at some point before they left for New York. The remaining furniture, evidently of high quality, was valued at 200 Reichsmarks. The "Aryanization" of Adolf Eisenmann und Sohn was also noted.

The IKG charged 2,500 Reichsmarks as a fee to facilitate emigration. The Reich exit taxes amounted to 32,500 Reichsmarks, paid, interestingly enough, by the new owner of the business. Though this was a large sum, it was still much less than the full value of the business.

The site interviewer wrote: *Applicant has been living on sale of house furniture and other house goods and has been able to cover ship tickets and IKG fees by liquidation of four life insurance policies for which he received 4300RM.* Anatol noted that 4,300 Reichsmarks was a considerable sum, more than most Jews in Vienna had by this time.

The life insurance policies Julius had bought for his children and himself and Anna had been put to necessary use. I was surprised that the Gestapo had allowed him to keep any of this money. But the unacknowledged manager of Adolf Eisenmann und Sohn and his wife and daughter would have had to live on something. Perhaps Makovsky, the Aryan owner, made this comparatively gracious situation possible, in the interest of keeping the factory operations running smoothly. I marveled again at Julius's excellent negotiation skills.

My mother had her own blunt thoughts on how their final escape came about. *Somehow or other . . . he must have made a deal with them. It's the only thing I can think of. Because we had no money at that point. We got a train ticket to go to Trieste and he got a boat ticket.*

The site interviewer noted that the family would take with them four to five pieces of luggage, which could include clothing, underwear, linens. No valuables were permitted.

In the "summary section" the interviewer wrote: *Applicant makes a very good impression: industrious, a sense of duty, all his life he has been dedicated to work and family. Information (see documents attached) was given in a clear and open way. After a long deliberation S declares possibil-*

ity that he is able to increase the necessary sum to 5000RM! The ship tickets shall be valued at this rate!

Anatol noted the unusual exclamation mark, indicating the interviewer's genuine surprise that Julius was willing to pay more than what was being requested. Had Julius still had some money left? My mother didn't think so. Perhaps the promise of Teddy Mann's financial generosity and the hope that he would soon be able to extricate his family from the terror in Vienna had allowed him to feel generous on this interview day. Julius understood that whatever extra money the IKG received from him could be used to assist other families who had no money at all.

After Anatol finished his rough translation, I cried hard for my dear grandfather. I could not understand how Julius had managed to preserve his faith in the goodness of people and his sense of generosity toward those so much less fortunate than his family. He did, and I wanted to believe that someone else's family made it out as a result.

———

THE VIENNA POLICE stamped the exit visa (at a fee of eight Reichsmarks) on March 14. It was valid till April 25. The family didn't linger in Vienna that long. On March 22, a Viennese official stamped Julius's and Anna's passports with a ticket number for the journey from Vienna to Trieste.

———

THE LAST ENTRY in Eva's keepsake book was added the day before the Singers left Vienna. Martha Altenberg, presumably related to "Onkel" Jakob Altenberg, wrote,

> Now you sail across the large ocean,
> Though I hope our farewell will not be hard,
> Because soon I too will come to that land

And you expect me then waving on the shore.

I wish you and your family good luck for the trip

And furthermore lots of success in every way!

Your loving cousin Martha

Easter Sunday, the 24th March 1940.

Was there a small gathering of family and friends to celebrate the Singers' departure? As a Catholic, cousin Martha Altenberg recorded the Easter holiday, and yet she hoped that she, too, would go to America.

Jakob Altenberg died in Vienna during the war years. When I made contact with his great-granddaughter in Berlin, she didn't know about a Martha Altenberg. She said that the cause of Jakob's death remained a mystery, though officially he died of natural causes. But she added that by 1944, even the converted Jews like Jakob who had married Christians were no longer safe and many committed suicide in despair. Jakob's daughter Adela safely emigrated to England, but without the friendship of Julius and Jakob, the close bond between the two families did not survive the war.

— *EXIT* —

I DIDN'T KNOW what time Eva and her parents boarded the train from Vienna to Trieste. Michael Simonson at the Leo Baeck Institute quickly helped me track down a train schedule from 1939, part of an archive posted online. Yes, amazingly, there were people who collected items like war-era train timetables.

In my imagination Eva and my grandparents took a slow night train with multiple stops on the way to Trieste. The 1939 schedule Michael sent me did list trains that left at 9:20 and 10:50 in the evening. By 1940 there were wartime curfews for Jews, so I imagined that the long walk from 22 Weimarer Strasse to the South Station must have taken place earlier in the day, when the city was still awake. And I imagined that they must have made this dangerous trip to the station escorted by Sylvester Mazura, loyal factory foreman to the end.

MARCH 25, 1940. In a photograph that could not possibly exist, Julius, Anna, and Eva step out of their apartment. Anna pulls the door closed, quietly, so as not to alarm the other families in apartment 5 or rouse the Steppans across the hall. Mazura is on the landing, his familiar blue uniform peeking out below his coat, a canvas satchel slung over his shoulder. He is wearing a Nazi armband.

Earlier in the afternoon, Mazura brought the two trunks down to his ground-floor apartment for safekeeping. Father, mother, and daughter are a solemn procession now as they follow Mazura down the staircase. Eva hesitates a moment, listening to the tapping soles of the others. She presses her hand on the wooden railing, soft as satin, and counts off the stairs like she has every day since forever.

Her father steps into the courtyard and takes a last look at the factory. This happens as cold late-afternoon rain settles over the city. No one speaks. It is time to leave. Their train will leave at 9:20 and they have a long walk ahead.

Herr Mazura opens his apartment and the trunks are just inside in a small cart normally used to deliver boxes from the factory to local clients. Her father unlatches the heavy wooden door to number 22, her home, and they are outside. The street trees shiver, underdressed in the early-spring days after such a long winter, but it is a comfort to see that they have carried on with their growing in spite of the terror of the last two years. In the last months she hasn't been out of the apartment at all except to go to school. And since the end of the last school term in December, there has been no good reason at all to leave the relative safety of their rooms. As she steps onto the sidewalk, she feels like a bear leaving a cave after months of hibernation. Or maybe this is how a zoo animal would feel after its release from captivity: excited and jittery and also frightened and unsure. Icy raindrops sting her cheeks. How small she feels, just a dot in this city that has been her home. The next home is still an ocean away, entirely unknown, and unreal. As Eva walks with her mother, under their last tattered umbrella, she wonders when she will return.

Her father falls in alongside Herr Mazura, who insists on pulling the cart. They know every small street in Vienna. It will take longer to walk the smaller streets, but they will be less visible. It is too sad for conversation, and they must conserve energy for the long walk, and what is there left to say? Herr Mazura will manage everything, as he always has. He will pass on farewells to the factory staff and they will understand why they were not told in advance. The cart wheels rumble across the cobbled streets, and with the sound of their footfalls on the pavement Eva hears a rhythm that reminds her of the skip-rope games she used to play with friends in the park, when Jewish children were still allowed to play in the park. Down Währinger Strasse, then through smaller streets, zigzagging toward the station. Stores have already closed for the day, but a few cars pass by, splashing through pools of rainwater and slush. They cross a small street near Mariahilfer Strasse, where "Onkel" Jakob ran his gallery, where her mother took her to buy her last new coat, but that was years ago. She remembers a millinery shop her mother used to frequent, cafés, a men's haberdashery where her father ordered hats and custom suits, including the one he is wearing today. She looks up at the windows of apartments on the upper floors, where families are getting ready for dinner, wondering if anyone up there is looking down at her family now.

There is the last of the thin daylight, the clouds break, and the air chills in the blue gloaming. Even under the umbrella, she feels naked and exposed when a few people pass by, and she imagines that they are staring, but if they have some thoughts about the four walkers with a cart, they must be reassured by Herr Mazura's swastika. When they reach an empty street, Mazura stops and offers them a drink from his water flask and they catch their breath. Her father checks his watch. They move on.

At last the roofline of the train station appears. Just another block or two and they will be there. Her father turns around to check on Eva and her mother. Eva watches him pat his coat to check again for the passports and ship tickets.

Finally they are at the huge station, joining the streams of other travelers. Mazura escorts them to the correct track, where they will wait for the night train to Trieste.

Mazura opens his satchel and withdraws a package, carefully wrapped in the brown paper the factory workers use to wrap up boxes. "For you, Frau Singer," he says, handing the package to Anna. "Sandwiches. And a few apples."

Anna wonders where in the world of Vienna Mazura found those apples. Fruit is like gold now. "Rosa saved some from last fall," he says, as if anticipating her question. "And this, too," Mazura says, handing her a tin water canteen.

They are going to Italy again, under circumstances so different from the joyful family holiday just two years ago. That time at Cesenatico seems to be from another lifetime, lived by a woman she can no longer recognize as herself. Her boys are gone; she hasn't heard from them much in recent months. Worry overwhelmed her. Then she spent days in the apartment with Evalein, reading or listening to records, trying to keep busy. In the evenings she sometimes realized with alarm that she hadn't thought about Fritz or Dolfi during the day because they felt so distant, as if they had never lived with her at all. Somewhere in London they are now nineteen and sixteen, two years older than the boys she sent away. Today the three remaining here are beginning a journey that will take them thousands of miles away from Vienna and her boys in London. A wave of sorrow washes over her, flames up into her throat, and then sinks into her belly like stone ballast. She clasps her daughter's hand, cold and small. The child is exhausted. "Sit, Evie, take a rest on the trunk, there is still time before the train." The train cannot get here soon enough. They cannot get away from here soon enough, even though the future terrifies her.

Eva curls up on one of the trunks, closes her eyes, and tries to sleep.

The chill cramps her legs, and she hugs her knees as close as she can. A million sparkles shimmer inside her eyelids, she listens to the humming in her ears and the muffled sounds of the station. In what feels like only minutes, her mother shakes her shoulders awake gently, but she can tell some time has passed while she slept. The train is coming soon. She is thirsty. Her mother seems to understand this and passes her the tin canteen. A distant whistle startles her. She rubs her eyes, dislodging the crustiness of sleep. The waiting is over.

Julius and Mazura shake hands. *Auf Wiedersehen.* Until we see each other again. Julius becomes conscious of a heavy metal weight in his coat pocket—his set of apartment and factory keys, so useless now—he forgot he still has them. He pulls them out and hands them to Mazura, who accepts them with a nod.

"Thank you, from all our family," Julius says. "You have been so good to us."

"Herr Singer, be safe. At the border I hear they will search even inside your clothing, to be sure you have nothing. You understand."

Julius understands. He will have to do something about the small amount of paper money hidden in his jacket. He cannot think what, but he must figure something out once they board the train. His heart races again, as it has during this long walk.

"Farewell, Frau Singer," says Mazura, taking her hand. "May you all travel safe."

Eva feels Herr Mazura squeeze her shoulders. But she wants a formal farewell, and extends her hand. Herr Mazura smiles and presses it between his rough palms. "Goodbye, Fräulein Eva. Be good, child. Be safe."

This is the end of their lives in Vienna. The train pulls out of the station, metal wheels screeching as the engine picks up speed. Familiar buildings soften and blur. The nighttime city bleeds into the countryside with fleeting silhouettes of farms. Inside houses are people unaware of the train chugging by them with its cargo.

Eva is wedged between her parents in a packed compartment. They are lucky to have seats at all. The passengers sit in tense silence.

Through the closed window, the clatter and clank of the wheels on the tracks measures out the minutes. The air is stale. Despite her anxiety Eva grows drowsy again. Her head drops and she tries to rouse her body, but the weight of her head pulls her down against her mother's arm.

The train climbs the mountains, on its well-worn route from Vienna to Trieste. Julius knows it well. He traveled it for business. He and Anna took this same train on their honeymoon, so long ago. Once, the strip of Friulian land hugging the Adriatic Sea was part of the great Habsburg Empire, and Trieste a prized seaport serving a landlocked capital. Now Trieste is the way out to the wider world.

The hours pass. They will be at the border soon. He reaches into his coat pocket, as if searching for gloves. He rises, startling his daughter to alertness, and slips out of the compartment.

"Where's Papa going?" Eva asks blearily. Anna hugs her daughter close. "Just to wash up, Evie. He will be back soon."

Julius presses his way down the narrow corridor packed with passengers and luggage. At last he is on line for the lavatory. When it is his turn, the passengers behind him heave forward, their force shoving him into the cubicle. He locks himself inside. There are no cupboards or closets, no crack in the wall or under the sink. Since he is here, he unbuttons to urinate. He rinses his hands, flicking away water droplets rather than use the grimy hand towel. He rips off a section from the roll of coarse toilet paper to finish the job. This paper, wartime paper, rough as cardboard, nothing he would ever have used at the factory, worse than even that crappy stuff at Café Taube. He can see threads of wood pulp in the sheets.

Someone knocks on the door with urgency. "One moment, please," Julius calls out. "Just a moment." He unrolls a few sheets as an exploration and then with energy born from a sudden inspiration, he unwinds the paper almost to the end of the roll. He quickly tears the short seam Anna made in his jacket lining and takes out the modest sheaf of paper money hidden inside, and flattens the bundle against the edge of the sink. He inserts the bills one by one into the roll, maintaining tension on the paper as he rewinds. If there is one thing Julius understands, it is paper, even the most humble: its composition, fabrication, its optimal tension, and its breaking point.

Another knock on the door, louder this time. "Just one more moment," Julius says. Sweat pricks at his brow and drips down his neck, dampening his shirt collar. He inspects the roll from all sides. It will have to do. He hopes the people waiting outside the bathroom won't use up all the paper before they reach the border. At least the money isn't in his pocket. He unlocks the door and exits, smiling at the woman waiting next in line. He makes his way along the packed corridor to his compartment. Once inside he closes the door and takes his seat next to Anna. "Well, so be it," he whispers.

The sky is still as dark as midnight when the train halts with a screech and moan of brakes. Nazi guards stalk through the cars, ordering passengers to remove coats and scarves and stand rigid while luggage is searched. A young one, pimpled, barely out of his teens, rifles in a distracted way through the contents of the Singers' trunks, missing the silver spoons, the menorah, Elijah's wine cup, and the silver opera glasses hidden in the plain white linens and embroidered piano shawl. Another one, also young, is more thorough with Julius, pointing with his weapon to the spot where he wants Julius to stand. Roughly, he pulls Julius's jacket, tugs out coat and jacket pockets, pats him down, all the way to the bottom hems. The train gasps and whistles. The high mountain air chills Julius's sweaty neck. Mazura was right. Thanks to him Julius has nothing to hide. The soldiers leave at last, moving to the next car. More waiting until the train lurches forward again, and at last, at last crosses the border out of Austria. Julius remembers their last Passover dinner, somber in the apartment at 22 Weimarer Strasse. *Bright as the light of day the darkness of the night. All miracles occurred at midnight.*

THE SINGERS WERE the lucky ones. Anna already had family well established in the United States. Julius had something of value to leverage, and his persistence and cleverness may have won brief reprieve from the Nazi police. The synchronicity of a shared passion may have been the deciding factor for a sympathetic U.S. vice-consul.

Sadly, the experience of her childhood deliverance did not leave my mother with an abiding faith in good fortune. Rather, it was the opposite. As I knew her she remained always vigilant and cautious. The sky was always falling, a heavy load. She did so many things expertly: her work, caring for her family, cooking, gardening, needle-point, sewing, small microcosms she could design and control. My impression was that the larger world presented unpredictability and possible fear. She never learned to drive. I blamed my own aversion to driving on growing up in New York City. I had the strong feeling that she did not want me to excel in this most average skill, perhaps from a feeling of protectiveness. Maybe it wasn't my inexpert driving she worried about as much as the unpredictable and unknown other drivers on the highway. It was a dangerous world out there. She was hard on herself and she saw me as vulnerable, in need of toughening. *Be prepared. Don't go soft.*

Her worldview was not an optimist's. But about some things my mother could appreciate absurdity and lightness. That last bit of paper money that Julius hid in a toilet paper roll and later retrieved aboard the train to Trieste provided comic relief, a family story often told, no doubt embellished over the years. To my disappointment, my mother did not share this story with her young Austrian interviewer, the one who went on to a law career. Too bad: it would have been a good ice-breaker.

––––––––

MY MOTHER SUMMED up what she had been told of the fate of the extended family of Singers and Nichterns during her Leo Baeck interview. Most families never found out what had happened to their relatives and it remains unclear to me how my mother received her information. But these were her stories and she told them to her interviewer. Wherever her relatives ended up, they never returned home.

Our family, my mother's family, there were five brothers. Three of them went to America. One of them [the remaining two brothers] *was a journalist with the* Neues Wiener Tagblatt [a major Viennese newspaper], *you know, big time. He thought that nothing would happen to him. Yes. Well. He went to—I think Dachau. And there was a younger brother who also didn't want to leave and he also went to Dachau and they both were lost. The rest of the family that I know of was my father's brother's widow. She didn't want to leave. She didn't go to Dachau. She went to Buchenwald. Same end.*

A Visit to the City by the Sea

*In my mind Jews and Trieste go together, and the long and fruitful
association of the two has made the city what it is—or at least, what
it seems to me to be in those moments, ten minutes before the hour,
when the idea of it bewitches me.*

—Jan Morris, *Trieste and the Meaning of Nowhere*

MARCH 2019. I had hoped for a poetic train ride to Trieste,
but I discovered to my disappointment that there was no
longer direct rail service from Vienna and that the few trains
available ran at night with connections in Ljubljana, Slovenia. Though
I'd always imagined that my mother's trip to Trieste had taken place at
night, I wanted to see the landscape in daylight, so I booked a van trip
that departed from Vienna's central station.

The driver was a tall and sullen-looking young man with a narrow
face and cavernous cheeks. He grabbed my heavy luggage (so much
paper) and heaved it into the back. I handed him my violin case with
some trepidation, but he placed it atop the luggage as if it were made of
glass. I liked that: a man of contrasts.

Besides myself there were three young women, one young man,
a man/woman couple in their forties, and another man of middle
years. There was no conversation for the next four hours in any language. Not one of the young people made an attempt to interact with
their peers; headphones and iPhones ruled. As they occupied their time

with streamed shows and online games and high-speed thumb texting, I turned away to look out at the landscape whizzing by: the outskirts of Vienna, greening hills and valleys and flatlands with farm villages of white houses on one side, snow-covered mountains in the distance on the other. In the dusky light of an overcast morning the snow glinted like polished steel. I saw a fairy-tale castle perched on a hillside. No one else looked; I had the feeling that these were repeat travelers for whom a castle no longer impressed. At a rest stop off the highway, we all stood apart eating sandwiches or salads from plastic containers. One woman made a call. The others texted.

Back in the van, headphones plugged seven sets of auricles. No, I was determined not to succumb, even though at home my family had complained about my phone obsession. Liza was right: iPhones did suck out human brains. As one of the young women texted pink hearts to an unknown recipient, I mourned a lost time of random encounters with fellow travelers, people I had met just once on a train or a boat but would never forget.

I returned my gaze to the landscape outside. Across a broad valley, a white forest of revolving wind turbines stood proud. Far off, a bank of clouds had blown into a scrim of concentric arcs, suggesting rain up ahead. We passed an industrial complex: DHL and DB Schenker warehouses, stacks of shipping containers, a colony of distribution centers. We crossed into Slovenia and two of our group left the van at a rest stop.

I could feel the change immediately: the text on road signage was now such an impenetrable combination of packed consonants and too few vowels that I couldn't even pretend to sound out anything. Soon enough—Slovenia being a tiny nation—we were pulling into Ljubljana. Gray blockish apartment complexes, a reminder of the Communist era, contrasted with billboards announcing an upcoming Sting concert, the latest cell phones, sneakers, sunglasses, discounted clothing, the nearest McDonald's, a Walmart-like chain store called Big Bang (I wondered if it was inspired by the TV show). All the proletarian glories of decadent capitalism. The remaining five passengers departed at a bus depot. Somewhere, not far away, I knew there was a historic city center, but I wouldn't get to see it on this trip.

Now the driver found his voice. "You are the only one for Trieste," he said. "In ten years with this company, I never go there."

Relieved to have conversation at last, I moved to the shotgun seat. The driver told me that many young Slovenians had full-time jobs in Vienna and returned home to their families and friends on the weekend. "It is a small country," he said, "we are only famous for Melania." Ah, yes, of course, that Melania, our cryptic mannequin of a first lady. "You can have a good life here, not so expensive as Austria. But the good jobs are there."

His phone rang, a friend on the other end; he chatted away and I understood not a word. I took out my iPhone to capture the snow-capped mountains on three sides, clusters of yellow farmhouses nestled into the hillsides, the tilled fields of earth as dark as crumbled anthracite ready for planting.

We crossed the border into Italy at the small town of Opicina and I sighed with relief. I could read the signs again, in my favorite language. The houses looked different right away—now stone and stucco—and the people on the narrow streets dressed like Italians, somehow more put together than rumpled Americans, even in jeans and T-shirts. I had missed being in this country, but I could already tell this was not the Italy I knew from many trips in the past to Liguria and Tuscany and Umbria: there were no palm trees, no Mediterranean light. This was not gilded Florence or Rome or Venice or Verona or the colorful coast of the Cinque Terre. The landscape here was rocky and rough; the trees that clutched the steep hillside were hardy evergreens and deciduous varietals that resembled those in my Hudson River town.

The roadway carried us up and up and at the crest I glimpsed the sea. I rolled down the window and inhaled a gust of salt air as a wide panorama spread out below us: the Adriatic, laid out like rippled silver, undulations of the last peninsulas of Italy, and beyond those, hidden behind a screen of low-hanging fog, the few miles of Slovenian coastline, and still farther on, Croatia. Far out across the sea was a pileup of heavy cloud and mist that reminded me of overcast days in Maine. A familiar blended scent floated in the air: sea brine with whiffs of fuel oil and car exhaust and cooking that reminded me of New York. A pang of home caught in my chest and I breathed it all in deeply. I loved this place already, before I'd set one foot on the pavement. Soon we were making our way down narrow twists and turns of residential streets onto the busy harbor road of Trieste, and I saw the famous Piazza dell'Unità, familiar to me from photos I'd seen. A mountainous hulk of glittering white cruise ship was docked at the passenger pier, the same one where Eva and her parents had boarded the *Saturnia* to sail to New York in 1940. After two years of research and planning, I was here at last.

EVERYTHING I KNEW about the city of Trieste had begun with Jan Morris's evocative travelogue *Trieste and the Meaning of Nowhere*. I'd first heard about the author as the subject of a 1974 *New York Times* profile when she transitioned from male to female. This was big news; I remember reading the story as a teenager and being mind-blown that such a thing as gender dysphoria existed. She'd been a successful travel writer as James Morris, and she carried on after transition. After reading *Trieste* I searched for an author photo and found a friendly British woman of a certain age, a smiling face surrounded by windblown curls, like a character in a British cozy mystery. By the time of my reading, Jan Morris was retired in Wales, having announced at the end of *Trieste* that it would be her final book (fortunately, she later changed her mind).

Morris describes the city, nestled in at the top of the Adriatic Sea, on a skinny tongue of land in the easternmost part of Italy. Bordered by Slovenia, Croatia, and Bosnia-Herzegovina, it is surrounded by a fortress of limestone cliffs known as the *Carso* in Italian, or the Slavic *Karst*. On a clear summer day the color palette was hot chalky white against blue sea and sky, but the city center itself had been built in dif-

The 1938 Lehmann Vienna street guide listing residents at 22 Weimarer Strasse. Fanni Eisenmann, widow of Adolf Eisenmann, appears at upper left. Jakob Ehrlich, board member at the IKG, appears at bottom left. Julius Singer is listed at bottom right. Sylvester Mazura, his factory foreman and building concierge, appears above. Steppan was the family name of the Nazi-sympathizing neighbors across the hall from the Singers.

Singer/Merz family archive at the Leo Baeck Institute, NYC

Julius Singer in his World War I uniform.

Adolf Eisenmann und Sohn sent this invoice to Stanislav Ilakovac, owner of a pharmacy in Zagreb.

Courtesy of the archival collection at the Division for the History of Medical Sciences, Croatian Academy of Sciences and Arts

Julius and friends hiking, location and date unknown. Julius appears in upper left carrying a walking stick.

Singer/Metz family archive at the Leo Baeck Institute, NYC

Five minutes after I sent Franz Novotny the photo at right, wondering if he could identify the location, he sent back this 1910 postcard of the famous Alpen-Gasthof Preinergschaid, located near the trailhead of the Rax-Schneeberg Group mountains, a short trip from Vienna and a good place to stop after a hike for beer and sausage.

Singer/Metz family archive at the Leo Baeck Institute, NYC

Julius, perched on a ladder with walking stick, his best friend and climbing companion Jakob Altenberg, and a young woman who might be Jakob's daughter Adela in the Hohe Wand, a mountainous area not far from Vienna. Dated lower right May 20, 1928, when Julius was 53 years old. By then he was father to two sons, with a daughter, my mother, on the way.

Anna Singer's 1938 membership card for the Alpenverein Donauland, the Jewish mountain climbing club founded in 1924 after the main Austrian climbing club expelled all Jewish members. As late as January 1938, two months before the Anschluss, Julius planned on more mountain trips with his family.

Commercial illustration of the *Pulverkapseln:* fifty folded and glued paper sheets that open to reveal a fan shape. Powdered medicine was inserted into each opening.

Anna Singer, née Nichtern, as a young woman, possibly wearing her wedding ring.

Anna on her way to one of the many costume balls that were popular in Vienna.

Anna, Fritz, and Julius Singer, 1924/1925.

Fritz, Eva, and Dolfi Singer, late 1928/early 1929.

Dolfi, Eva with her much-loved stuffed bear, and Fritz, early 1930s. According to my mother, Dolfi (who became a vascular surgeon) later performed surgery on this stuffed bear.

Eva with an elderly relative, early 1930s.

Dolfi, Eva, and Fritz, sometime in the mid-1930s.

In October 1945, as a Private First Class in the U.S. Army, Paul Ehrlich, son of Jakob Ehrlich, took this photo of Rosa and Sylvester Mazura, who did so much to safeguard the Singers between 1938 and 1940. When I made contact with the Ehrlich family in late 2020, I discovered that Rosa had been Paul's nanny. Rosa and Sylvester stand in the courtyard of 22 Weimarer Strasse in front of the U.S. Army jeep that Paul drove to this reunion. The windows of Julius's factory are on the left.

Julius Singer's and Anna Singer's passports, dated July 21, 1939.

A page from Eva's *Poesiealbum*, dated January 12, 1939.

DONALD WINCHESTER BROWN, Jr.
Born on May 14, 1910 at New York, New
York. Prepared at St. Mark's School. Home ad-
dress: c-o Guaranty Trust Company, 524 Fifth
Avenue, New York, New York. In college three
and one-half years as undergraduate. Dunster
House. Harvard College Scholarship, 1931-1932;
Cercle Francais, 1929-1931; Mountaineering
Club; Hasty Pudding-Institute of 1770; Signet
Society, President, 1931-1932; Spee Club.
Field of Concentration: Intended Vocation:
Anthropology   Law

Donald
Winchester
Brown, in
Harvard's 1933
yearbook.

Donald Winchester Brown (*left*) with a
hiking companion. Penelope Brown W.
wrote: "I think this is the earliest—
maybe even still in college?—based on
his face looking younger than in the
other two pictures—and from the
amount of hair he has."

Donald Brown in his thirties. He
would have looked something like
this when he issued visas for the
Singer family.

Penelope scribbled this on the back of the third photograph: "I'm sure this is the latest. The boy is my brother who was born February 1940 and don't you think he looks about ten?"

Cosulich Company third-class passenger housing on Via Italo Svevo as described in a company brochure: "While waiting for the departure of the ship from Trieste, passengers are housed free of charge in the 'Casa degli Emigranti' of the Company, a large building of 5 floors, surrounded by a park near the sea shore. The building has 25 dormitories and 2000 beds. A second building below, connected to the first, contains the enormous refectory and the chapel."

Nell' attesa della partenza del piroscafo da Trieste, il passeggero è ricoverato gratuitamente nella „Casa degli Emigranti" della Compagnia, grandioso edificio di 5 piani, circondato da un parco, in riva al mare. La casa ha 25 dormitori e 2000 letti. Un secondo edificio più basso, unito al primo, contiene gl' immensi refettori e la cappella

Courtesy Italianliners.com Archives, Maurizio Eliseo collection, Trieste

Brochure printed by the Cosulich Line, advertising the *Saturnia* as the largest and fastest ship in the world.

Postcard showing the *Saturnia* in Trieste, at the dock still in use located across from the Piazza dell'Unità d'Italia.

Third-class cabins aboard the *Saturnia*.

One of the third-class lounges aboard the *Saturnia*, designated as a music room.

The *Saturnia* passing through the Strait of Gibraltar.

The *Saturnia* in New York City, 1934.

Singer/Merz family archive at the Leo Baeck Institute, NYC

The newly arrived Singer family poses in front of the Ford Pavilion
at the 1940 World's Fair.

20

This Is Your City
TOURS AND TRIPS INTRODUCING NEWCOMERS TO AMERICANS AND THE AMERICAN WAY

Arranged by the New World Club, Inc., in cooperation with the Division
for Social Adjustment, N.R.S., Inc., and Reconciliation Trips, Inc.

Leitung: Hans Hacker

Alle Führungen sind, soweit nichts anderes vermerkt ist, ohne Voranmeldung
zugänglich. Im Falle der Voranmeldung müssen Teilnehmerkarten mindestens
einen Tag vor der Führung schriftlich bestellt oder im Büro (New World Club,
Inc., Dept. of Group Excursions, 67 West 44th St., VA 6-3168) gelöst werden.
Bei schriftlichen Bestellungen ist Voreinsendung des Spesenbeitrages unbedingt
erforderlich. Mindestalter bei Betriebsführungen: 16 Jahre. Für Unfälle irgend-
welcher Art wird keine Verantwortung übernommen.

Teilnehmergebühren: Wochentags: Mitglieder 10 Cents; Gäste 15 Cents.
An Samstagen, Sonn- und Feiertagen: Mitglieder 10 Cents (Mitglieds-
karten vorweisen!); Gäste 20 Cents. Erhöhte Spesenbeiträge werden ge-
sondert bekanntgegeben. Ausflüge sind den Mitgliedern des N.W.C. bei
Lösung eines monatlichen Zusatz-Tickets von 15 Cents frei zugänglich.
(Zusätzliche Fahrtspesen gelten immer ab Treffpunkt.)

Sonntag, 30. November, 9:25 a. m.: "The Deserted Village" — Trail-Wanderung durch die Watchung Reservation

Ein bergiges Waldgebiet in New Jersey. Der "Indian Trail" durch
das verlassene Dorf. Die Geisterschlucht im Tannenwald am Blue
Brook. Viele schöne Panoramen. (Photoapparate mitbringen!) Rast
am "Surprise Lake". Grosses Lagerfeuer (Lunch mitbringen!). Geh-
zeit: 4-5 Stunden. Heimkehr: 7 p. m. Zusätzliche Fahrtspesen: 75c.
(Tax 4c.). Gute Schuhe! Treffpunkt: Eingang Lackawanna Ferry,

A 1941 advertisement from the pages of *Aufbau* ("Reconstruction"), a newspaper for
German-speaking immigrants.

RHEINGOLD
BIER
Extra Dry

Gut gehaltene Weine

Restaurant
NEUGOESCHL
Hotel OXFORD
205 W. 88. Str.--SC 4-7700
DINNER ab 6 P. M.
Samstag u. Sonnt. LUNCH

Jeden Samstag nach 9 Uhr:
Treffpunkt der gemütlichen
Wiener.   BERTL WEISS

NEUGROESCHL AT HOTEL OXFORD
205 West 88. Str.   SChuyler 4-7700

Verkauft   SCHALET, KUTTELFLECK, BEUSCHEL,
            Container **35¢**
            BISCHOFSBROT, LINZER TORTE,
            SPEZIAL BUTTER COOKIES ....Pfd. **85¢**

Serviert   u. a. ein FULL COURSE DINNER ......
            GANSL IN RISIBISI ODER GRAUPEN .. **$1.00**

Übernimmt   HOCHZEITS-DINNER und PARTIES — in und
            ausser Haus.

VIENNESE RESTAURANT
at Hotel Oxford, 205 West 88th Street - SChuyler 4-7700
Formerly NEUGROESCHL
Management: JULIUS SINGER und ADOLF DRESSLER
ALLE WIENER SPEZIALITÄTEN
DINNER: Daily 5 to 9 p. m., except Monday
Sunday and Holidays 12-9 p. m.

Advertisements for Neugroeschl Restaurant from the pages of *Aufbau*. "Meeting point for cozy Viennese," where hungry émigrés could eat a full-course meal for $1.00 in 1941. Eventually the partners split their two locations, and Julius took over one with another partner.

Frank during his
army service, 1944.

Eve, a glamorous young American,
visiting Nichtern relatives in Florida,
around 1945-6.

Anna, Eve, and Julius
at Bear Mountain, NY,
summer 1947, with Frank
behind the camera.

Eve takes a favorite
pose in a photo taken by
Frank's art school friend
Seymour Mednick.

ferent hues. During the height of the Austro-Hungarian Empire, Trieste, "one of the great achievements of Habsburg imperialism," had served as the warm water port for this inland empire and it was their architects who had laid out the city center in monumental grid formation with buildings as solid and grand as those in the center of Vienna.

When I'd first mentioned my interest in traveling to Trieste a year earlier, my father and his wife had recommended a detective series set in the city titled *The Inspector Vivaldi Mysteries*. I binge-watched with the avidity of a vicarious traveler. I couldn't wait to see the city for myself, but for the moment I settled for a dated TV show—flip phones and outmoded boxy computers. The opening scenes were everything I could have hoped for: it is winter, our hero's rain-soaked trench coat flaps in a fierce bora wind that whips the sea into treacherous choppy bands, blowing off a thick fog of salt spray.

The bora had always been a player in this city, not to be messed with, and a source of civic pride. Jan Morris looks out her window one day "delighted to see the old monster whipping through the trees below, sending the leaves scudding madly across the sidewalks and boiling the lethargic sea." The image recalled a time I'd been walking in Red Hook, Brooklyn, on a wintry day so fierce it felt like unseen hands were hurling me across Conover Street toward the river. Trieste looked like my kind of place. I wondered if my mother and her parents had encountered the bora in late March of 1940.

THIS CITY BY the sea had always drawn people of many nearby nations—Hungary, Austria, the Slavic area of Istria, Slovenia, and Croatia. Eager to secure a presence of merchants in Trieste, the Habsburgs had actively encouraged Jews to move there and many had done so, and of that population many had thrived, enough so that the community had built a large synagogue. Unlike the central synagogue of Vienna I'd visited in 2012, hidden on a narrow side street, this lavishly Byzantine-style temple had been constructed as a proud freestanding building.

The rise of shipping companies had created an escape opportunity for Jews who chose not to stay in Europe, even in relatively laissez-faire Trieste. Throughout the 1920s and '30s, ships left here for Palestine, points east, and America. In 1938, as the Jews of Vienna fled to any nation that would accept them, Trieste was one remaining route to safety. My uncles traveled west through France to England, but as this route was no longer possible once Britain declared war on Germany in September 1939, the port of Trieste became all the more important.

My friend Stefan's side-by-side translations of Julius's and Anna's passports had revealed that Eva and her parents had spent about nine days in Trieste after arriving on March 26, 1940, until the *Saturnia* departed on April 4. With so little money—given the Nazi currency restrictions enforced on departing Jews—how had they managed to find shelter and food during their stay? Morris describes how the Triestine Jewish population mobilized to assist transients on their way out of Europe starting in the 1920s, an effort that included establishing a hostel and a small adjunct synagogue on Via del Monte.

I wrote a fan letter to Morris, care of her literary agent, as soon as I read the last page, and to my delight she replied, suggesting that I contact the Jewish Museum of Trieste, housed in that same building on Via del Monte. Director Annalisa Di Fant replied, telling me that she would be glad to welcome me if I ever made a trip to her city. Annalisa in turn directed me to Stelio Zoratto, the librarian of the Maritime Museum, who responded to my queries.

During this period of research I reached the limits of my Italian and began working with a tutor. Business correspondence in Italian requires use of formalities that are not intuitive for English speakers: a singular person is addressed in the feminine third person singular *lei* and a group of two or more is addressed using the third person plural *loro*. I did not want to begin my relationships with faraway resources by coming off as a crass American, even after Annalisa and Stelio had begun emailing me in English.

ON MORRIS'S TUMBLR page I saw a post with a photograph of Trieste's Piazza dell'Unità illuminated at night, tagged by someone named Emiliana—in English. I needed Emiliana, someone who could represent me for a while until I could get there myself, someone bilingual who evidently loved the city as much as I did already.

I hated the way social media glued us all to our smartphones as we rummaged for news or gossip or new shoes. Social media sucked, until it didn't. I sent Emiliana a message and she wrote me back. She was a young woman, a former student at the University of Trieste, now living in nearby Udine, where she had grown up. With her dark hair and glasses, and her earnest energy, she reminded me of someone—a thirty-years-younger me.

In our first Skype conversation I mentioned that until its surrender to the Allies in 1943, Italy had been a relatively safe place for Jews, compared to Germany and Austria.

"Do you think Italians were less enthusiastic Fascists?" I asked.

Emiliana sighed. "We Italians are just kind of lazy."

"It couldn't be just that," I protested.

She shrugged.

Over the course of several months, Emiliana interviewed professors on my behalf, including Annalisa Di Fant, translated newspaper articles, visited the Bora Museum in Trieste (yes, there was one), and researched photographs of some of the accommodations for travelers like my mother's family. The Jewish community of Trieste hostels were simple places with bunk beds in large open rooms, dormitory style, and they served meals. No luxuries, but at least there was a place to stay and food to eat. Julius, Anna, and Eva must have eaten a lot of pasta and bread.

Tragically, the Jewish community of Trieste that fed and housed refugees had been slaughtered after 1943. When Italy surrendered to the Allies, the German army swept in to claim the valuable port city and wasted no time rounding up the Italian Jews of Trieste. They were held in a salt factory building on the edge of town called La Risiera, now a memorial, before being deported east to concentration camps. The Nazis moved south and west, gathering up Jews in other cities where they had thrived. Giorgio Bassani wrote about the destruction of his Jewish community in Ferrara in a series of novellas, most famously in *The Garden of the Finzi-Continis*.

———————

I WATCHED OLD film footage of the bora in action, showing people struggling to cross the street, wind-battered cars sheathed in ice. Emiliana located and translated a positively melodramatic weather report from the Triestine newspaper *Il Piccolo* from one of the days my mother and her parents had spent in Trieste, during which the bora had blown hard.

> 29 March, 1940. Yesterday was one of those bizarre days that sometimes happen in the month of March, in which it seems like the weather changes at least twelve times within the span of a single day. We had menacing clouds, clear weather, the sun shining, a raging wind, scorching heat, bitter cold, summer downpours, rain that seemed to turn to sleet; which was all reflected by the temperatures—after rising to 17C the other day, last night it dropped to about 5C. . . . We are still in March, a month certainly accustomed to these eccentricities, perhaps spurred on this year by the intense electromagnetic storm that was unleashed in the previous days by the Earth's atmosphere. We hope that the weather will let up eventually, since last week Spring looked well on its way, bringing with it the awakening and flowering of plants, shrubs, and trees. . . . On the threshold of April, the weather was perhaps trying to indulge itself one last time, to put its signature on a winter chapter of uncommon

rigor. These last few days there was an intermittent drizzle, but the temperature remained mild. Yesterday rain and Bora formed an alliance and—at about 7pm—there were violent spurts of growing intensity, severely testing the resistance of umbrellas and raising the issue of coats and raincoats. The culmination of the bad weather was around 11pm when some kind of hail started to fall, perhaps an appendix of the exceptional hailstorm that hit Venice last night. A bad night indeed, with bitter cold and with some lashes of icy water on the face that would make you reconsider your plans for tomorrow. But we are in full equinox and March has always been crazy. Maybe the rain will be defeated today by the Bora; and even if we don't have ideal weather, we can hope for a few sparse, playful sunrays. Snow is falling on the Karst, and many cars from the Fiume have their hoods sprinkled in white. At about 2pm, the streets have been swept by the Bora, the asphalt clean and dry.

AND NOW I was in Trieste, settled into an apartment near the Piazza dell'Unità. I took my first walk along the harbor, riveted by the sea and the Carso and the distant inlets draped in mist. Silhouetted against the sky, a few kayakers crossed the harbor, their paddles sweeping aside water in perfect synchrony. I noticed African immigrants trying to sell books and trinkets, mostly rebuffed by tourists. I saw a few Muslim families; the women covered with at least a head scarf. I knew that the wave of anti-immigrant xenophobia had risen in Italy; politics here had veered sharply to the right. Silvio Berlusconi, discredited but still popular, was threatening another run for office. Mussolini's great-grandson was running for office in the south, hoping that his infamous last name would be an asset.

Most alarming was the rise of Matteo Salvini, another far-right politician who became prime minister in June 2018, with a goal of reducing illegal immigration into Italy. Echoing Donald Trump's infamous speech about Mexican immigrants ("They're bringing drugs. They're bringing crime. They're rapists. And some, I assume, are good people"), Salvini claimed that Tunisia only sent convicts to Italy, prompting the Tunisian government to issue a statement declaring its "profound amazement at the remarks of the Italian Interior Minister regarding immigration." Undeterred, Salvini continued on, announcing the closing of Italian ports to migrants. As a result, a ship operated by Doctors Without Borders and SOS Méditerranée with six hundred migrants aboard was refused entry, stranding the passengers at sea until Spanish prime minister Pedro Sánchez accepted the vessel. In late September 2018, the Italian Council of Ministers approved the "Salvini Decree" aimed at abolishing a number of protections for migrants and making it easier for the Italian government to deport them to their countries of origin.

In the past I had been quick to critique the ever-volatile drama of Italian politics, but now I felt ashamed to be a citizen of a country whose president had launched a full-on rejection of refugees fleeing their countries for so many reasons, from the results of American foreign policy to civil war to the environmental devastation caused by climate change.

As the sun dipped lower, I walked across the flagstones to the sprawling Caffè degli Specchi in the piazza and settled into one of the chairs facing the square. The waiters were unhurried, but one noticed me eventually and I ordered a prosecco with fresh strawberry juice. Surrounded by elegant Italian women and selfie-snapping tourists, I succumbed to that particular exhaustion that follows a day of travel and the promise of a good night's sleep ahead.

I wondered where and how Eva and her parents had spent their first evening here, the beginning of a week of waiting, unable to truly revel in the miracle of their escape from Vienna. I wanted to think that they had been able to sit in this very same *caffè*, take a walk along the seawall and admire the great ship *Saturnia* they would board soon for New York. I wanted them to have slipped into the same sleepy relaxation I was feeling as I nibbled on the potato chips (treats I rarely ate at home) and mini sandwiches that arrived with drinks here, but I knew this could not be how it had happened. Not at all.

———————

IN THE MORNING I followed my iPhone map to the Antico Caffè Torinese, stop number one on my historic Trieste *caffè* itinerary. I'd read that the interior of this jewel box had woodwork designed by the same architect who had created the upper-class interiors for the *Vulcania* and the *Saturnia*. The ceiling was a sunburst of intricate diamonds varnished and aged to a honey gold. A chandelier mounted in the center caught the morning light, as did the curved bar, edged with foliage-embossed brass and polished to a shimmering patina. The coffee was syrupy and packed a wallop, jolting me into the bright day.

In search of a high view, I made my way up the narrow canyons of ancient streets older than the Habsburg center until I found myself at the top near the Castle of San Giusto. Cherry trees were already in full bloom here, petals skittering across the square surrounded by peach and tawny stucco houses. The high sun had bleached the sky to a pale forget-me-not blue washed with streaks of cloud, and low fog softened the cliffs to the northwest, location of a hike I'd signed up for the following day. Like a flock of white birds, a flotilla of sailboats soared out into the bay, their white sails reaching for the wind. I'd been here less than twenty-four hours, but already I was desperate at the thought that I would have to leave this place too soon. How easy you are, I told myself. Some blue sea and sky and a pink building or two and you fall in love. But there was something more here, something familiar. This city smelled like home, enveloped by a body of water that looked like it could mean business when it wanted to. Open, yet enclosed, gentle and fierce. There was beauty and industry and history and neglect. This was no pampered city like Paris or Vienna. This was my kind of place.

———————

AFTER A STROLL around the open-air Saturday market along the canal I found a sunny spot on the long stone pier called Molo Audace, killing time till Emiliana was due to join me in the early afternoon.

Which turned into midafternoon.

Like always in Italia, my train is late, she texted.

I was happy to people-watch fellow visitors and the locals, well-bundled in a rainbow of goose-down puffery, some trimmed in sparkles and pearls. I'd missed Italy, even the excesses, especially the excesses. My ear was tuning itself to the familiar music of this language, one I could speak, sort of. After a week in Vienna, where I'd understood almost nothing of the language I heard on the streets, I had the feeling here of being both at home but also, hopelessly, a foreigner, just another American tourist who could never fathom the complexities of this city's history. I was determined to keep my focus narrow: to find out as much as I could about what might have transpired here for the trio of my grandfather, grandmother, and my mother, Eva.

Late afternoon. *I'll be there soon,* Emiliana texted.

I spotted her in the piazza at last and we hugged as if we were old friends. She guided me on a walk along grand tree-lined boulevards—Mussolini oversaw the planting of those trees—and then we went to dinner at the elegant seafood restaurant she'd chosen for us. Later, we walked back to the piazza, now lit up in its evening display. She pointed out a stone set into the square, illuminated with its own spotlight:

Il 18 settembre 1938 Mussolini scelse questa piazza per annunciare l'emanazione delle leggi razziali antiebraiche, macchia incancellabile del regime fascista e della monarchia italiana.
Comune di Trieste 18 Settembre 2013

On September 18, 1938, Mussolini chose this piazza to announce the emanation of the anti-Jewish racial laws. An indelible stain of the fascist regime and the Italian monarchy. City of Trieste, September 18, 2013.

Under pressure from his Nazi allies to institutionalize anti-Semitism to Adolf Hitler's standards, Mussolini had chosen this famous square to make his announcement because it was in the center of a city that had such a thriving Jewish community. But when Eva and her parents arrived here in March 1940 this city was still something of a sanctuary, and a way out.

Emiliana told me that in the aftermath of the Fascist rule, the Italians had not only killed their once revered leader Mussolini, they had also expelled the royal family. In the recent decades, Italy had swung to the right, so I was not surprised that it had taken Trieste so many decades to install this plaque to acknowledge the destruction of its Jewish community.

Close to midnight, Emiliana and I parted with plans to meet up the following afternoon.

I'D ARRANGED A Sunday morning walking tour to get a taste of the Carso. Michele, my guide, picked me up in his car and soon we were off to the north and west of the city, still in the Friuli-Venezia Giulia district. We stopped in several villages and walked hillside paths edged with small terraced fields of olive trees and vineyards. I learned that the prosecco I'd been drinking was the name of a town, not a description of the wine's dry flavor, as I'd thought (*secco* means "dry" in Italian). Michele told me that most prosecco was made in Veneto now, using a somewhat different method from the classic Friulian style of fermentation.

Spring was further along here than in the Vienna cemetery I'd explored a few days earlier. As we walked through a new-leafed deciduous forest I caught the same two-note descending birdsong I'd heard in Vienna and another bird chimed in with a metallic *tat-tat* cry.

"Are you okay with heights?" Michele asked before we climbed the rusty stairs of a water tower built during the Habsburg era. At the top we had a 360-degree view of distant mountains, the limestone cliffs, the entire peninsula of Trieste and Istria beyond. Our next stop was a cliff-side fortification originally constructed as a redoubt for German soldiers during World War I, used again during the Second World War. From here we could see the steel-blue choppy sea, and in the distance a whorl of low-hanging smoke-gray clouds. Rain was on the way. It was a day I'd hoped to see, a taste of the monster that Jan Morris had described. The wind was made visible in bursts that raced along the heaving sea, marking the surface with jagged row after row of frothy whitecaps. The olive trees swayed and the new grasses bent like flattened hair. My own hair whipped around, catching bits of errant leaf and twig.

"This is just a mini bora," Michele said. It felt like a day in the Maine islands I knew and loved, at the tail end of a late-summer hurricane.

We stopped for lunch at a farmhouse known as an *Osmica* in Slovenian/Croatian. The proprietors served an inexpensive meal of cheese, bread, pickled vegetables, and cured meat at communal tables, along with carafes of local wine. Triestini loved visiting Osmica and often drove to Slovenia anyway for cheap gas and other supplies. The local dialect, which I heard at the long tables but couldn't understand, included many words adopted from Slovenian. On the way back to Trieste, Michele drove along the coastal boulevard, another of the many modernizations of the Mussolini era. Miles of paved walkway on the ocean side was packed with visitors in spite of the dodgy weather.

"Here is where Triestini come for the day," Michele said, "to this hard beach of concrete." This felt just like New York to me, and I loved it.

————————

EMILIANA AND I were seated at the Caffè San Marco, which was stop number two on my coffeehouse itinerary. This place was huge, with high ceilings, tables and booths as well as a bookstore. The pastry cases were filled with strudel and Linzer torte, also New York–style cheesecake. Espresso drinks had uniquely Triestine names. My afternoon decaf *macchiato* was now a Capo Deca in B (served in a *bicchiere*, or glass). Emiliana spoke about the lingering recession in Italy and the resentment Italians felt toward Germany, the powerhouse that had set the economic standard for the European Union. There was growing sentiment that Italy should leave the EU and return to the lira, an idea that made me nostalgic for my first trips to Italy as a student but seemed like one more stake in the heart of a unified Europe. How long Italy could struggle was a reasonable question, but if everything began to fall apart there was the risk of conflict that had nearly destroyed Europe and the world twice in the twentieth century.

We left for a last walk together along the harbor, the wind still blustery, whitecaps curling and jumping like flying fish, swells bashing against the Molo Audace and sweeping over the top like lip-smacking tongues. Some seagulls bounced along, enjoying the surfing sport, while others coasted on the air currents above the turbulence. The clouds were breaking up and now a refulgent shaft of sunlight raked across the sea, casting a spotlight on the Carso, where I'd walked that morning. Emiliana said that after a bora, the air would be washed clean. After she left to catch her train home to Udine, I waited till sunset, watching the layers of cloud thin out and speed away to the south. As the sun dropped, the bowl of light above us was a clear indigo, the mist at the horizon lifted, revealing the snow-covered Alps across the Adriatic, backlit against an afterglow of apricot. How I loved it here.

———————

THE FOLLOWING MORNING all was bright and fresh as I made my way up the narrow Via del Monte toward the Jewish Museum at number 5. Annalisa Di Fant, director, and my longtime email correspondent, greeted me warmly.

After I explored the exhibits, I found Annalisa again in the open area that served as office and event room. She told me she was from a small town in northern Friuli, and like most of the academics I'd met in Vienna she was not Jewish. She had begun her career investigating anti-Semitism in the Catholic Church and then switched to Jewish studies.

And then, as if on cue, a man entered, a representative of the Catholic Church. He began a discussion with Annalisa, arguing that this Jewish Museum did not properly credit the work of the Catholic Church in saving Jews in Trieste. Finally he left, looking less than satisfied. Annalisa, graciously hiding her irritation, said that in reality there were two Catholic newspapers in Trieste during the Fascist era and both were very anti-Semitic.

"You were very polite," I said.

Confronting revisionist history was undoubtedly one of the challenges of her job, something that grated on me daily back at home as our president ranted about "fake news." I understood that today's Italian Catholics might resist facing the reality of their church's wartime Fascist collaboration. History could be brutal that way.

Annalisa said that in Trieste it was the Jewish community that did the work of saving Jews.

One hundred fifty thousand Jews from Central Europe had made their way to Israel in the years between the First and Second World Wars, supported by a Triestine Jewish community of about 5,000 Italians and 1,600 foreigners from places as far away as Poland and Corfu. There were wealthy families in the Jewish community who had funded the construction of the synagogue and the immigration committees that provided housing and food for travelers, including people like my mother's family. Wealthier refugees stayed in the fine hotels near the ship docks. There was a small hostel in this same building on Via del Monte that catered to the Orthodox families who required kosher food. Other refugees arrived at the Trieste station and were immediately sent onward by a tram that traveled the length of the harbor, dropping off passengers at smaller hotels or the Pensione Cosulich, a facility operated by the Cosulich shipping company that owned the Saturnia and other ships. In a moment of connection that did not seem to be isolated, the designer of the Trieste synagogue had also designed the second class of the *Saturnia*. I wondered where the Pensione Cosulich had been located; if this was where Eva and her parents had stayed.

———————

IN THE AFTERNOON I walked toward what is now called the Porto Vecchio, the Old Port, once the New Port when it was built by the Habsburgs. An expanse of buildings long abandoned, this was once the site of active shipping, receiving, and fabrication. Trieste's success had been built on its status as a free port: raw goods arrived and could be assembled into finished products in these spaces and then shipped onward without being taxed for the duration of their stay in Trieste. The buildings of the Old Port were barricaded behind high chain-link fencing, but as I walked along the access road I could peer through into surreal scenes of crumbling nineteenth-century grandeur. The stone buildings were now darkened, entries were missing doors, windows were missing panes, empty lots were overgrown with high grass and wildflowers and littered with beer bottles and other trash, suggesting that some Triestini had found a way inside. The empty buildings seemed ripe for something innovatively postindustrial, like the business incubators and sound stages and food halls and performance spaces and showrooms that had exploded at Brooklyn's waterfront, but Emiliana had suggested that while there was much talk of what to do with these structures, immovable bureaucracy impeded solutions. I walked the length of the Old Port and then back, trying to imagine the noise and bustle of the port in its prime. Eva and her parents might have caught a glimpse of this place from their train as they pulled into Trieste. As a businessman, even, as he was by then, a businessman without a business, Julius would have admired such industry. Perhaps for a moment he wished he could stay here rather than heading off to unknown New York City.

———————

THE STREET-LEVEL DOOR to the offices of Thalia Marine Services was well-concealed in a dark passageway, but upstairs the rooms were light and the ancient parquet floor gleamed like the interiors of the Italian Line ships, the lifelong obsession of Maurizio Eliseo. Maurizio designed and retrofitted cruise ships, but he also operated the website called ItalianLiners.com that I'd stumbled upon a few years earlier.

The Cosulich Line had built and launched the diesel-powered *Saturnia* and her sister ship, the *Vulcania*, in 1925. They were not the bloated floating condo developments that are today's cruise ships, like the one I'd seen in the harbor when I'd arrived in Trieste. The sleek *Saturnia* cleaved the sea like a finely honed chef's knife, flaying back arcs of water at her bow. She was 632 feet, almost 80 feet at her widest midsection. *La più grande e veloce motonave del mondo*, the introductory brochure proudly announced, the largest and fastest ship in the world.

The name of this ship came up occasionally in our family, but in another context. My father had always loved telling the story of the crossing he, my mother, and my grandmother Anna had made to France in 1951 on the French ship SS *De Grasse*. Anna, by then widowed, had offered the trip as a belated honeymoon present. "First class, not like when your mother came here on the *Saturnia*. The food . . . the pastries made fresh every morning. You could smell the buttery croissants. . . . Unbelievable." When my mother was still alive, at this point in the telling she always sighed and a smile warmed her face. I'd seen a black-and-white photo of the three of them lounging on the deck of the *De Grasse*. My mother was the epitome of 1950s chic in a trim cardigan, hair wrapped in a scarf, eyes hidden behind sunglasses, lips painted a deep red color, nearly black in the photo. Apart from the Marx Brothers' *A Night at the Opera* I'd seen as a child, I had no other understanding of these classic cruise ships, only that they were all members of a long extinct breed, from a time when wealthy people routinely changed into evening wear for dinner.

Years later, Mario Pulice, a graphic design colleague, had mentioned that he was a collector of vintage ship memorabilia and that his collection was on exhibition. What a curious obsession, I'd thought at the time. When Mario and I began a correspondence as part of my research into the *Saturnia*, I discovered that there was a world of people just like him who knew everything about these ships and collected all sorts of artifacts, from photographs and posters to tickets and menus, much now searchable online. Mario told me that his grandfather had also sailed to the United States from Naples on the *Saturnia*, just a year or so before my mother had made her journey. Mario marveled at the coincidence. For me, the coincidences had been piling up so fast that this latest one had a feeling of inevitability.

Mario found a third-class menu from 1929 online. The food had been simple but plentiful: cream of barley soup with croutons; *fritture* of liver *à la Venitienne* with shirred eggs (my mother loved liver); roasted young turkey with mixed salad. Desserts included ice cream, wafers, cheese, and fruit. And of course there was wine. A *Saturnia* third-class luncheon menu from 1934, during the Depression, was not shabby. An antipasto of mortadella di Bologna was followed by a choice of pasta, gnocchi, or Portuguese rice and bean soup. The main course was *stracotto di bue*, beef stew, followed by fruit for dessert. Three lighter courses were presented for dinner. The Italian ocean liners had standards to maintain.

Mario sent me a *Saturnia* luggage tag, a circular design in olive green with bold lettering in tomato red. The handsome leather strap and buckle, still intact, would have secured the tag to a suitcase. The leather was still pliable and smelled like a pair of good Italian shoes. Such tags were for the upper-class passengers. But I knew my family had traveled third-class.

Most of the images I'd found of the *Saturnia*'s interior showed the extravagant first-class accommodations: grand carved staircases fit for a baroque castle, wood-paneled dining rooms, elegantly furnished salons, smoking rooms, and sleeping cabins, all fascinating as a cultural document of the wealthy classes of the 1920s and '30s, but not at all what my mother would have experienced.

At last, I'd stumbled upon an archive of photographs—the collection of the obsessed collector who turned out to be Maurizio Eliseo—

and found an undated photo of a cramped cabin and another of the third-class dining hall. No wood-paneled glory here. Rows of long wooden tables were bolted to the floor. On either side of the tables, wooden swivel chairs were also bolted to the floor, a necessity for so many people packed into one space during a rough journey on the open Atlantic. The ceiling of the space was strung with piping for water, waste, and ventilation. I could imagine the cavernous dining hall packed with European refugees, a cacophony of different languages adding to the desperation of the fearful travelers.

———————

MAURIZIO WAS SLENDER, with an ageless face and the satisfied smile of a man who had been fortunate to discover his passion early in life and follow that through.

"I fell in love with ships very young and started collecting all this memorabilia as a child," he said. And *certo* he knew my design colleague Mario Pulice, because this circle of avid collectors was tight.

Maurizio formally introduced me to Nicolò Capus, the young architect with whom I'd arranged my appointment online. Handsome and fine-featured with chin-length dark curly hair, he looked like a figure in a painting by Jacopo Pontormo. Maurizio and Nicolò pulled out boxes of original publicity brochures, beautifully designed and printed in Trieste, and photographs of interior cabins. To my relief, Maurizio told me that the *Saturnia* had undergone a complete renovation in the mid-1930s at the shipyard of Monfalcone, just north of Trieste, and even the third class was redesigned by 1936. The new lounges and dining areas were simple and modern. Photographed empty, the third-class cabins were hardly luxurious, but humane in proportions, a great improvement compared to the photos I'd seen earlier. In April 1940, the ship would have been filled to capacity. *The ship was crowded and the food was terrible*, my mother had reported in her Leo Baeck interview. I imagined a lot of bread and pasta.

Maurizio knew all about the immigrant hotel run by the Cosulich company. "This was where the third-class passengers stayed until their ships left, with about two thousand beds and meals provided on site."

He showed me a photograph of the building with travelers lined up outside and told me that the building was still standing and in use as a public school. A caption below the photo described the use of the building and its private enclosed park area. Nicolò pointed to the address on a city map: Via Italo Svevo 15, along the harbor but a good ways out from the elegant center of the city. The street was named after the celebrated Triestine Jewish writer whose career began when he befriended James Joyce, his English-language tutor.

I was starving as I prepared to leave. Maurizio glanced at his watch and seemed to understand what I needed. "But if you are hungry, you must go into the small piazza just around the corner and you will find a good place right there." After walking around twice in a circle I managed to find the restaurant, where I ate a dish of pasta with radicchio and melty Gorgonzola cheese. Fortified, I walked to the train station and boarded the number 1 bus. I asked the driver to let me know when we got to Via Italo Svevo, and then watched the blue dot on my iPhone as we wound through the neighborhoods I'd walked with Emiliana and onward to increasingly residential areas. Here the buildings were homelier than in the grand imperial center, representations of the impoverished postwar period in a stuccoed patchwork of pastel colors. Matchbox-sized *caffès* and local shops lined the street level, and locals were out and about, running their afternoon errands. It was three p.m. and schoolchildren were collecting at bus stops. I hoped I wasn't too late to get inside the school.

As the bus turned onto Via Italo Svevo, I recognized the building immediately from the photograph Maurizio and Nicolò had shown me: broad and ochre yellow with light colored trim, clearly built in the earlier grand era. This was the place. I darted across the wide street and pushed open the heavy door, entering a high-ceilinged lobby. There were no students around. I walked with purpose toward a central staircase, resting my hand on the smooth wooden banister that looked original to the building. My mother and grandparents had held this banister and walked up these stairs. This was the place. I could feel it. Light shone down through large windows on the first landing. There were kids' drawings on the walls with quotes by Martin Luther King and Mahatma Gandhi, about fighting for truth and doing good deeds for one's fellow man. So many desperate people had stayed here and now the building was filled daily with young children, a fitting repurpose. I was weeping by the time I reached the second floor, overwhelmed by the presence of so many ghosts. From the window on the landing I could see the resplendent ocean, the faraway mountains, and the orange and yellow cranes and stacks of shipping containers in the new commercial port. I stood there for a while, spacing out.

A woman approached and I tried to collect myself and explain what I was doing here without permission.

She was gentle in her reprimand—only students and school personnel were allowed on the upper floors. "But everyone in the school is aware of the previous purpose of this building. You are not the only person who has shown up over the years looking for the past. Come, follow me, I will show you something."

She led me downstairs to view a photo display of the building in its previous incarnation, like the one Maurizio and Nicolò had shown me, with crowds of refugees lined up outside. This was the place.

I thanked her and took a last look at the lobby and the grand staircase. Outside on the street I saw that there was a walled-in outdoor space for the schoolchildren and I wondered if my mother and her parents had spent time there on days when the bora wasn't blowing. I crossed the street to the bus stop and took a last look at number 15 Via Italo Svevo, and in that moment I understood that Eva and my grandparents had arrived here on that day in late March, exhausted after a terrifying exodus from Vienna, and most likely did not leave these premises until they took the tram back to the center to board the *Saturnia* on April 4. There were no stories to tell and my mother may have forgotten her nine days here as soon as she got to New York, for by then new challenges subsumed the memories of a strange week in a dormitory in a foreign city. A waiting period, a pause; this had been her experience of Trieste.

A number 1 bus was waiting at the stop and I grabbed a seat. By now it was past four and the bus quickly loaded up with parents carrying groceries and children carrying knapsacks, and chatter grew all around me in the dialect I couldn't understand. It was comforting to feel part of an everyday afternoon, to imagine their evenings of meals and homework and bedtime.

Back in the center I made a beeline for the Caffè degli Specchi, where I drank two glasses of prosecco and ate two plates of mini sandwiches and all the potato chips that came with them and slowly calmed down. The ghosts of Via Italo Svevo had flown off and in a tipsy euphoria I watched the sky turn dusty rose and the Alps mauve. Darkness fell and the piazza lights came on. I stayed for a long time, until I felt I was fully returned to the present.

ANNALISA HAD GIVEN me the private email of Stelio Zoratto, who had worked for over thirty years at the Trieste Maritime Museum. I'd corresponded with him and had planned to visit the museum, but he'd retired in the last year, much to Annalisa's sorrow. His mind was like an encyclopedia, Annalisa said, and no one would ever have so much knowledge as he had amassed. I sent him a message and he offered to take me around the city. So instead of visiting the museum, I opted for a morning with a man who was like a living museum.

By the time I met Stelio for a coffee at ten o'clock, I'd already enjoyed a latte under one of the ornate cream-colored arches inside the Caffè Tommaseo, stop number three on my list. He was a tall man with long graying curls, a sprinkle of salt-and-pepper mustache, and a dash of soul patch, his eyes squeezed nearly shut against the sun behind square glasses. Ripples of cheek dimpled when he smiled, which was often. He drove us through residential streets into the industrial areas at the city edge, past the enormous Illycaffè headquarters and into the Carso just south of Trieste. We talked about my research in Trieste and his years at the Maritime Museum in an easy flow of my rough Italian, his elegant Italian, and English, his musical and accented with all vowels pronounced. We stopped at a churchyard that offered a view of the entire harbor of Trieste.

I searched for the yellow building on Via Italo Svevo, but it was hidden now behind shipyard cranes and a LEGO-colored Chinese container ship. Following along the harbor I called out the landmarks that were now familiar to me: the piazza and the Molo Audace, where I'd walked and napped and watched sunsets.

"There is a story about the Molo Audace, do you know it?"

Of course I didn't know any such story.

"Underneath the *molo* there is an old ship."

"A ship under the *molo*?" I thought I'd misheard him. "Under the stone?"

Stelio smiled, clearly satisfied to have a Trieste newbie.

"It was called the HMS *Cumberland*, and was built in 1695 by a woman named Ann Wyatt, who owned a shipyard."

"A woman owned a shipyard?"

"Yes, it was like that, made in Scotland. The ship, it was *quarantadue metri*—forty-two meters—long. Then this ship was lost to the French in 1707 in the Battle at the Lizard."

"Wait," I said, quickly passing him my notebook, "you'll have to write this all down for me."

Stelio took my book and carefully noted the dates, writing the numbers as my mother had taught me to, crossing all his 7's.

"Then in 1715, it was sold to Genoa," he continued. "And then two years later, 1717, it was bought by Spain. They renamed it *Principe de Asturias*. But then in 1718 it was lost to the British in the Battle of Cape Passaro in the south of Sicily, and then it went to Menorca and then to Naples in 1720, and then finally it came to Trieste in 1734 because the British were allied with the Austrians, and Trieste was part of the empire. And it was docked there. It was called the *Quai San Carlo* then."

"And then?" I asked, like a kid listening to an adventure story. I imagined battles at sea, sailors perched in lookouts shouting to crew on the deck, ships aflame and sinking below the waves. And perhaps some of the sailors on the *Príncipe* ended up staying here in Trieste. And why leave? After just a few days I was already loitering in front of realty offices, pricing apartments.

"*Allora*," Stelio said, "the ship was taking water and people were pumping, but still it was sinking. And so in the end, they let the boat sink and they built *il molo* right over it. And now that ship is there, inside the womb of the quay. This is like the story of Trieste, so many people of so many countries have been here and the history remains."

"I would never have guessed when I was walking on it that there was a ship under my feet."

"Nobody does," Stelio said wistfully, "people have forgotten. Take a look at it now," he said, extending his long pointer finger. "*Il Molo Audace*, it sticks out like this finger pointing toward the sea, saying, *This is your destiny*."

Even from our high post above the city, the smell of commerce, salty and funky and acrid, floated toward us, molecules of scent suspended in the perfume ester of sea mist. I imagined that it smelled just as funky here in 1940, long before the arrival of gargantuan container ships. So many people like Julius, Anna, and Eva had passed through this city, and taken in deep draughts of Triestine air: fractured families like mine or lonely travelers running away from the old country, wondering what would be on the other end of their journey in the new country. The finger of the *molo* led the way westward, toward New York.

BACK IN TOWN, Stelio and I ducked into the Caffè San Marco just as the weather shifted and a cold rain splattered against the windows like handfuls of tiny pebbles. Over lunch and more coffee we compared notes on politics in our two riven countries. Stelio said he had been glad to work in public service, but after leaving his post, he was worried that a sense of civic pride had been lost and that something ineffable in the society of Trieste seemed to be breaking down. A coat of many colors was unraveling at the seams, just like American identity, built on assumptions of greatness and endless prosperity, was fraying amid partisanship. And yet there was an important difference between our two nations. Here was a man who had never made a fortune doing work he loved, but it was all fine, because he had been able to retire knowing that there was still some reasonable safety net and a standard for what constituted a good life. I had always observed that, in Italy, people didn't talk endlessly about their work. They made time for friends and good food and an aimless hour spent discussing the world over coffee and cake.

"You have not seen enough," Stelio *tsked* in dismay when I told him I would be leaving in two days. "If you are free tomorrow I will take you to Muggia, and we will have lunch, no? Just a simple place, with fried fish, but I think you will appreciate it." I was moved by Stelio's intense love for his city and that he would clear two mornings to spend time with me, to share something of normal daily life with a near stranger.

Time seemed to pass more slowly for me during travel because every experience was exceptional; I knew I would remember these days more vividly than he might. Yes, I agreed, let's meet tomorrow. "You should be here *almeno un mese*," Stelio said. Yes, a month here would suit me wonderfully, I thought, even though I was missing my family acutely.

———————————

IT WAS STILL rainy as I walked from the Caffè San Marco to the synagogue, joining the group waiting for a four p.m. tour to be led by the Orthodox rabbi, whom I'd met briefly at the Jewish Museum.

I had never been anything close to Orthodox. I recalled the resentment I used to feel in Brooklyn on Friday afternoons, when pods of conservatively dressed Orthodox young women and men would approach me to ask, "Are you Jewish?" I brushed by them quickly. Of course I'm Jewish, I'd mutter to myself. Just not that kind of Jewish. For me the visit to this temple would be like going to a museum, but it was also important to me, even as a nonobservant Jew, to feel that there was a living community of Jewish life in Trieste.

Inside, I admired the high vaulted ceiling glittering with Byzantine-style mosaic work, a marvel of craftsmanship. The rabbi was blunt in acknowledging that the Orthodox congregation was dwindling to just a few hundred mostly older people. Unfortunately, he had no interest in building bridges to the potentially broader population of Reform Jews who also lived in Trieste. It seemed inevitable that the Orthodox population would die out, leaving behind a temple that would perhaps become a museum operated by the government, while the Reform Jews of Trieste had no place to worship at all.

As I left the synagogue I did my best to stuff down a feeling of indignation. There was not just one way to be Jewish. That kind of thinking had brought us the current immovable political situation in Israel, and all manner of hypocritical political alliances in the United States. Even as a committed nonbeliever I felt more Jewish than ever as I walked away into the late-afternoon mist, hoping that at some point a more open-minded leader could gather up the Jewish community of this city.

———————

STELIO COLLECTED ME the following morning and we drove again through the industrial areas and into the hills toward the village of Muggia. We ate lunch at a small fish restaurant whose picture windows offered a view of the Triestine commercial port and the bay and hills beyond. During the drive back to Trieste, Stelio said he was pleased that I had visited Via Italo Svevo. He promised to send me more photos he had in his archives at home.

"Come back as soon as you can," he said as I stepped out onto the street. And then, at one with the city's flow, he accelerated into the traffic along the harbor.

I sat for a long while on the Molo Audace. A light fog obscured the horizon, painting the dome above and the water the same shade of blueish gray so that only the soft banding of waves clued the divide between sea and sky. The Carso was gray and forbidding, a fortress wall. I was not alone on the Molo Audace. Kids were bopping up and down to music on their iPhones. Tourists were snapping photos. A young gull paddled by, leaving no wake, scanning the harbor for scavenge.

From here I could see the passenger dock where the huge cruise ship had been docked the day of my arrival. The weather on April 4, 1940, had been overcast like today. The *Saturnia* motored out of Trieste harbor toward a union of sea and sky.

MY LAST EVENING in the grand square. I'd met Annalisa for a drink earlier and was a bit tipsy as I walked to the Molo Audace for a last night view of the sea. The piazza was lively, filled with packs of celebratory university graduates, whose heads were crowned with wreaths of fresh green laurel tied with ribbon. The evening wind smelled briny and buffeted me with an intense longing for New York, my home, and a sorrow to leave this place that I felt could be home.

Had I found enough here in the old country to recapture a lost week of my mother's lost childhood? I was alone and yet I felt observed by all the unknown spirits who had passed through this city. I longed for one conversation with my mother to tell her that maybe now I knew her more intimately, having been in her home city and here in this city by the sea. I could have stayed there all night just to watch the waves break against the stone pier; reluctantly, I pulled myself away and returned to my rented apartment to pack.

AT THE TINY Friuli airport I ordered a sandwich and fresh-squeezed blood-orange juice, already in mourning for the food culture I was about to leave behind. Fresh blood-orange juice, at an airport concession. I couldn't get over it.

During the second leg from Munich to Newark I watched bad movies and dozed until the captain announced that because of a storm we would be rerouted to another airport. We parked on the runway and I texted Clark, who was in Manhattan and found us a hotel room. I repeatedly checked the weather in Newark, wondering how long we would wait.

A few rows ahead two white middle-aged couples edged into a conversation about their recent cruises. This somehow detoured into complaints about the socialist creep of the American left, singling out the recently elected Alexandria Ocasio-Cortez, who was by now enough of a celebrity that even they called her "AOC." How long would I have to sit here, trapped in a metal tube listening to Trumpies? Five minutes was already too long. I'd avoided most news from home while away, but the Mueller Report was due any day. The couples kept at it, having found that they were aligned in philosophy. Socialized medicine was next on their list of evils, though they were all retirees, old enough to be on Medicare, i.e., socialized medicine. My head was on fire as I got up out of my seat.

"I grew up in New York," I said to them, my voice hard and bitter. "And anyone who grew up there can tell you that Donald Trump has always been a money-grubbing sexist racist crook who belongs in jail, along with the rest of his corrupt family. So I'm going to insist that you shut this down, like, right now."

To my relief, they did.

The fortyish man next to me smiled as I settled back into my seat. For the first time in eight hours of travel we spoke to each other. He was Bosnian, returning from a visit to see family and friends. He'd already missed his connecting flight back home to St. Louis, but seemed sanguine enough about it. I had the impression that he must have been through some hellish times getting out of Bosnia, but I didn't want to pry so soon.

I asked him how things were in the old country.

"It's terrible there," he said, shaking his head. There were food shortages, no jobs.

He'd been living in the United States since the early nineties, having arrived as a war refugee along with his brother. First they were sent to Salt Lake City, Utah, and he'd liked living there, as the mountains reminded him of the landscape he'd left behind. But then he and his brother had learned that there was a large Bosnian community in St. Louis, thousands strong. And so they'd moved to St. Louis. By now he was married to another Bosnian and had two young children. He and his brother had started a trucking company and were doing well. He knew he was one of the lucky ones who'd made it out and now he was an American.

"And what's it like living in St. Louis?" I asked.

"It's good," he said. "It's very flat! I miss the mountains, but it's good that we are so many all together. It's a community. And you know," he said, with a shrug, "there are many Serbians there also."

"Really?"

"Yes," he said. "And so it goes to show. We got along all right before the war, and now we are living together again and it's okay. You know, it was the politicians that made us hate each other."

The Crossing

*Little is more extraordinary than the decision to migrate, little more
extraordinary than the accumulation of emotions and thoughts which
finally leads a family to say farewell to a community where it has
lived for centuries, to abandon old ties and familiar landmarks, and
to sail across dark seas to a strange land.*

—John F. Kennedy, *A Nation of Immigrants*

DAY ONE ***Thursday, 4 April 1940. Trieste-Gravosa.
Sky overcast. Choppy sea, with wind from the SE. Normal
navigation, inspection rounds completed.***

I WASN'T SURE what I'd find in the envelope of photocopies I'd
ordered from the archive in Trieste. I'd spent a year with my tutor,
Rosella, brushing up my Italian, struggling to master the subjunc-
tive well enough to write a letter to the museum archivist. I'd read
my short letter many times, fretting over subject and verb agreements
before I clicked Send, hoping that during the language-mangling I'd
committed I'd at least communicated the essentials. The archivist had
written back to say that I could order copies of the original handwritten captain's log for the April 1940 trip of the *Saturnia*, but I would
have to send money for the photocopies by mail in advance, twelve

or so euros, a pain in the neck, requiring a trip to a bank to exchange currency. At last the envelope arrived and I tore it open, wondering what secrets would tumble out.

The forty-odd pages of the captain's elegant Italian cursive kept mostly to the weather and sea conditions. This was not at all what I'd expected of an April journey: cherry trees in the park, buds breaking, *dear greetings from springlike Vienna sends you*. The journey along the Adriatic coast, into the Mediterranean, and then across the Atlantic, was another story entirely. The captain reported rough seas, the ship pitching and rolling, nearly continuous overcast skies with wind and plenty of rain. For most of the two weeks at sea, the doors to the outer decks were sealed, and passengers remained inside, waiting it out.

As I read the first log entries, I recalled a ferry trip out to a Maine island some years earlier, just Liza and me, with waves so steep that as we dipped into the troughs we could see only a wall of water in front of us. At each crest we caught air, like a flying surfer, before slamming down into the next valley. I cursed my decision to take this ferry instead of the one that left from a town farther down east. We were approaching the island from a different angle, making for a shorter but miserable crossing. Passengers were retching all around us. I was usually happy on a boat, but without a flat horizon to focus on, I couldn't settle my stomach. After ten minutes or so of this, I was too terrified to look at the oncoming waves. *We're gonna die today*, moaned a gloomy voice inside my head. I closed my eyes and clutched Liza's hand, taking comfort that she seemed thrilled by our roller-coaster ride, wilder than the Cyclone at Coney Island. Overcome with nausea, I rested my head on my knees, inhaling deeply, willing the journey to be over. When I peeked, the captain and his assistant looked relaxed—calmly eating sandwiches as they piloted. We would get there just fine, the captain reassured us, with just twenty minutes' delay. It was, after all, a clear August day, a Maine sparkler, not a wind- and rain-swept crossing on the open Atlantic under wartime blackout.

I wondered how it was that I'd never asked my mother to describe her exodus from Europe in detail. The train trip from Vienna to Trieste, the days in that city, and then the two weeks on a wartime crossing aboard the *Saturnia*. I think I was too afraid—of her sorrow at being forced to leave her home. I imagined the fear and despair I would have felt at the age she was then—not quite twelve. She had said goodbye to her city, the Viennese relatives who had either chosen to stay or couldn't leave, her friends, and most of her childhood belongings. She was old enough, and had seen enough by then, to wonder when, or if, she would ever see her city again. All she had left of her former life was in her keepsake book, the one she would keep hidden in a drawer for the rest of her life.

What did the Singers bring with them to begin their new life in America? The two trunks, each about the size of the one I took to summer sleepaway camp, were made of something like thick cardboard or thin wood, covered over in rough canvas cloth. Inside were linens and clothes. The Passover wineglass, etched and decorated with splashes of red and blue enamel. A small painting from Jakob Altenberg showing a group of musicians in a quaint outdoor setting. The invaluable photograph collection. The few forbidden items that the border guards on the train had not discovered: a small silver menorah, a pair of silver and mother-of-pearl opera glasses, a few silver serving pieces, and some of Anna's jewelry, wrapped up in the embroidered shawl that had once covered the piano in their living room on Weimarer Strasse.

One of the trunks remained in a closet in my parents' Connecticut weekend home until the summer of 2014, slowly crumbling to dust so many years after crossing the Atlantic. Before disposing of the remains of the trunk, my father mailed me the third-class label. Julius had carefully hand-printed his name and destination, New York.

In her interview, my mother began her account of their rough voyage. *We left on the last boat that ever left Italy to come to the United States, called the* Saturnia, *and when it got to America it was never allowed to go back. It was already war, so everything was blackout. And we were petrified of submarines.*

My mother often told the story of sailing "on the last boat" from Italy and I had embraced it as family lore, a miraculous escape against all odds. But further investigation showed that the *Saturnia* did return to Italy after the April 1940 crossing and made several trips after that to repatriate Italians before being temporarily renamed and converted to a hospital ship. Other ships with Jewish passengers left from Genoa until July 1940. So, the true story, barely less harrowing, is that the *Saturnia* sailed in April 1940 as the window for escape was closing. I understood how much my mother needed that story during the rest of her life and how I had needed it, too, as a way of understanding my mother's childhood trauma until I was ready to let it go. It felt disloyal to give up this version, but I decided that I could still value it as emotional truth even as I corrected the facts of the narrative. This was just one more reminder of the fallibility of memory and how the stories we hear as children can stay with us as totems of the past.

DAY TWO *Friday, 5 April 1940. Gravosa to Patras. Strong cold winds from the S, choppy sea moving in the same direction, light pitching and rolling of the vessel. Anchoring in Patras initiated at 7:48 hours. 45 passengers disembarked, followed by inspection for clandestine passengers and contraband. 20 sacks of mail have been taken aboard at Patras and 1 diplomatic pouch. Remainder of the day overcast, wind shifts from W.*

THE SEA ISN'T so rough and every seat is filled. Such noise—the clatter of cutlery on china and so many conversations in so many languages besides Italian, German, and of course Yiddish, words layering on top of each another. Exhausted from travel, her father speaks little. Eva begins to see him as others might, stooped with heavy bags under his eyes. Her mother is always beautiful, her hair carefully pinned up, her dress neat, though she also looks tired. Her dress still smells of rose water, the very last from the bottle left behind. Waiters bring food. It is bland, but there is enough. And the waiters do not appear to care where passengers come from, what language they speak, or if they are Jews.

DAY THREE *Saturday, 6 April 1940. Patras to Napoli.*
Cloudy and rainy, strong winds from the S, sea moving
in same direction, light pitching and rolling of the vessel.
Occasional spray over the decks. All doors sealed.
All guards at their assigned posts, normal rounds and
navigation.

WHEN I WAS eight and my brother Simon, six, our parents took us to a Maine island for the first time. They had been there many times on their own, before they became our parents. I loved looking at a photo of my mother and my grandmother Anna, relaxing on a rock ledge, smiling into the sun.

This was our first trip. We were old enough to appreciate it, my mother said. My father drove us from New York City to the town where we would board a ferryboat, a two-day trip. My brother and I were packed into the back seat of the family station wagon (no air-conditioning), where we bickered over territory or dozed off, sedated by the hot wind and the whiz-thrum of the highway, the odor of sun-melted tar oddly intoxicating. A one-night stop at Race's roadside motel outside of Wiscasset and a lobster dinner served on the pier at Pemaquid Point were new adventures for us—with the novelties of normally forbidden American treats—potato chips and Coke—and so much more TV than we ever got to watch at home.

During the car trip my parents told us about the upcoming boat trip, how exciting it would be to cross over to the island in the open ocean. We lived on the upper end of the island of Manhattan, but as a child I was only vaguely aware of the ocean somewhere way downtown, where the Hudson and East Rivers met the sea.

My parents were outdoorsy within limits. By the time of this trip they owned their weekend house in rural Connecticut. This is where they gardened on weekends, their efforts there focused on taming nature. Weeding was religion. Neatly edged flower beds, well-mulched to inhibit the native flora from popping up among the peonies, dahlias, and the roses my mother loved. The native fauna—slugs, rabbits, squirrels, moles, rabbits, raccoons, and deer—ruthlessly excavated bulbs, and nibbled daylily buds, lettuce, and rhododendrons. My parents retaliated by stomping down mole runs and setting traps. A muskrat set up house in the embankment of the pond where Simon and I dog-paddled and caught frogs. My father spent a day armed with a gun left over from his army days, waiting for the animal to appear, but this muskrat had good reconnaissance. After a long hot afternoon my father gave up that battle and shortly after that he got rid of the gun, a relief, as it was hard for me to imagine him killing anything larger than a wasp. Meanwhile Simon and I made up our own adventures in the woods that enclosed the property, armed with homemade bows and arrows. This kept us busy while my parents planted vegetables in neat rows.

We did not hike mountains. We did not go on camping trips: my father had experienced his lifetime quota of camping during his stint in General Patton's infantry during the Battle of the Bulge. My mother did tell those stories about hiking in the Vienna Woods with her father, the summer camp in the Austrian Tyrol, and Julius and Jakob's ambitious hiking trip after the First World War. I understood, without asking, that the time of those beautiful places had come to an abrupt end, not to be revisited. This boat trip ahead of us was a wild adventure I could never have imagined for our family.

The town where our journey ended turned out to be a tiny fishing village out on a spit of julienned coastline. The ferryboat was vintage 1943, built as a patrol boat during World War II. After the war she was brought to Maine, first as a lobster-hauling vessel. She was eventually refitted to service the tiny island community of year-round dwellers and the throngs of summer visitors. She was painted tan and white, many coats layered on against the salt water and wind.

It's a rough ride, my mother said, *but you'll love it.* She was wearing her summer uniform of Bermuda shorts, striped T-shirt, Keds sneakers, and sunglasses, her dark bob restrained in a knotted bandana. She took out windbreakers for herself and my father, but she made us put on our thick yellow rain slickers, though the day was clear and bright, a real Maine sparkler.

Fully loaded with travelers, luggage, canvas mailbags, and box after box of supplies for the island grocery store, the boat nosed away from the pier and out of the safe harbor. Most of the passengers huddled on the seats inside the rear cabin, but once we hit the first big swells, Simon and I rushed to the bow, because this was better than any adventure game we'd ever invented in the woods or in our bedroom, bouncing up and down on a hill of pillows. Wave after wave smashed against the bow, pitching the boat back and forth, into the troughs and up again, splashing us each time with frigid salty spray, tangy on our lips. As we shrieked in surprised delight, my normally cautious parents beamed, especially my mother, who smiled into the wind during the entire crossing, her salt-speckled sunglasses reflecting the sun glare. Up and down we rode until a low hump of land came into view, like a paper cutout through the veil of sea spray. I knew so little of my mother then—her pleasures and sources of pain—but I remember her joy on that crossing.

DAY FOUR *Sunday, 7 April 1940. Permonenza to Napoli. Anchored at 11:00 hours. Completely overcast, heavy rain, cold wind from WSW, rough seas, with continuous pitching and rolling of the ship.*

WHAT APPALLING WEATHER. A few days trapped in the third-class cabins aboard the *Saturnia* would have made even the hardiest traveler seasick. And at this point the ship was still in the relatively sheltered waters of the Mediterranean Sea. I can imagine that all aboard dreaded what would happen in a few days, when the *Saturnia* aimed her bow into the open Atlantic.

DAY FIVE *Monday, 8 April 1940. Napoli to Genova. Calm, clear, light wind from North, normal navigation, coast visible, flags illuminated. Later in day, mixed cloud cover, wind from the East. Preparations underway for next arrival in port. Arrival in Genova at 10:00 hours, docked at 10:07 hours, engines off at 10:48.*

A CALMER DAY as the ship moved north along the Italian coast. Perhaps passengers were able to step out onto the decks, get some fresh air, and admire the gorgeous rocky coastline. Some of this seacoast was familiar to me from my trips in Tuscany and Liguria. In the fishing villages I knew, pastel-painted houses were stacked like children's blocks against the cliffs, and on a breezy day in April the whipping palm fonds were already green.

DAY SIX *Tuesday, 9 April 1940. Genova to Gibraltar. Light winds, variable sky, light wind from the NE. Pitching and rolling of vessel, with waves breaking over the decks. All doors closed, inspection rounds completed. We have taken on a new cook in Genova.*

14:00 hours the Balearic Islands came into view. Waiter #3B Savori injured as he tripped while exiting a refrigerator. Safety drill from 16:15–17:00 hours. Passengers in all classes gathered in their assigned emergency meeting places. In the evening, choppy seas, wind variable from SW.

BACK TO A turbulent sea. Even a seasoned waiter was having difficulty keeping steady. What a day for a safety drill, the passengers crowded together at the exits, listening to instructions . . . in Italian? Broken English? Mangled German? Eva and her parents would have felt dislocated without the familiarity of their language. The ship was like another country, just a hint of what was to come when they reached the Tower of Babel that was New York.

DAY SEVEN *Wednesday, 10 April 1940. Genova to Gibraltar. Clear skies, light wind from NW, normal navigation, gentle movement of the ship. Flags illuminated. Two airplanes spotted overhead. All in order and secured in preparation for landing at Gibraltar. Renato Zarubon, waiter in the Third Class dining room, slipped and fell at 13:05 hours, suffering contusions on his left elbow.*

ON ONE OF my hunts for memorabilia, I came across a postcard of the *Saturnia* heading past the Rock of Gibraltar on her way to open ocean. I kept the postcard near me as I imagined my mother's journey. I found myself examining the details: the lifeboats, the portholes, the tiny ant-specks of people on deck who appeared to be waving toward the distant photographer. I tried to materialize Eva's perspective of this sight, the iconic rock heaving out of the Mediterranean like a tidal wave, and how fearsome that cliff would have appeared arrayed with British military hardware.

DAY EIGHT *Thursday, 11 April 1940. At 16:35 hours. British Customs agents, plainclothes officials, as well as nine British sailors boarded ship to check the mail and passenger lists. They removed the mail from Germany: 57 insured packages, 102 regular mail. Altogether 13 sacks of mail were opened, with all mail from Germany removed from the ship for further examination. 23 sacks of mail were brought on board for Lisbon, 2 for New York. Altogether on board are 91 sacks of mail, 87 for New York and 4 for Lisbon. 23 new passengers boarded in Gibraltar, 23 for Lisbon and 2 for New York.*

Customs agents interrogated 15 passengers whose journeys originated in Germany. This included eight of German origin, five North Americans, one Argentinian and one Brazilian. Their cabins were examined as well but nothing of a suspicious nature was discovered. The interrogations concerned the passengers' route and destination, reason for travel, and various questions concerning their stay in Germany. The customs agents completed their visit at 21:20 hours.

MY MOTHER LOVED to tell the story about a spy who was discovered on board ship at Gibraltar. *We had to go through Gibraltar, which I don't know if you've ever seen pictures, it's all stone, rocks, and it was full of guns. It was very frightening. We went through, we got through finally, and then a boat came after us and made us go back, and they found a spy on the boat. So then we were allowed to go.*

There was something authentically childlike about her memory of the stopover in Gibraltar, the vivid image of the guns on the famous promontory, and the story of the spy.

I imagined the cliffs shimmering hot orange, sunlight glinting on the mounted artillery as bright as flames. A cluster of storks passed overheard, white feathers tinted peach, black tail feathers irridescent as if made of precious dark metal. As the ship docked, up rose a noise like the collective wail of a thousand shrieking newborns, followed by a swarming whirlpool of dark wings. The starlings gathered overhead, the murmuration shape-shifting as they swooped and then darted back to their nesting posts, small dark stains on gray stone.

This was the gateway to freedom, though in the open Atlantic more dangers awaited. I loved my mother's spy story as a child and accepted it in the same way as the story of Julius's arrest. It was only when I read the captain's log that I discovered, to my disappointment, that my mother was a slightly unreliable narrator, likely a result of shipboard rumor, a story that transformed like the game of telephone I played at birthday parties as a child. Eva was still a child who would accept a rumor her parents overheard. The captain had no reason to exaggerate or suppress the truth in his log, or did he? After some days trying to reconcile the conflicting narratives, I chose to side with the captain's record. The detained passengers with German-sounding last names were likely fleeing Jews, just like the Singers. It was spy rumors like this that fed into the xenophobia in America, where anti-immigration politicians refused to increase the quotas from Nazi-dominated countries, based on the fear that Jews were Nazi spies instead of a persecuted minority.

When I examined my *Saturnia* postcard again, I noticed that the

Rock of Gibraltar had the look of a theatrical backdrop. The light-house and the tiny houses perched at the base of the rock were in the same sharp focus as the ship in the foreground, which wouldn't have been possible with a camera. My postcard looked like a retouch job, created for the unquestioning tourist, the kind of visual sandwich easily rendered in Photoshop. Back then the visual elements would have been pieced together with a sharp razor knife and a fine brush dipped in gouache. I hadn't noticed the trickery right away, because I wanted to believe the postcard's narrative.

———————————

DAY NINE *Friday, 12 April 1940. Lisbon to New York.* *Sky overcast, brisk wind from the NW, rough seas. Normal navigation, doors sealed. Rounds completed. Approaching Lisbon. In port at 14:36 hours. Injured waiter B. Savori taken off ship at 15:40 hours. 75 passengers disembark. Altogether there are now 863 aboard including crew and passengers. Departure from Lisbon at 23:45 hours. Wind from North, choppy sea moving in same direction, significant pitching and rolling of vessel. Doors sealed. Position 38 degrees 30 north. Orders to sail without lights due to wartime regulations. First sighting of a convoy with four ships under blackout. Appeared at first to be warships, but proved to be a convoy of four mercantile ships.*

———————————

THE CONFECTIONARY FACADES and terracotta roofs of Lisbon dissolved into the mist as the ship pulled out to sea. The *Saturnia* was now a true island. By now, after nine days at sea, it was a city in motion, alive with its own social order.

After two years mostly confined to two rooms in an apartment, a small third-class cabin must have felt as tight as a cage. Julius, exhausted from travel, may have spent his time reading whatever newspapers were available. Sociable Anna may have sought out the company of other German-speaking women to pass the time and to soothe anxiety. There must have been many other children on board, but after the last winter in Vienna, Eva was out of practice and fearful. Children are often so adaptable and make friends in all kinds of unlikely conditions, but this was no pleasure cruise. Parents were on edge, and somewhere out there was the very real threat of German submarines looking for prey. But just the presence of other families like hers might have been some kind of comfort in this strange and desperate community created by the randomness of last-minute visas and ticket purchases. For a moment, perhaps, she could forget about the war in Europe, her faraway brothers, everyone and everything left behind, and whatever awaited them in New York.

I thought about the encounters I'd had on trains and planes and boats in my own solo travels, and how I could recall conversations with fellow passengers even decades later. I had never been in life-threatening circumstances during these journeys, but I'd often felt lonely and grateful for company and a bit of conversation. Sometimes on a ship headed out to an island I'd felt vulnerable, just a pin dot on the ocean, and I had been saved by a few kind words from a stranger who also wanted to feel connected in that moment to a fellow traveler.

———————————

DAY TEN *Saturday, 13 April 1940. Lisbon to New York. Flags illuminated. Doors remain closed. Maintenance and security check. Normal rounds. Variable skies, mostly overcast, with light winds from the East, choppy seas. Light pitching and rolling movement of the ship. All guards at their posts.*

———————————

OUT ON THE open Atlantic the seas were rough. Had Eva been allowed out on the decks, the view would have been nothing but water in motion and an endless horizon.

_____

DAY ELEVEN *Sunday, 14 April 1940. Lisbon to New York. Overcast, wind from North, rough, normal navigation, doors sealed. Guards in their positions, rounds completed. At daybreak mixed clouds and sun. Cleaning and maintenance completed. Throughout day, variable skies, brisk wind from NE. Significant pitching and rolling of vessel. Waiter Eugenio Gropazzi discovered a stowaway passenger, Jose Sofrez, aged 37, from Arcos de Valdevez, Portugal, in cabin number 646, third class, occupied by a Portuguese/American passenger. Following interrogation, Jose Sofrez stated that he had boarded secretly in Lisbon and claims not to have allies aboard ship, though it is evident that he must have had assistance in gaining access to the ship. Passenger is being held and will be interrogated further.*

_____

MY MOTHER HAD told us the story of the stowaway. As I read through these pages of the captain's log, I was reassured that the family narratives of my grandfather's rescue at the train station and the family's escape, even the money hidden in the toilet paper roll on the train to Trieste, had truth in them, even if the shipboard spy story did not. I'd never considered how much these stories had meant to me. Anyone who managed to survive that time would have such stories. The Nazi net was wide, but grasped tightly as time passed. For those who escaped, there was some miraculous series of events that must have seemed fantastical as they unfolded, even more so later once there was time to reflect. Perhaps it was during those days of the crossing that Julius, Anna, and Eva began to tell their stories in a new way. The worst danger was behind them; the future was unimaginable.

DAY TWELVE *Monday, 15 April 1940. Lisbon to New York. Overcast sky wind light but chilly from the SE, choppy seas. Considerable pitching and rolling. All guards at their posts. Rounds. Ventilation check in freezers and refrigerators. Chilly winds from SSE, continued overcast, agitated sea, considerable pitching and rolling. Doors remain closed.*

DAY THIRTEEN *Tuesday, 16 April 1940. Lisbon to New York. Rain and wind from the west with fog, very rough seas, and considerable vibrations from the pitching and rolling of the ship. Strong sea swells with frequent waves washing over the decks. Checking to make sure that there are no leaks or damage to the holds. Doors sealed. As the day proceeds, violent pitching and rolling. In the afternoon rain abates, but wind continues to be forceful from the NE with rough seas. Illuminated flags, regular rounds.*

DAY FOURTEEN *Wednesday, 17 April 1940. Lisbon to New York. Completely overcast. SSE. Flags illuminated. Have ordered guards to continue to check for any other clandestine passengers and to complete a full check of passengers on*

board, cross-checking with official passenger lists from
each port of call. Preparations begin for arrival in New York.

I WONDERED HOW my mother felt as the *Saturnia* arrived in
New York Harbor. In my online searches I found a photograph showing the ship's deck packed with passengers eager to see the famous vertical skyline, so different from the classical proportions of old European cities, not to mention small villages many of the travelers had left
behind. In another photograph, the *Saturnia* is set off against that skyline, on a misty overcast day not unlike the one when Eva arrived with
her parents. The air would have been pungent with the maritime aroma
I'd identified in Trieste that had reminded me of New York—dank
salt air, fuel oil, a whiff of the refuse the city scuttled into the working
harbor—but also with sounds of scavenging gulls, tugboats pushing
barges. As the ship prepared to dock, the music of Italian spoken on
board was interwoven with voices of dockworkers calling out in the
new language that would have to be mastered as quickly as possible.
English was still a foreign language. American culture was a mystery.

The Singers knew only they would be living with their relatives in
a Jewish neighborhood in Brooklyn. They had no plan except to find
work and a safe home living among other Jewish refugees in a city of
immigrants.

DAY FIFTEEN *Thursday, 18 April 1940. Lisbon to New York.*
Completely overcast rain and light wind from NE. Consider-
able pitching and rolling of vessel. Heavy fog. Rounds com-
pleted. Guards at their posts. At 2:36 hours ship passes by
Fire Island and through Ambrose Channel. Anchor dropped
at 5:10 hours near quarantine station of Staten Island. At

6:00h, we proceed at slow speed with limited visibility towards Pier 92 with light rain falling. At 7:15, assisted by four tugboats boat is guided towards Pier 92. Engines off at 7:42 at Pier 92. Four Gangplanks extended to dock. Beginning commercial operations. US Immigration Service officials boarded, began immediately the verification of passengers, checking each single passenger before debarkation is permitted. Afternoon, light rain, overcast. At 12:00 hours passengers disembark. Twelve passengers are sent to Ellis Island: one from first class, two from tourist class and nine from third class including the stowaway passenger Jose Sofrez discovered in page 63 of this journal. Normal maintenance continues until 17:00 hours.

IT IS RAINING and rain should feel the same everywhere, but here everything feels alien. Julius and his family are aliens. Skyscrapers rise up in the distance: nothing he or Anna or his young daughter have ever seen except in photographs or imagined they ever would see even after reading the letters Anna's brother Theo had sent from Brooklyn. A location once remote and unpronounceable, Brooklyn is now so close, just across the water. He cannot suppress the exhilaration of this arrival, after so many struggles. At last they are here and safe. Soon Theo will be here and they will begin life in New York. All is uncertain. It will be hard. But it will surely be easier than what they have already lived through. He feels in his coat pocket for his camping utensils in their pouch. The vice-consul Brown said there were mountains nearby.

"Passports," the customs officer barks.

"Vetter is beautiful in New York!" Julius tries as he hands over their documents. The customs officer stares at him like he is an alien.

Julius persists, hoping to lighten the mood on this gloomy day. "But is bad for hatz!"

The customs officer looks over the documents and then peers at the group of three. Old man, tired wife, young girl. Three more. When will they stop coming?

"Singer. Any of you speak English?"

Eva steps forward. "A little," she says. Something is happening that doesn't feel right.

"This is your father? Is he well? Any medical problems?" The officer pores over the passports again, as if he could read the German. "He's how old?"

She has never thought about her father's age. "Papa," she whispers in German, "how old are you?" He tells her that he is sixty-five. So old!

"My father, he is sixty-five, sir."

"Did he work in Germany?" the officer asks.

Eva wants to explain that her father ran a printing factory and to describe the *Pulverkapseln* and the complicated folding machine that her father helped design, and that they were from Vienna, a beautiful city that was once the capital of Austria, a country that no longer exists.

"Yes," she says, searching for words. She remembers how Herr Mazura used to joke that one day she, Eva, would be *der Chef* of her father's business. "Yes, my father was chef of important factory for paper."

"Important, was it?"

MY MOTHER HAD told us the bitter story about what happened as the Singer family prepared to disembark the *Saturnia*. Probably beside himself with relief and joy at having arrived safely to America, Julius made a mistake, attempting a lighthearted joke in his limited English with the customs officer, and it must have been seriously lost in translation. Whatever happened in those first minutes in America, the encounter went very badly. The Singers were three of twelve passengers who were sent to Ellis Island.

It took fourteen days to get from Trieste to New York. We arrived at

the pier in New York City and an American immigration officer looked at
my father and decided he was senile. My father was not senile. So we spent
fourteen days on Ellis Island looking at the backside of the Statue of Liberty.
It was terrible because we were coming to this country of the free and then we
went to jail. They kept saying that I could get out. I could go stay with my
uncle. And I said, "I stayed in Vienna with my family, I'm not going to leave
them now." Eva was a forceful young woman, even at not quite twelve.

Ellis Island had once been the gateway for all immigrants arriving
in New York City, but by 1940 it was a prison island for detainees, with
the real possibility of deportation back to their countries of origin.

Of course, deportation at this point would have been a death sentence for my mother and her parents, as it was for many of the passengers
aboard the *St. Louis*, a ship that sailed from Hamburg, Germany, to Cuba
in May 1939. Almost all the 937 passengers aboard were Jews fleeing from
Germany. The plan was to arrive in Cuba and wait for admittance to the
United States. Cuba and the United States refused to accept the refugees,
with the exception of a very few who already had valid visas. The rest
were sent back to Europe. Some were accepted by England and Belgium,
but 532 passengers were unable to escape Western Europe before the May
1940 German invasion. Of those, almost half died during the Holocaust. In
describing the decision by President Roosevelt not to accept the emigrants
on the *St. Louis*, the United States Holocaust Memorial Museum website
reports, "A *Fortune Magazine* poll at the time indicated that 83 percent of
Americans opposed relaxing restrictions on immigration. President Roosevelt could have issued an executive order to admit the *St. Louis* refugees,
but this general hostility to immigrants, the gains of isolationist Republicans in the Congressional elections of 1938, and Roosevelt's consideration
of running for an unprecedented third term as president were among the
political considerations that militated against taking this extraordinary
step in an unpopular cause." The story of the ill-fated *St. Louis* was widely
reported. The fear of deportation was ever-present for the Singers during
their time on Ellis Island. All they could do was wait and hope.

There were people from New York who came from Jewish organizations and they brought us books, and for the women they brought needlework to keep us busy and to make clothes. My mother was a good seamstress. She made clothes for me. And people came to entertain us. Wonderful Jewish entertainers, and they brought food with them. The food at Ellis Island was all right, but first of all there were people who were kosher and wouldn't eat the food, but also, it was prison food. So they would bring food and they would sing and they would talk to us and they tried to make it easier. And then finally, after fourteen days, we were released.

They were not deported back to Europe. They were admitted to the United States as war refugees, during a time much like our own, when there was enormous antipathy toward foreigners, especially Jews, a facet of entrenched fear and racism. The attitudes of the majority of Americans were fixed: these Jewish immigrants were spies; they would steal jobs from Americans; they were altogether undesirable.

THE FAMILY'S AMERICAN adventure began. *My mother's oldest brother was living in Brooklyn in a small apartment. He came to pick us up from Bowling Green, and we went on the subway and I was frightened to death, but anyhow we went on the subway and we got to Brooklyn.*

ONKEL THEO IS a friendly face in the sea of men and women rushing along the streets beneath the skyscrapers. Theo says he has no idea why this place is called Bowling Green. Just one more mystery in this confusing city. For Eva and her parents, the English language is still familiar letters forming mostly meaningless words. As Eva looks up, the buildings seem to be moving against the background of clouds, as if they might fall forward on top of her.

Onkel Theo is changed, thinner, clean-shaven, and his trousers are of a different style. It is a drizzly morning and a scattering of flowering trees near the ferry terminal are still in bloom. Eva tries to remember the cherry trees in Türkenschanzpark, half a world away. The hum and whine of this strange new city is pitched louder than Vienna. Cars bark at each other like animals with barely contained fury. Theo and Julius carry one of the trunks. Eva and her mother manage the other one. Theo leads the newcomers along the sidewalk and explains how they will travel by underground train to his family's apartment in Brooklyn. As they descend into the dark tunnel, the roar of a train barreling into the station swallows his voice. On the platform, the subway doors open, expelling a surge of busy New Yorkers on their way to somewhere. People push and shove and all this motion of people draws the Singers inside. The doors close and the train lurches out of the station. Eva looks out the smudged windows as the train gathers up force. She wonders how she will live in this city that looks and smells and sounds so different from the one she left behind. All around her people are speaking rapidly in English. She picks up a word here and there, but it is mostly a blur of a strange new music, muddled by the mind-numbing din of the wheels clattering over the rails. She is hungry and thirsty and so tired, but her parents still need her, so thirst and hunger and sleep will wait a bit longer. The train emerges from the darkness of the river tunnel into the light of the elevated rails, and daylight blasts the water droplets on the windows into prisms. Eva takes in the view of blocks and blocks of row houses and factories and warehouses as the train makes its way toward her next home.

PART FOUR

The New Country

And once you're here, you're ready to give everything, or almost everything, to stay and play a part in the great theater of belonging. In the United States, to stay is an end in itself and not a means: to stay is the founding myth of this society.

——Valeria Luiselli, *Tell Me How It Ends*

NEW YORK CITY doesn't exactly set out a welcome mat for newcomers. The Singers stayed with Onkel Theo for a week or so and then the hunt began for an apartment cheap enough for the two families. Julius was unable to find work, which would be just as hard today for a sixty-five-year-old new immigrant with poor English skills.

And we lived together with my uncle and his wife and his two daughters and my parents and myself in a small apartment because that's all the money we had. My father somehow had a little bit of American money—maybe it was the money from Switzerland. I'm not sure. My father was rather private about his money.

Franz wrote that according to immigration documents, Julius declared 6,000 in US dollars. This was a small fortune, and must have been a gift from Teddy Mann. Julius would have held this money tight, unsure how long his state of unemployment would last. He needed to find a new business opportunity, worthy of this capital.

FOR EVA, THE first challenge was to learn English. *I went to school here. In Vienna we had had a woman who tried to teach us English, all three of us, and of course you know how children are, we never paid any attention, but somehow or other I must have picked something up in the back of my head because when I came here I spoke English more or less within two or three weeks. I have a gift for languages. At home my parents insisted that we had to speak English because we had to all learn English. My mother went to work in a factory where they made children's clothes. My mother had never done that kind of work, but we needed money.*

My mother always called it a sweatshop. Anna, like those in generations of immigrants before her, was grateful for work that most Americans didn't want. By the 1940s working conditions in clothing factories had improved from previous decades, thanks to unions, but Anna and Theo still worked long hours. At some point Anna left the children's clothing factory to work at a company that made hand-crocheted dresses that were popular at the time.

We used to buy food in the Jewish neighborhoods on Friday. You know, before the Sabbath, they closed the stores and everything was cheap, so my mother and I would go and buy food for the week. But we ate and it was all right.

My father was very depressed. And then he had a heart attack. I think all the Sturm und Drang *in Vienna caught up with him. He had a heart attack but it wasn't very bad. He was in bed for a while and then he decided that he had to get up because we couldn't live on what my mother made.*

My mother often used that German phrase "*Sturm und Drang*" to describe any kind of drama at home or abroad. The phrase translates as "storm and stress" and was the phrase given to the German early Romantic literary movement that brought Goethe and Schiller to prominence. It was the only German phrase my mother used in her interview. I was struck that she slipped back into her native language to attempt to describe her father's mental and physical collapse for which there were no English words at her command even so many years later, long after his death. A mouthful of angry guttural consonants, this expression was a sealed package for feelings she wanted to keep locked up in the past. She would refer to my adolescent outbursts in this same way—*Sturm und Drang*. Her own teenage years had given her no preparation, or language, for my very American coming-of-age rebellion, one that caused us both so much shock and pain.

————————

TWO PHOTOS THAT do exist document an outing that took place in those first months in New York City. The Singers embarked on a most American adventure: they went to see the World's Fair in Queens. In one, the family poses in front of the Ford Pavilion, a tight trio, as always, with Eva in the middle.

In spite of their straightened circumstances, the family dressed formally, as they would have in Vienna, in clothing that suggests late summer or early fall. Julius and Anna wear suits, Eva a dress and jacket. Anna wears a trim hat. Eva's hair is still girlishly bobbed. She has just turned twelve. Soon enough they will adopt more American clothing and hairstyles, but here they haven't yet embraced the informality I saw in family photographs from subsequent years. They look like strangers in a strange land. The trio of Singers is small. The image is really about the Ford logo, so clean and modern and centered in the frame and the poignancy of the three survivors, literally "fresh off the boat," standing before this American icon at an exhibition devoted to the promise of the future.

The second photo from the same day has the same faded sepia hues and scalloped edge. A man stands in the center, wearing a stylish double-breasted suit, white shirt, tie, and a perfectly crimped fedora. His polished shoes catch a gleam of sunlight. As the shutter clicks, he is stuffing his mouth from a box of concession stand popcorn. With his olive complexion and large dark eyes he looks like someone who could be a family member, but when I showed my father the photo he could not name this person. The camera probably belonged to this prosperous-looking mystery man. And whoever he is, he doesn't look like an immigrant fresh off the boat. He is already an American.

After two years hiding out in their apartment on Weimarer Strasse, unable to use public transportation, afraid for their lives, this family engaged in the simplest of American freedoms. Mystery Man accompanied the family on the subway out to Queens just for fun. Life, liberty, and the pursuit of happiness.

––––––––––

A FAMILY TRAGEDY unfolded in numbers typed on a four-by-six-inch card: in March and April of 1941 Anna sent payments totaling $900 to an agency called the American Jewish Joint Distribution Committee in hopes of saving her brother Saloman, his wife Gertrude, and their daughter Gisela, who were still in Vienna. The card lists Saloman's address in the 8th district of Vienna and leaves space for the name of the ship that would bring the family to the United States. In this way, Anna was trying to pay forward the help she had received from Mr. Nichtern of Detroit and Teddy Mann and her brother Theo. On factory wages this couldn't have been easy. At some point after April, the agency lost track of Saloman and his family. Perhaps they were moved into one of the few remaining Jewish-occupied apartments. By 1941, for those who ended up in the predominantly Jewish 2nd district, deportation was imminent. The agency refunded the total amount of Anna's savings on October 21, 1941. At that time, Anna would not have known anything about what had become of the family.

Michael Simonson at the Leo Baeck Institute established that Saloman and his family were sent to Theresienstadt, the notorious transit camp in Czechoslovakia, on October 1, 1942. Saloman died there of pneumonia on February 3, 1943, perhaps weakened by slave labor and inadequate food rations. Gertrude and Gisela remained in Theresienstadt until they both were deported to Auschwitz Birkenau on October 9, 1944, on a transport of 1,600 people crammed into cattle cars. They arrived at Auschwitz three days later. From here their fate is uncertain. Most likely they were sent immediately to the gas chambers along with all but about 180 of the transport. It is possible that one or both of them were selected for slave labor and lived for a few days or weeks or months. I could not imagine Anna's grief and guilt when she finally understood their fate after the war ended. She'd done her best, but it wasn't enough.

———————

BY MARCH OF 1941, the Singers had saved enough money to relocate and were probably eager to claim some space for themselves after the cramped circumstances of life with Theo and his family. They moved from Brooklyn to an apartment on the Upper West Side, the one my father had pointed out to me on a walk home from one of our evenings together during my mother's illness. The residential streets and small shops lining Broadway had something of the feeling of residential neighborhoods in Vienna and many Austrian refugees had settled there. What may have spurred the move was a business opportunity made possible with the money from Teddy Mann.

My father finally found a man whose father had had a restaurant in Vienna, a very well known restaurant called Neugröschl's, and he wanted somebody to handle the money. So the two became partners and they had a very successful restaurant. It was on the Upper West Side, where there were a lot of Austrians, and they had Austrian cooking, and during the war when meat was sort of hard to get in New York they, because they were a restaurant, they were allowed to buy.

Neugröschl's had been a famous restaurant in Vienna, both for the food and the cantankerous character of its original owner. In 1939, Neugröschl's son had fled to New York and wasted no time reestablishing this familiar Viennese haunt. I could imagine what a comfort it was for so many immigrants to rediscover the transplanted smells and tastes of home, and for Julius this would have been a happy reunion with a place he had patronized before the war.

I traced the struggles and ultimate success of the refugee community through the advertisements in the pages of the newspaper *Aufbau* ("Reconstruction"), a publication established in the 1930s for

German-speaking immigrants. Articles focused on the tragedy unfolding in Europe. *Wien ohne Juden?* (Vienna Without Jews?) asked one op-ed, echoing the title of Hugo Bettauer's famous 1922 novel *The City Without Jews*. As in the novel, the Jews of Vienna had accepted their second-class status, continually striving, ever hopeful, only to be rejected again and again. In 1941, it looked like the anti-Semites had succeeded after all. It must have been horrifying for the Singers to read about the war from the safety of New York at this time, when it was not at all clear that the Allies would succeed in pushing back against Hitler's conquests.

All the more reason to adapt to a new reality, and Jews sought ways to integrate into their new country. I found a notice for tours of New York, designed to help new arrivals adjust to "Americans and the American Way." At this time, the American Way included a savage dose of Klu Klux Klan and other pro-Hitler activity that had led to attacks in New York City and Boston. The America First Committee was still promoting xenophobia. But compared to what the Jews of Europe had left behind, the Upper West Side of New York City must have felt like a piece of heaven.

At first, *Aufbau* reached out to a mostly impoverished community of new refugees. The advertisements were small and crudely designed: pumpernickel bread, shipping services to soldiers and families in Europe, English-language classes, driving schools, discount clothes, accountants, travel agents, tailors, fresh eggs and chocolate (essentials for any self-respecting Viennese home baker), cheap apartments for rent, and always, multiple ads with the headline " *WANZEN*" (pests) for exterminators to evict the hordes of roaches and other scavenging creatures that colonized them.

And then, as the immigrant population began to find work and thrive, small ads appeared for hotels in the Catskills offering relaxation and fresh air. These ads multiplied until they populated entire pages, like a typographic crazy quilt. Designers of fine men's and women's clothing began to purchase half-page advertisements. By 1945, as the war drew to a close and Bess Myerson became the first Jewish Miss America, there were ads for perfume and men's aftershave, surely a signifier of a growing middle class with disposable income.

In every edition of *Aufbau* there were pages of ads for teahouses, cabarets, concerts, musical theater, and restaurants promising home-cooked Viennese food. It was among these printed mosaics that I finally found a few small ads for Neugroeschl's or sometimes Neugoeschl's, varied Americanized spellings for the restaurant's name. Perhaps this was an innocent typo, but as a graphic designer, I observed that including the "r" would mean reducing the size of the type, resulting in less visibility. Herr Neugröschl's son might have prioritized size over accuracy. Whether a choice or a typo, what the restaurant offered hardly needed advertising: a home away from home, "*Treffpunkt der gemütlichen Wiener*" (meeting place for cozy Viennese). Ultimately, there were two separate restaurants located in the lobbies of neighborhood hotels: one for catered events like weddings, holidays, and bar mitzvahs, and the second dining room for daily meals. My father told me that when he met my mother in 1947 and first started visiting the restaurant, there were always long lines of regular patrons waiting outside. From an edition of *Knife and Fork in New York* comes this mouth-watering review:

> Located in the Hotels Standish and Oxford, these large restaurants are noted for their extra good Viennese cookery served in bountiful portions. The roast goose is really something to carry home in one's gratified tumtum. In addition, there's roast duckling, boiled chicken, pot roast, boiled beef, breaded carp, liver steak, goulash, broiled rib steak, and Wiener rostbraten. Full line of Viennese pastries, cakes, etc. Cocktails, wines, beers. Patrons are mostly Central Park Westers and Riverside Drivers.

Reading the review reminded me of the glass jar of goose fat my mother kept in the fridge—the best medium for panfrying veal schnitzel. Until their doctor advised them to modify their diets in the seventies, my mother made all the dishes mentioned here and I loved them all, with the exception of the liver steak. There were various tiers of veal schnitzel; sometimes she bought the fanciest, and we felt like royalty. When I smelled liver cooking in onions I knew liver wouldn't get any better than this, and it still made me want to retch. On those evenings I so wished we had a dog. But back then, my mother and father delighted in all this fatty plenty, the antidote to my father's Depression-era childhood, my mother's last hard years in Vienna, and the first in New York City.

ELISABETH KÜBLER-ROSS WROTE about the five stages of grief: denial, anger, bargaining, depression, acceptance. For Julius, the phases of denial, anger, and bargaining were in the past, left behind in Vienna. Following his heart attack, his attempts to find work at a standstill, Julius must have despaired about how the rest of his life might unfold. And then, somehow, he met Neugröschl's son, the embodiment of happier times. Darkness lifted. He wanted to be useful, and now he had a new purpose.

Julius began his time at Neugroeschl much as he had at Adolf Eisenmann und Sohn so many years earlier. He started as a bookkeeper; eventually he was manager and partner, thanks to Teddy Mann's financial support. Anna left her sewing work and became the pastry chef at the restaurant. At some point, Julius and Neugroeschl parted ways and my grandfather found a new business partner, another Adolf, to run his Viennese Restaurant. Many of the displaced Vienna Jews hated New York and dreamed only of returning home, but the Singers settled in. This was acceptance.

I POSTED SEARCHES for Neugroeschl online, hoping that someone had a photograph or a story about this restaurant. One woman wrote back to me, a Dr. Neugroschl at Mount Sinai Hospital. A few days after our first emails, she told me that a man named Herbert Sinclair had just contacted her, noting her last name. A year younger than my mother, Herbert grew up in Vienna and remembered eating regularly at the original Neugröschl's as a child. Dr. Neugroschl was startled by this out-of-the-blue coincidence. *Amazing how the world works*, she wrote, sending me Herbert's phone number. When he and I connected by phone, he told me that while he could not remember much about what he ate at Neugröschl's (except that the food was delicious and plentiful), he did remember his own exodus from Vienna in 1940. Thanks to yet another wealthy American uncle who paid for their passage, the family fled to France and then made their way to Seville, Spain, in the spring of 1940, where they boarded a cargo ship. The journey to Havana, Cuba, took thirty days across the Atlantic, dodging German submarines all the way. He remembered that there were cows on board the ship, slaughtered one by one to provide food for passengers and crew. "Thank God for my uncle, without him I wouldn't be here today," Herbert said. The family stayed in Cuba until 1943, when they moved to New York.

Herbert asked me to remind Dr. Neugroschl that he wanted to enroll in her memory loss study, whose posting initially caught his attention while he was getting one of his thrice-weekly dialysis treatments.

"Honestly," I said, "you don't seem to have any problems remembering things at all." I was so struck by the vivid details he shared with me in just fifteen minutes.

"It's exhausting," Herbert said, of his dialysis. "I tell my girlfriend and my daughters, I don't know whether I should continue, but without dialysis I wouldn't be here."

"I think you should stick with it," I said. "Don't give up yet."

————————

AFTER MY MOTHER died, I inherited a pile of white cloth napkins, some stamped by a professional laundry. When I used them I imagined my grandfather directing the staff as they set up for the evening rush, and my grandmother in the kitchen, humming melodies from Viennese light opera as she stretched paper-thin strudel dough. My father told me that Anna had a fine singing voice and an unfailing warm personality, miraculously preserved in spite of everything the family had endured.

And business was good. People loved the food and the free-flowing unrationed meat. The restaurant's success allowed for comforts and even a few luxuries. Among our family photos, I found one of Julius and Anna from the late 1940s. Anna's shoulders are draped in a fur stole, just like the one she'd worn in Vienna in easier times.

———

BY 1942, THE family was immersed in New York life, but the war was still raging in Europe. In January of that year, while Julius and Anna worked at Neugroeschl's and Eva entered ninth grade, high-level Nazis met outside Berlin at the Wannsee villa to discuss the implementation of the Final Solution.

For the remaining years of the war, there was grim news of battles in Europe and the Pacific, until the tide turned leading up to the Allied invasion. My father entered the army as a nineteen-year-old private in a mortar battalion, landing on Omaha Beach in the fall of 1944, following the successful D-Day landings. He fought in the Battle of the Bulge under General Patton, ending his tour in Germany. On V-E Day, in 1945, he and his fellow soldiers fired celebratory shots in the air and hoped they would soon be home.

———

GERMANY AND VIENNA were in ruins. The *Aufbau* front page was jubilant on V-E Day, but there were also the horrifying revelations of the Nazi concentration camps. The lucky refugees in New York now understood the fate of those relatives who couldn't, or wouldn't, leave.

My father's days as a soldier were also over, and he returned to Philadelphia. His father picked him up at the train station and bought him a set of civilian clothes. During his deployment, Frank decided that if he made it through the war alive he would enroll at art school, and now he was able to fulfill that goal.

ON SEPTEMBER 6, 1945, at the age of seventeen, my mother, now Eve, became a naturalized American citizen along with her parents. There would be no going back to Vienna. The Singers were in New York City to stay.

THE INCOME FROM Neugroeschl's meant that there was enough money for Eve to take a trip to Florida, where she visited Nichtern relatives who had settled there, including her cousin Erika (now Erica). The beautiful young woman who gazes at the camera is an American, who watches her share of Hollywood movies and reads the latest fashion magazines. She knows how to pose seductively for a camera—on top of a car or leaning against a rock in a flowery one-piece—to make the most of her curvy figure. Her arresting face is framed in waves of dark hair. Her mouth is painted deep red with a manicure to match. Here is the same steady gaze from her childhood photo from 1938, before the Nazi terror began, when life was simpler and she was innocent. That little girl has grown up. Eve is worldly now and she understands her beauty (not a few of the young men in Florida must have been tripping over themselves as she strolled the avenues of Miami Beach in her platform sandals). She has experienced fear and despair and has rebounded and learned the ways of her new country, but she takes nothing for granted. "Never again" could happen tomorrow.

JULIUS HAD SAVED his family, reclaimed his life, and now he tried to reclaim something of his material losses. *After the war my father tried to find out and sue and get compensation and we were told by the Austrians who were "victims" that "all the factory was shipped to Germany and therefore they were not responsible." Unquote. He never got any money.*

Recently the Austrian government has tried to compensate and the three of us [Fritz, Dolfi, Eve] *we did get some money. Not specifically for the factory, but for everything that we lost.*

In 1947, the Austrian government was still in denial. My father said that Julius was a calm man, but if anything could make him angry, it would have been that denial of responsibility.

Eventually, Eve and her brothers received Austrian pensions. It would take till 2005, the year before my mother died, before there was any other financial recovery, and this money came not from Austria, but from a Swiss bank. After the war ended in 1945, all Swiss accounts were frozen. Once the freeze was released, survivors came forward to make claims, but Swiss banks deliberately withheld or misstated account information. The final resolution letter was issued by the Claims Resolution Tribunal for Holocaust Victim Assets Litigation, Case No. CV 96-4849. The gifts my mother had given to me and my brother the year before she died were a portion of the total compensation she and her brothers received sixty years after the end of the war, a tiny fraction of the value of my grandfather's company.

––––––––––––

AFTER HIGH SCHOOL, my mother attempted a year at CUNY School of Engineering. *I was one of the only women that year and I just couldn't do it. I tried to smoke and drink beer with the men, but after a year I gave up.* I appreciated that she gave engineering her best shot, given the forces set against her at that time. Eve recalibrated quickly, enrolling at the Traphagen art school in New York, where she took courses in fashion illustration. A few of her drawings survived, elongated figures of women in the styles of the time. A skilled seamstress like her mother, she would have made a fine dress designer if she hadn't fallen in love with bookmaking. At Traphagen, my mother met a woman named Inez from Philadelphia. Her boyfriend was enrolled in art school there and had made a friend named Frank, a recent war vet who was hoping to meet an interesting young woman. Inez thought that Eve would be a perfect match.

This was the young woman my father met on a blind date one weekend in 1947 in New York City. Eve still had a strong Austrian accent that would soften over the years. By the end of the weekend, they both knew something big was happening. Soon enough, Frank was a frequent guest at the Singer apartment on 104th Street furnished with some of the Biedermeier furniture Julius had somehow shipped from Vienna. Everywhere in the neighborhood Frank heard people speaking German. Eve and her parents were great music lovers and Frank often went with them to see performances of German-language operettas. Eve especially adored Beethoven's master opera *Fidelio*, a story of political imprisonment, the quest for freedom, and the power of love. For her the story must have felt personal.

———————————

DURING THAT FIRST summer, Frank accompanied the Singers to Bear Mountain. He took a photo of the trio—Anna, Eve, Julius—centered in the frame, squinting as they faced the camera. They dress like Americans now. Anna wears a relaxed summer dress, short white socks, and spectator shoes. Julius has adopted the short-sleeved button-down shirt of the period, open at the collar, tucked into his high-waisted trousers. He looks his age, no longer the vigorous man who climbed Hohe Wand at the age of fifty-three. My mother wears a peasant blouse and a full circle skirt that would look just as adorable today as it did on that hot summer afternoon. She tips her head and smiles flirtatiously at my father, a most come-hither gaze. Among many revelations for my father, who had grown up with unhappy parents in a tension-filled home, Julius and Anna were loving with each other, and open-minded about premarital sex. Anna took the same shot with Frank in the frame, dressed in trousers and a white T-shirt. The family had embraced him and he was glad to have been embraced. The mountain behind them beckoned but remained a backdrop to an easy afternoon of sandwiches and chilled tea. This ancient dome was nothing like the craggy Alps

Julius and Donald Brown had climbed, but it was a beauty. I wondered if Julius brought his folding utensils along on this excursion.

———————

MY FATHER TOLD me that when he'd first met my mother he asked Julius why they hadn't left Vienna sooner. I imagined the two of them talking together in the apartment on 104th Street and Broadway.

"I was an Austrian citizen," Julius told my father. "I thought it would pass. I loved my country." Vienna, in Julius's mind and memory, appeared personified, like the love object in an affair that matures into a successful marriage. In this marriage of the Vienna Jews with their city, the anti-Semitism they experienced, whether overt or subtle, was just part of a complex relationship. Vienna wooed them, accepted them, and then, like a cruel lover, she rejected her most loyal citizens. Julius did not give up on love of place. He transferred his devotion to New York City.

———————

IN MY FAVORITE photograph of my parents as a new couple—a two-inch-square print taken by one of Frank's art school friends—Eve sits cross-legged on a picnic table in a wooded park. She wears a crisply tailored white blouse, black cropped trousers, loafers with white socks, like Katharine Hepburn on a day off. Her arms are raised to shoulder height, hands under her chin in a stylized pose she must have enjoyed, as I'd seen similar photos of her in my parents' album. I'd never been able to interpret the gesture; perhaps she was copying a film star or model of that period. My father, wearing round glasses, a white shirt, high-waist pleated trousers, and a lopsided goofy smile rests his hand on her shoulder. The photograph captures an inside joke, long forgotten.

Frank and Eve managed two years of long-distance romance, filled with misunderstandings and a separation before they married. One impediment to their relationship was that Frank's parents did not approve of Eve. They did not like her difference, her European ways, and they especially did not like that she lived in New York City, far from the family lumber business they assumed my father would join. There was a power tussle, but eventually Frank left art school and pulled away. He moved to New York and married Eve in February 1949. For a short time they lived with Julius and Anna before finding their own apartment in the neighbor- hood. My father loved his in-laws, a fact that created further distance from his own family. When it became clear that he would never return home, his family disliked Eve more, blaming her for their son's flight north.

HIS HEALTH IN decline, Julius confided to my father in another of their intimate conversations that he regretted that his weak heart now prevented him from making love with Anna. By then he was nearing seventy-five, not so old now, but Julius had lived hard and wartime had taken its toll.

On a morning in October 1950, Julius went out for a walk to buy a newspaper. When he didn't return, Eve and Frank accompanied Anna to the local police station. They were sent to Bellevue Hospital, where they identified his body. The official report stated that Julius had col- lapsed from a heart attack on Ninety-Sixth Street and had died in the arms of strangers. I saw his hat blowing into the street as he fell to the pavement, but unlike my imagined morning many years earlier at the Café Taube in Vienna, this time the hat was lost, carried off by an autumn gust rushing in from the nearby Hudson River.

ANNA MOVED TO a smaller apartment a bit farther downtown from 104th Street. Eve and Frank found an apartment nearby and tried to fill the void left by Julius's sudden death. Even during my parents' brief foray into suburban living just north of the city, they would bring Anna up for weekends. My father told me that when they sold their tract house and moved back to an apartment on the Upper West Side less than a year later, he got down on his knees and kissed the sidewalk. By then he was already a true New Yorker.

Frank, Eve, and Anna vacationed together. They all sailed on the *Degras* to Europe, and my mother made that first trip back to Vienna. In the summer, they all went to Maine. In one photo taken by my father on Monhegan Island, Eve and Anna sit close to each other on a rock in the sun. They both face the camera, but there is connection and ease between them. I had friends who referred to their mother as their best friend and I felt sure that Eve thought of Anna this way. My father told me that Anna adored Monhegan, and was still an energetic walker, singing Austrian tunes as they hiked the island trails. In another photo Frank relaxes on a lawn chair with Eve and Anna on either side. Anna was so much younger than Julius, so she must have given some thought to what was likely to be a long widowhood, and could now take comfort in having her daughter married to a man she could love like a son, especially as both Fritz and Dolfi were still in England. Eve must have imagined then that she would have many more years with her mother.

New York, 25 May 1956

I hereby petition for your benevolent help for the reimbursement of our erstwhile "Phoenix-Insurances." My husband, Julius Singer, born 6 September 1875 in Vienna, died since 5 years here in New-York, had then undersigned at least 2 if not more insurances with single premiums, which he paid in cash in advance with the Phoenix Insurance company. In the year 1940, March, we were forced to emigrate and after one had taken away our entire assets for the Jewish property levy, we had to give away the insurances for 1/3 of their real value. The money was transferred to the Israelite Kultusgemeinde in

Vienna and for it we received 3 shipping tickets for my husband, me and our then 11 year old daughter. When the full amount had been paid in advance I took it for granted, that I would have the right to demand the rest of the amount that was due to us. Unfortunately I had not received any numbers at all for the insurance policies as we had to hand over the insurances and I am writing at the same time to the "Austrian Insurance plc," Vienna I, Freyung, in order to get the data clarifying this issue.

In looking forward to your kind news, I take my leave.

Yours sincerely

Anna Singer

In 1956, Anna typed the letter above to the state finance office in Vienna, in an attempt to reclaim the lost value of the insurance policies Julius sold under duress in 1938. The letter is stamped at the bottom by the office as "received." Anna's tone is infuriatingly deferential and polite. She should have been screaming, instead she was pleading. As I read the letter a second and third time, I felt an urge to time-travel back to 1956 with a particular female friend of mine who happened to be a kick-ass lawyer in New York City who could surely have fixed this injustice for my grandmother. But in the real 1956, nothing happened and Anna's request was unanswered.

ALSO IN THE spring of 1956 Frank and Eve made a trip to Vienna. My mother had been in touch with the nurse who had cared for Julius during a long-ago illness. In her Leo Baeck interview she described a comforting reunion with the nurse, who was glad to see Eva, now Eve, after so many years. At some point during their stay my parents visited one of the famous wine gardens located on the outskirts of Vienna. My mother's voice broke—the only time I heard this during her interview—as she described the arrival of a group of young children who performed traditional songs for them, tunes my mother probably remembered from her own childhood.

IN 1958, ANNA died six months after a diagnosis of colon cancer. She was sixty-six. I often wondered how things might have been between my mother and me if my grandmother had been part of my childhood. Anna had managed to preserve a sense of exuberant joy in life through her many hardships. For Eve, the untimely loss of her mother just a few years after her father's death was a blow that must have confirmed the inescapable harshness of life, its unfathomable cruelty and suffering. As she would often tell me, first comes laughter, then tears. *I have trouble with my God*, she said during her Leo Baeck interview, when the young Austrian asked if she still practiced Judaism. Words spoken like a skeptic, who continued to light candles during Hanukkah and make Passover dinner, perhaps hedging her bets in case there really was salvation at the end of her life's journey and a scenario where she might be rejoined with her parents. By May 1958, Anna was gone, and at the age of not quite thirty, Eve was orphaned and her brothers remained far away. She did have Frank, but as it happened, their marriage was in crisis.

I FIRST LEARNED about this time when I was sixteen or seventeen. My father and I were eating lunch in a French bistro on Madison Avenue at a small table packed close to others inhabited by perfumed ladies and their handbags, a world away from our apartment across town on the shabbier Upper West Side. It must have been during a school vacation, when my father often took me on treks to his favorite art galleries, our common ground. He was telling me a story I did not want to hear. Perhaps it was the red wine talking.

We were an odd couple at this restaurant. I was an anxious,

nail-nibbling teenager dressed in a vintage frock and clogs, twirling an errant brown curl to keep my hands busy since chain-smoking wasn't an option here. My father wore his curly gray hair swept back, with long bushy side whiskers and large wire-frame glasses. His sartorial choices, as well as his strong design opinions, had always been stand-outs. Even then, when everything about my family was mortifying to me, I was proud of the way he worked a mash-up of olive-green paisley tie and a red-and-blue-striped shirt with such bravado.

My father continued his story while my toes worried the soles of my clogs, as if seeking a hideaway from my acute embarrassment. I listened, painfully aware of every mechanical action of my teeth and jaw. Gripping my fish knife, I was poised to attempt the deboning of the broiled trout that gazed at me through one cloudy eyeball, as if sizing up my skills. My parents were big sticklers for four-star-restaurant table manners and this was no time to slack off. I poked my knife under the delicate spine, tugged and twisted, marveling as the curved architecture separated neatly from the flesh. It was something to do. I was not the most self-aware teenager, but even I could see that what was happening here was paradigm-shattering: the moment when I understood that my parents were imperfect humans with secret longings, weaknesses, and, most shocking of all, complicated sex lives.

How had our conversation turned to this? However desperately I wanted to back out, it was too late. The story was on a roll. It was about a time, some years before I was born, when my father and mother were struggling. I didn't like talking about my mother. She and I battled nightly. Almost anything could set us off, including my daily miseries at a school she felt I did not appreciate. I knew my parents had been a young couple once. I'd seen the photos from when they'd met and married. She was so beautiful, with wavy chestnut hair like an English movie star, posing behind a lacy curtain for my father, hidden and yet present. You could feel his gaze reflected in her eyes. I didn't want to listen to my father's story, but this was where we were.

Several years into their marriage, my father said, vaguely, they'd met another couple, and my father's infatuation with the other woman nearly broke his life apart. This other woman sounded like the opposite of my mother. I pictured a cool blonde, scarlet lipstick staining her cigarettes, perhaps something like the highly polished mothers of some of my classmates at the private school I attended, also on the Upper East Side, not far from the restaurant where we sat.

My father paused to take another sip of wine. "She smelled so good." He said this, and right there in the restaurant I caught a whiff of what that scent might have been: delicate floral, infused with the heady musk of old money.

"Did anything happen?" Was I really asking my father this question? Would he even tell me the details if there were any?

He shook his head. He and my mother had married so young, he said by way of explanation. In the end he realized that the other woman wasn't what he wanted at all and then it was over, but not without some damage done.

"But it was always the great romance with your mother," my father said, concluding his story with a mouthful of the good red wine. He was an early rebel against the white-wine-with-fish rule.

I let my father's story end there. On that day it was already too much information to process, a jarring dissonant note in my family narrative. And that's the last he and I would speak on this subject until a few years after my mother died, when I felt brave enough for a revisit. By then he'd remarried. At eighty-two, he wasn't ready to give up on love.

WHEN I WAS born in June of 1959, Eve was still mourning the loss of her mother. Her grief was free-flowing in so many directions: the lingering trauma of the Nazi occupation, her exile from Vienna, the lack of acknowledgment and restitution from the Austrian government, the obvious toll the family's ordeal took on her parents' health. Her father had saved her and his effort had taken years from his life.

Her adored mother also died too soon. She was left with the profound loneliness of becoming an orphan, a searing pain at whatever age it occurs when one loses beloved parents.

———————

DURING THIS DECADE of the 1950s, Frank and Eve launched their careers through a combination of accident and determination. In "Making Books," a 2004 profile for the *Washington Post*, they described their years at Simon & Schuster, the company comprising the imprint that published this very book. Determined to find a way to live in the worlds of art and commerce, Frank apprenticed at design firms. In 1950, he found his way to a job at Sandpiper Press, the children's book division at Simon & Schuster. Four years later he rose to become the art director. In late 1957 he was tapped for the art director position in the adult trade division and he stayed there for the rest of his working years as the company grew.

In the interview, Eve spoke almost mystically about the path that had led her to a career in publishing. *When I was a child in Vienna, my father had a factory that did lithographs from large flat soap stones. I often went to his shop, which was just down the street from our elegant 19th century apartment house. I would watch him work and smell the ink. It was then, I think, that my future was written.* She had taken some typography classes as part of her coursework at Trapaghen art school, and in 1951, while between jobs, she was offered a freelance project revising an art book for Simon & Schuster. Soon she joined the full-time staff.

Until they retired in 1995, Frank and Eve continued to build their careers. When I was young it was still unusual to have a working mother, but I remember feeling proud that she had a job in an office. My mother bought us a picture book titled *Mommies at Work*, which I loved poring through. Imagine having a firefighter as a mom! The picture book did not include an art director mom, but I got the message. Work could define you and make you self-sufficient, and win respect. You could buy your own Ferragamos if you saved up your pennies.

Over dinner, in addition to office gossip, my brother and I might hear of meetups with famous authors. I wrapped my high school textbooks in some of the celebrated book jackets my father art directed: *All the President's Men*, *The Handmaid's Tale*, *Catch-22*, and the psychedelia of Carlos Castaneda's memoirs. I learned to identify typefaces at a young age, appreciated a good balance of positive and negative space on a page, and I always loved the smell of ink on paper.

––––––––––

AS AN ADOLESCENT, my parents were the weird, annoying obstacles to my secret plans. But all that time they were leading their secret work lives, hours when they didn't have to think about their weird, annoying teenagers.

Recently, I spoke with several women who worked with my mother during those later years, beginning with Bonni, who began her career at Simon & Schuster around 1985.

We met for lunch in New York City's financial district, where she worked. We were about the same age, both small Jewish women, with the same head of incorrigible curly hair. As we perused the menu, we bonded over the lack of frizz-sedating hair product in the eighties. Back then almost every day was a bad hair day.

Bonni's Jewish family had not been directly touched by the Holocaust, as her grandparents had all arrived in the United States decades before the Second World War. She was proud to be Jewish and when she left the safe "bubble" of a Long Island town to attend art school in Manhattan she remembered being surprised that the rest of the world wasn't all Jewish.

I laughed when she said this because to the rest of the country and the world, New York City is often identified as Jewish, just like "Red Vienna."

Six months after finishing her degree, Bonni interviewed with my mother. "And I remember exactly what I was wearing because years later she said, 'I can't believe I hired you because you were wearing a denim miniskirt.' She was very put together. Her bun, Ferragamo shoes, you know, perfect. I was so young and not worldly. I sort of bullshitted my way into this interview. I didn't know how to spec type. I had no idea what I was doing."

Bullshitting or not (and I have definitely bullshitted my way through plenty of interviews), Bonni was a quick study, convinced that she could learn the job. She remained amazed that my mother had hired a kid right out of school to whom she immediately delegated responsibility and offered independence. And then, looking at me sincerely, as if asking for acknowledgment, Bonni added, "She was tough." A beat. "She wasn't always the nicest person."

I nodded. The tough woman Bonni worked for was the tough mother I'd known. Brusque. Blunt. Not always the softest. It was tough being a working mother in the 1950s. Until President Clinton passed the Family and Medical Leave Act in 1993, there was no such thing as the paid maternity leave Bonni was able to take when she had her two children. Before that, working women saved up their vacation days. My mother took off two weeks after my brother and I were born.

As a freelancer, I also began working again just a few weeks after giving birth. I missed plenty as I attempted to balance parenting and career, including my daughter's first steps, but I was home during working hours most days, able to feed my baby lunch and play with her during work breaks. On a quiet afternoon I could take Liza to the playground. I wondered how it felt for my mother to leave her children behind with a full-time babysitter so soon after giving birth. And then years later watch Bonni manage her parenting life with just a bit more balance. I can imagine my mother thinking this was just one more layer in a harsh unfair world.

As Bonni spoke, I wished I could tell my mother how much I had always admired her work, that my advice to young expectant mothers was still "Never quit your job." For all the progress women had made, it was still hard to win respect. Work had defined my mother's life, and truly it had also defined mine. I had the sense that my mother's steely toughness with Bonni was her way of showing caring, to remind a younger woman that a career was hard to build, but easy to lose.

Bonni seemed to sense something of my mother's inner conflict about her religion, that "she was Jewish, but she wasn't, you know what I mean?"

I thought back to the end of my mother's interview for Leo Baeck when she said, *I have trouble with my God.*

Bonni recalled my mother speaking about her childhood in Austria. "She had a distinct accent. It was lovely. It wasn't strong. It was subtle and very proper. There was anger at leaving her beloved country, because they had a beautiful life there." I was struck by the way Bonni described my mother's accent, the one I'd never noticed during her lifetime, and how my mother had preserved the memory of her lost childhood.

"She talked about you a lot," Bonni said.

"I hope it was nice things," I said, feeling suddenly awkward.

"Oh, yes," she said. And that made me want to cry.

———————————

"SHE WAS A strong presence as head of our all-female department," Kathy wrote in an email. "She fiercely protected us, our work, and the department. I think she loved teaching and sharing and I was (and still am) an eager student. I've loved books since I was a kid and I was thrilled to learn everything I could about book design. As a side note, I always thought it was cool she got to have her initials in 'em-dash.'"

Ah, another hard-core typography nerd.

Kathy overheard plenty in the office. "I remember a very loud argument she had with Carl Bernstein—they were both in her office and I was across the hall at my desk—while she was working on the book design for his CIA book, *Veil.* I can't recall what it was about, but, Carl Bernstein!"

Perhaps my mother and Carl Bernstein were arguing about type height or leading or margin widths or the size of his name on the title page. More typography nerd stuff. Now I knew where I got my short

temper and my intolerance for ugly page layouts. A woman assert-
ing herself was still a notable challenge to the status quo. My elegant
mother was trying to walk the delicate line between claiming her
power and being labeled a mean bitch. In her department, she was
playing the publishing world version of the "strong female lead" Brit
Marling described in a recent *New York Times* op-ed: a woman who can
vanquish foes while looking hot. Sometimes she had to do some yell-
ing to stake her territory. Sometimes female superiors created the most
obstacles, because this is what happens still when women are forced to
compete for respect.

Kathy recalled some words of wisdom that made me laugh out
loud with surprise. "She said a lazy person will figure out shortcuts to
finish a job and that could be a good thing." I could not imagine my
mother (the least lazy person I knew!) offering work-arounds. Maybe
it was more like: she was a woman with a demanding career who also
really needed to be able to leave her office at five o'clock so she could
buy groceries and cook dinner for her family and do laundry and help
her kids with homework and still have an hour to herself to read in bed.

"I was a shy kid," Kathy wrote, "and I loved her ability to be so
outspoken and strong with her opinions. She probably didn't know it
but she was a role model for me."

"I'm going out to get a bowl of soup," my mother would tell Kathy
at lunchtime. Is love of soup genetic? Until it closed, whenever the
woman at the lunch spot across the street from my house saw me coming in the door she would ask, "A bowl of soup?" and I would nod.
Maybe I have turned into my mother after all.

PEI GREW UP in suburban New Jersey in a Chinese family that had
moved from Malaysia in the 1960s. She arrived at Simon & Schuster
with no experience in bookmaking since this isn't really taught in art
schools. "I learned on the job," she said. "Your mom held my hand

during some of those first layouts. She was very maternal . . . but I personally didn't mind that."

Songhee, who was born in Korea and moved to the United States with her family when she was six, arrived a year or so after Pei. She recalled that Eve asked her to do some math problems at her job interview. The usefulness of math became clear soon enough. She told me that Eve could tell how many pages a book would be just from the heft of the paper manuscript. "I said, really? You're a magician?" But now, after thirty years in publishing, Songhee has learned that skill.

Like Bonni and Pei, Songhee appreciated my mother's hands-off management style. "This is how I think management should be, because of her. If you needed help she was open and gracious with her time to teach you and show you, but otherwise she left you alone. If you wanted to come talk to her, just to chitchat, she was always open. And she liked to talk about her own life."

Some maternal-type wisdom was dispensed during these conversations, including the proper way to iron a shirt and how to manage other household tasks, lessons I also received.

Both Pei and Songhee noticed the ways that Eve tried to find some balance in her life as a career woman and mother, despite the fact that the work world was hardly accommodating at the time.

My mother worked and managed our home life, the infamous "juggling" that my contemporaries and younger women are still trying to master with equal parts guilt and multitasking. How she did it all was a mystery; she always seemed to be in motion.

———————

MY FATHER SHARED this story from my parents' last trip together to Vienna in 1996. Upon retirement the year before, Simon & Schuster honored my parents for their decades of service with a grand party and a gift of two round-the-world tickets. They decided to keep their traveling to the Mediterranean Sea. After many adventures on an elegant cruise,

Frank and Eve flew to Vienna, but when they arrived at their hotel they discovered that their travel agent had made an error: they were one day too early for their room. The apologetic concierge suggested that another hotel across the street might have availability. Off they went, and my mother explained their situation to the hotel manager in her fluent Viennese. The hotel manager, who had no doubt been expecting to speak in English to two American tourists, was startled. "Madam," she said. "Your Viennese is so wonderful. Do you live here?" She could not have anticipated what happened next as my mother replied that she had, indeed, grown up in Vienna and came by her dialect naturally. "And I would have stayed here if you hadn't kicked me out."

IN SPITE OF the good life my mother made for herself—as an American, wife to my father, mother to my brother and me, with a career at a prestigious publishing company—I do not believe now that she ever fully recovered from the terror of those last two years in Vienna and its aftermath. Deep emotional pain lasts unless the underlying causes are treated and this rarely happens for refugees of any war.

My father told me that when he first met my mother, she suffered from chronic migraines and startled easily at loud noises, a visceral reaction to the marching of black-booted Nazis in the streets of Vienna. The trauma lingered long after she'd found safety in New York.

My young parents shared this aversion to loud noises. During his time in a mortar battalion of Patton's Third Army during the Battle of the Bulge in the winter of 1944 he experienced the constant threat of the enemy. A snafu left soldiers without proper winter clothing and boots. They dug foxholes in the frozen ground of the Ardennes forest, in which two or three men would attempt to sleep while mortar shells rained down from the enemy lines. They ate cold food out of cans and smoked cigarettes when they could get them. Stretches of something like boredom were punctuated by hunger and cold and then terrifying blasts of enemy fire. He saw terrible things—the dead and wounded bodies of his fellow infantrymen and the enemy—and then it was over and he was returned to civilian life intact.

My mother experienced several bouts of colitis, a disease of the colon that is exacerbated by stress. During one episode, when I was about twelve, she continued working right through, returning home exhausted. My father would tell my brother and me that we had to be quiet in our rooms, while my mother retreated to my parents' bedroom to rest. It seemed that she had internalized the dark forces of her childhood and that sense of menace and danger had wreaked havoc on her bowels. I read a number of medical studies that linked the ordeal of Holocaust survivors to depression, anxiety, and related physical and psychological issues.

Now my parents, and possibly the entire generation of those who fought, fled, or miraculously survived the terror in Europe, would be diagnosed with post-traumatic stress disorder, along with the survivors of all the conflicts since then. In a radio interview, neuroscientist Rachel Yehuda, an expert in PTSD and the field of epigenetics, explained how the traumatic experiences of one generation can be passed on, even altering the way genes function. "Trauma changes people permanently and in an enduring way," Yehuda said. "We're trying to understand whether resilient people are born or made."

In a November 5, 2019, episode of one of my favorite podcasts, *Terrible, Thanks for Asking*, host Nora McInerny also investigated the legacy of trauma in an interview with Dr. Brian Lynch of the Mayo Clinic in Rochester, Minnesota. He spoke about the effects of toxic stress—consistent, long-term traumatic situations that can overwhelm a child who hasn't been able to adapt with coping mechanisms—and how this alters the child's brain as it develops and his/her biological systems. Toxic stress weakens the immune system, leading to increased risks for illness later in life.

War, famine, genocide, or a sudden devastating loss can literally change our DNA and our children's. There are generations of traumatized survivors in Rwanda, Burundi, Bosnia, Syria, Somalia, Sudan, Palestine, Iraq, Syria, and everywhere in the world where one group of people has assaulted another over territory or religion. There are millions upon millions of rape victims everywhere.

I listened to an NPR interview highlighting the lingering trauma to children from Mexico and South America who were separated from their parents by the Trump administration's "zero tolerance" immigration policy. Lulu Garcia-Navarro reported that a federal district judge in Los Angeles ruled that the federal government must provide mental health services to families who suffered as a result of this policy. Ms. Garcia-Navarro interviewed Cristina Muñiz de la Peña, a psychotherapist, about her work with children and parents, who described the lasting feelings of vulnerability, powerlessness, and vigilance that remain long after the trauma. She could have been describing victims of any war.

———————

MY MOTHER WAS resilient—she had survived, and in so many spheres of her life she had thrived—but the trauma of what she witnessed and personally experienced as a child left her changed, and forever, and left its indelible mark on me, and so many others in the second generation of Holocaust survivors.

I remembered times—especially as I entered adolescence—when I sensed my mother's deep bitterness about the tragic loss of her homeland and the theft of her innocence. I wondered if our close physical resemblance might even have caused her pain, if I reminded her too much of her younger self, the Eva she was before her childhood abruptly ended on a March morning in 1938. Her later American life was different from any she might have envisioned for herself as a child. My mother's sorrow was buried under the surface of a highly productive life. It was a sorrow I dared not penetrate as I was growing up, and for as long as she lived. For all the ways I had turned out to be quite like her—a shoe collector, a gardener, a homebody, an opinionated political cynic, a passionate lover of paper and ink, and books as objects and as a refuge—now I understood in a deeper way why it was never easy for us.

SOME PEOPLE ARE a marvel of survival and optimism. My grand-mother Anna was such a woman. As my father wistfully described her, she was the most unfailingly warm, loving, and optimistic person he ever met. Some of us, like my mother and me, are wired less cheerfully.

I also struggled with her lingering bitterness that infused my under-standing of how people could adapt and accept each other. That bitterness only grew after the election of 2016 exposed the persistence of the same "America First" thinking that had prevented the rescue of Jews during the Holocaust and was now demonizing people trying to escape despots and war in countries in the Mideast and below our southern border.

In 2018, a respite presented itself. Before my mother died, my parents had arranged a trip to Normandy, France, where my father had landed in the fall of 1944 as a nineteen-year-old draftee. When my mother became ill, the trip was canceled, but now my father decided to make new plans with Justine. When he mentioned this idea to me, I invited Clark, Liza, and myself along. In September of that year, we all met up in Bayeux, a medieval city that was miraculously spared during Allied bombing, and the following morning we embarked on an organized tour of the Amer-ican D-Day battle sites of Omaha Beach and Pointe du Hoc, and the D-Day memorial and cemetery. In addition to the five of us, there were three other Americans in our van. Our guide was a young Brit, one of many who have relocated to Normandy to serve the World War II tour-ism industry. The three other passengers seemed starstruck to be traveling with a World War II veteran, especially one with such deep knowledge and recall as my father. At Omaha Beach, Liza, Clark, and I walked to the water's edge. The tide was far out that morning, so we could experience the deep expanse of sand the landing troops saw when they arrived on June 6, 1944. In my mind, I tried to overlay the famous grainy black-and-white Robert Capa photographs onto the peaceful beach before us.

As we walked up the road from the sea my father recalled arriving with his battalion in October 1944. "The first thing we saw was the cemetery," he said with a sigh, referring to the temporary cemetery that held the bodies of the D-Day casualties until a final memorial resting place was built at the end of the war. A harrowing sight for a young kid headed off to battle in Luxembourg and northern France.

Later, as we walked through the rows and rows of white grave markers, we saw some with Jewish stars, but our guide pointed out that there were many more Jewish soldiers who did not want to be identified as such, in case they were captured by the Germans. My father was a lucky man to be walking through this grassy field and I was heartbroken that my mother had missed a chance to be there with him. They had both escaped Nazi Europe with their lives.

BY THE FALL of 2019, three years into the Trump era, I battled gloom every day as I read the newspaper, pondering the grim realities of our now: an American president who riled up supporters by attacking the press and promoting the xenophobic nationalism that had caused so much damage in the 1930s. As Tyler Anbinder, professor of history at George Washington University, wrote in the *Washington Post* on November 7, "Trump's nativism is especially striking for its comprehensiveness. Over the centuries, nativists have leveled ten main charges against immigrants: They bring crime; they import poverty; they spread disease; they don't assimilate; they corrupt our politics; they steal our jobs; they cause our taxes to increase; they're a security risk; their religion is incompatible with American values; they can never be 'true Americans.' Trump has made every one of these charges. No American president before him has publicly embraced the entire nativist worldview." Trump would have said the same about the Singers. He made exceptions for fashion models. Those he married.

Overseas, Europe was in turmoil not seen since the end of World War II. Britain was still in the last throes of Brexit, a not-so-secret attempt to keep out immigrants that also threatened to upend the UK economy. Marine Le

Pen had been defeated in the last elections in France but was hardly discouraged; her rebranded far-right party carried on. Hungary and Poland and Turkey teetered toward dictatorship. Matteo Salvini was still pursuing his relentless anti-immigration goals. On June 14, 2019, he had refused entry to the *Sea-Watch 3*, carrying fifty-three migrants it had rescued off the Libyan coast, insisting that the ship could not dock without authorization. By June 29, when the ship's captain chose to deliver the exhausted passengers to safety, the Italian government arrested her, prompting an international incident. She was ultimately released, but these events and Salvini's later motion of no confidence against Italian prime minister Giuseppe Conte made his political ambitions clear. In February of 2020, the Italian senate voted to force Salvini to face trial for these actions, but the outcome was far from certain and Salvini still retained substantial political support.

And then there was Austria. In May 2019, a series of scandals led to the resignation of members of the FPÖ, including Interior Minister Kickl, and the collapse of the coalition government. After new elections, a new coalition government was formed between the ÖVP and the Green Party. Despite these changes, the nationalistic trend in Europe remained a concern and refugees were still fleeing Syria with nowhere to go.

I had one personal cause for optimism: in September 2019, Austria finally passed the new citizenship law I'd discussed with Tim Corbett in Vienna that would make it possible for me, my brother, and Liza to apply for dual citizenship. This felt like a proper way to honor my mother and so many others who had been forced to leave their home, an overdue act of correction. How wonderfully ironic it would be, I thought, to have Vienna suddenly repopulated with Jews from the Diaspora carrying their newly issued Austrian passports. If my own country went down in flames, I would be able to run away to the country that had forced my mother to flee and Liza could become a citizen of Europe.

But aside from this prospect of escape, the fall of 2019 was mostly about the possibility of a presidential impeachment, with the country sharply divided, Republicans refusing to abandon Trump, and the prospect of a vicious election season.

I wondered what my mother would have made of this time. My family had been riveted in front of the televised Watergate hearings, as the sordid tale of Nixon's political machinations unraveled further each day. It had taken a while for those 1974 Republicans to come to terms with the corruption of the president and vice president, both of whom left office in quick succession. I knew my mother would have been disgusted by the right-wing rhetoric casually launched on Fox News and by white supremacists reviving Nazi themes of "blood and soil." Mostly, I was disturbed by the growing chasm between political affiliations. We were now all Others. And that kind of division in America has never led to anything good.

"DON'T WORRY," LIZA said over dinner one evening when I lamented the latest outrage from Washington.

Liza now preferred "they" as a pronoun. I tried hard to remember, but often forgot.

Of course I worried, about everything.

"Don't worry," Liza said again, with a sincere and steady gaze. "My generation isn't afraid of change. I'll protect you."

I thought about the future this young generation would inherit, with so many problems from the climate crisis that kept me up at night to the rise of right-wing despots. How many more wars and traumatized generations of refugees would it take? I knew how most revolutions turned out: one set of tyrants quickly replaced by another.

I wondered about all the other Evas, children forced to leave their countries because of war and drought, riding the *Bestia* train through Mexico, or waiting in refugee camps in the Mideast and Europe. The current era of anti-immigrant fervor was as harsh as the xenophobic time of Eva's childhood. I knew that most of the refugee children who were fleeing their homelands would not be able to bring anything with them to mark a more peaceful time, like my mother's *Poesiealbum* or the photograph from January 1938 that had startled me when I first noted the date written on the back. I knew that my family was privileged to have such historical artifacts, compared to the vast majority who had no documents or images to record their past lives or evidence of their displacement. They would be dispossessed, undocumented, and threatened with cultural erasure. They were truly Other in a world that did not care about the fate of those unable to make themselves visible.

I worried, but I wanted to hope, because without hope we would be lost. I looked at Liza, who in that moment had that same fierce gaze I'd seen in the photograph of Eva at nine, a fierceness our world needed to collectively find if we were going to survive.

IN MARCH 2020, the COVID-19 pandemic forced us indoors. My ninety-four-year-old father and Justine left the city for their house in Connecticut, the one where my mother had planted her rose garden. Simon and Mary lived nearby and could help them with groceries and other supplies. Liza, now twenty-three and a most loyal New Yorker, decided to stay in the epicenter. Clark and I were together in our Hudson River town. One of our tenants was a doctor at the local hospital, and he gave us reports on the local COVID-19 caseload. Like many, I was furloughed from a paying job. But unlike most of the millions of freshly unemployed Americans, I was fortunate to have some savings, a secure home, health insurance, and a reasonable expectation that my employment would resume in the foreseeable future. In many ways, life wasn't so different for me: I had spent most of my working life alone in a room, but now the street outside my window was noticeably quieter and the welcoming lunch spot where I'd eaten so many bowls of soup was closed, possibly for good.

During the months of quarantine I thought often of the two years Eva and my grandparents spent inside their apartment on Weimarer Strasse. They had been afraid to show themselves in public for fear of being attacked, as they had become aliens in what had been their country. I was afraid of going into public spaces for fear of catching a potentially lethal virus. They would have been grateful if a face mask could have protected them against the violence of an ideological virus.

Throughout this time when I could not see my family or most friends in person, I looked for comfort online (dear Randy Rainbow, always a bright light). I connected with friends around the world and with my new colleagues in Austria and Italy. How would this all turn out? Would this new reality last for months, or years? Would politicians who had succeeded in making Americans hate one another capitalize on this precarious time to unravel our democracy? Amid a thousand online voices I felt bewildered: Should I try to fake some happiness or allow reality to wash over me? I did not want to muster joy I could not feel. I wanted to hope that we could emerge from this time with some progress and lessons learned. I wanted tests and a vaccine, so that my father and his wife could return to the city they loved and my daughter could move forward into an independent adulthood without fear. I wanted my family and other families to be safe with jobs and guaranteed health care.

Emily Esfahani Smith, author of *The Power of Meaning: Finding Fulfillment in a World Obsessed with Happiness*, offered some answers in her April 7, 2020, op-ed for the *New York Times*, in which she wrote about the idea of "tragic optimism." This term was coined by Viktor Frankl, Holocaust survivor, psychiatrist, author of *Man's Search for Meaning*, and long-ago nature-loving member of the Alpenverein Donauland. As Smith explains, "Tragic optimism is the ability to maintain hope and find meaning in life despite its inescapable pain, loss, and suffering." It is the idea of a certain kind of resilience in the face of hardship, the ability to find the positive even in darkness.

The search for meaning would involve pain and effort but ultimately would help us feel part of something more vital and beautiful. As Smith concludes, we could not avoid suffering but we could learn to find meaning in both joy and sorrow. And in the future, we and our children and their children would be able to see how thoughtful people navigated this hard present moment, just as we now look back to that time of my grandparents and my parents and cherish their examples.

A LONG, SLOW spring unfolded, melting the last of the snow and ice in the mountains where we hiked on weekends. The magnolia and crab-apple and dogwood trees bloomed in our garden. On V-E Day, I called my father and we reminisced about our trip to Normandy two years earlier. We welcomed the beauty of the new season and hoped we would be able to see each other soon. After so much time indoors, the end of winter seemed especially vibrant, the clear air filled with birdsong. A starling built her nest in a broken eave of our house and I watched as she raced back and forth with mouthfuls for her screeching chicks.

Clark and I visited Liza via FaceTime. Even with artfully cropped bangs and bleached eyebrows I could see traces of my mother's face; the Singer/Nichtern genes were more than a match for scissors and hair dye. Liza described the daily 7 p.m. celebration of emergency workers in Brooklyn. "Our backyard goes very hard," they told us, with New Yorker pride. "One guy plays a tuba. People clap and cheer and bang on pots and pans. And then a dog starts barking . . . and there's a little kid, maybe six or seven, who starts screaming, not because he's upset, but as his . . . contribution. It makes me so happy." I laughed, imagining the rau-cous orchestra with dog and boy howling solo lines. Clark and I wished we could take a trip to the city to be witnesses. By mid-May, the evening backyard celebrations seemed to subside.

On a gorgeous afternoon, Liza decided to take a walk in Prospect Park. "I went to visit all my old spots," they began wistfully. "And it had me feel-ing some kind of way, remembering high school days in the summer in the park, when we ran around and it didn't matter that you didn't have any money." In the open meadows New Yorkers were sitting on blankets, safely apart but connecting with their neighbors. After weeks of quarantine, this sight was an inspiration. For Liza, even though these were frightening times, the city felt safe. As the day drew to a close, they ended at a favorite place, a waterfall tucked in secluded woods at the top of a hill, hidden from the park roads and the meadow below. Suddenly, thunderous applause and cheering erupted, and this music of thousands of voices seemed to be coming from everywhere. The air was electrified. "Everything lit up," Liza said, describing the feeling of being both alone and yet surrounded by unseen human joy. "It was magical." It reminded me of a line from Donald Brown's travelogue: *Familiar scenes become strange and the world changes.*

On this evening, New Yorkers had not forgotten the importance of 7 p.m., to honor the essential workers who were risking their lives daily, to mourn the terrible loss of life and mark the toll this had taken on the city and the country, and the world. It was just that the warm weather had drawn people out of their apartments, and now they were celebrating in the park. For Liza, it was both dystopian and hopeful. "Imagine if aliens came down to Earth right now. What would they think about people clapping and cheering during this terrible time?" Clark and I laughed. It was one of those moments where I was sorry that my mother had not lived to know Liza as an adult. I think Eva and Eve would both have recognized something of themselves in their grandchild. For now, the beautiful thing was that Liza had somehow found uplift and meaning in this crisis, and it had made them stronger to face whatever lay ahead.

I could not have imagined what would unfold just a week later. After the death of George Floyd, an unarmed Black man, at the hands of police in Minneapolis, something shook loose. This latest outrage, after so many others, was just too much to bear. The pandemic was a reminder of our common vulnerability to disease, but its toll among people of color also exposed social injustice and power imbalances in every aspect of daily life. The local protests that expanded nationwide within a news cycle coalesced into a global movement to protest racist violence and police brutality. As part of an informal cavalry of bicyclists, Liza joined daily protest marches in New York. My father told me this time reminded him of antiwar protests he and my mother had joined in the 1960s. As the activism continued, several cities pledged to reform their police departments. Statues exalting the Confederacy were coming down. Support for Trump was beginning to crack. Resilient people fighting back against prejudice were speaking loud and clear against the voices of hate and division. The pandemic had brought fear and despair and isolation, but now a new sense of world consciousness was unfolding, focused on what unites rather than divides us. While I could not travel to New York to be part of the protests, I still felt part of that shift. We still have work to do, and we can do this best when we strive to find the inclusive spirit of shared purpose that is the ideal source of American identity.

Quarantine days—mostly alarming but sometimes encouraging—began to feel like the beginning of an ending. With effort, it seemed possible that the latest ugly manifestation of America First would eventually be pushed back, replaced with a vision of decency and long overdue justice for African Americans and other minorities who have given so much to this country and received so little in return.

I thought often of the seemingly random connections of intertwined lives that came together while charting my mother's journey from Eva to Eve and how these stitched threads have helped me understand her life and mine. I lived with the ghosts of my mother and all those who touched her life during her family's ordeal: Anna and Julius, Sylvester Mazura, Jakob Altenberg, Donald Brown. My circle widened to include Michael Simonson, Franz Novotny, and the many scholars who helped me find my mother's story. I wish that these connections could happen for us all, that we could find these filaments that reveal how we are connected as part of the arc of history. When those who have suffered persecution feel that they belong, that their lives truly matter, we will all live more truthful lives.

As I close, from the current moment of calamity and hope, of confronting the darkest strains of American history, there's a sense of turning a corner toward a more just society. My journey here has unearthed a story of the will to survive in the face of unspeakable evil. If there's a lesson, threads to be pulled together, it is that I can draw strength from this year of darkness and light. It has changed my child, my family, and all of us, and forever.

Acknowledgments

*E*VA AND EVE began as an eight-hundred-word story called "Instructions," published in Larry Smith's anthology *The Moment*. I could never have imagined that reflecting on the loss of my mother would take me on a much longer journey.

This book came together with the help of individuals and institutions in many places. I am grateful for the tireless work of all those who study the past so that we can learn lessons for the present. Heartfelt thanks for research assistance and advice to: Michael Simonson at the Leo Baeck Institute in New York; Anatol Steck at the United States Holocaust Memorial Museum in Washington, DC; the Office of the Historian at the U.S. State Department; NARA.gov; the Pusey Library at Harvard University; and the American Alpine Club. Thanks to Eve's design team members: Kathy Kikkert, Songhee Kim, Peiloi Koay, and Bonni Leon.

I received essential support along the way from: Larry Bowne, Andrea Chapin, Alice Eve Cohen, Carole DeSanti, Marion Kaplan, David Konigsberg, Leah Lococo, Miranda Magagnini, Jan Morris, Crystal Patriarche, Peg Patterson, Suzanne Potts, Mario Pulice, Heidi Reavis, Stefan von Senger, Lisa Silverman, Sarah Tschinkel, Brooke Warner, and Sarah Wildman. Many thanks to beloveds who read drafts and gave me thoughtful notes: Leigh Giurlando, Mary Metz, Caroline Press, and Clark Wieman. Many thanks to the extended Singer/Nichtern/Adler families, the Brown family, Elizabeth Heichler and her family, Agnieszka Michalik and the Altenberg family, and Katy and James Ehrlich. Many thanks to all my friends and colleagues near and far for love and companionship while I worked on this book.

In Austria, *besonderer Dank* to Franz Novotny for opening the door to Number 22; Danielle Spera and the staff of the Jewish Museum in Vienna;

Martin Achrainer and Veronika Raich at Austrian Alpenverein; the Luka-vsky family at Jos Binder, Evelyn Adunka, Tim Corbett, Ronny Eppel, Johann Kirchknopf, Gerald Lamprecht, and Susanne Korbel at the University of Graz; Doron Rabinovici, Michaela Raggam-Blesch, Philipp Rohr-bach, and Hubert Steiner at the Austrian Archives; and ZAMG Central Institute for Meterology Geodynamics for their 1939–40 weather reports.

In Italy, *grazie mille* to Emiliana Tomba, Stelio Zoratto and the Museo del Mare, Annalisa Di Fant and the Jewish Museum of Trieste, Maurizio Eliseo and Nicolò Capus of Italianliners.com, Trieste City Archive, and the Bora Museum.

In Croatia, *posebna hvala* to Jasenka Ferber Bogdan and the archival collection at the Division for the History of Medical Sciences, Croatian Academy of Sciences and Arts.

I am grateful to the Virginia Center of the Creative Arts and the Corporation of Yaddo for the gifts of time and space to write.

My splendid literary agents Jane Dystel and Miriam Goderich took on this project with unfailing enthusiasm, and I am deeply grateful for their calm guidance.

It was some kind of crazy kismet that my book found its way to Rakesh Satyal at Atria, an imprint of Simon & Schuster, where my parents worked for over three decades. His encouragement and insight improved this book in every way. Thanks to Trish Todd, who brought me the rest of the way. Many thanks to Libby McGuire, Lindsay Sagnette, Loan Le, Liz Byer, Rob Sternitsky, Gena Lanzi, Milena Brown, and the creativity of James Iacobelli, Laywan Kwan, and Erika Genova, who helped make the stunning inside and outside of this book a reality during a pandemic.

My deepest thanks and love to my father, Frank, who patiently excavated the past with me, and to all my Metz family: Simon, Mary, and Justine.

Last and always, my endless thanks and love to Clark for so many fancies, songs, dances, and adventures during our years together and to my dearest Chimwemwe who amazes and surprises me in every way. *Nunc scio quid sit Amor.*

Selected Bibliography

Arendt, Hannah. *The Origins of Totalitarianism*. New York: Harcourt Brace Jovanovich, 1976.

Åsbrink, Elisabeth. *1947: Where Now Begins*. New York: Other Press, 2016.

Beller, Steven. *Vienna and the Jews: 1867–1938, A Cultural History*. Cambridge, UK: Cambridge University Press, 1989.

Berg, A. Scott. *Lindbergh*. New York: Simon & Schuster, 1998.

Berkley, George E. *Vienna and Its Jews: The Tragedy of Success, 1880–1980s*. Lanham, MD: Madison Books, 1988.

Breitman, Richard and Alan M. Kraut. *American Refugee Policy and European Jewry, 1933–1945*. Bloomington: Indiana University Press, 1987.

Churchwell, Sarah. *Behold, America: The Entangled History of "America First" and "The American Dream."* New York: Basic Books, 2018.

Clare, George. *Last Waltz in Vienna*. London: Pan Books, 1982.

de Waal, Edmund. *The Hare with Amber Eyes: A Hidden Inheritance* (Illustrated Edition). New York: Farrar, Straus and Giroux, 2012.

Eliseo, Maurizio. *Saturnia and Vulcania: Record Motorships*. London: Carmania Press, 2018.

Frankl, Viktor E. *Man's Search for Meaning*. Boston: Beacon Press, 2006.

Friedenreich, Harriet Pass. *Jewish Politics in Vienna, 1918–1938*. Bloomington: Indiana University Press, 1991.

Hall, Peter. *Cities in Civilization: Culture, Innovation, and Urban Order*. London: Phoenix, 1999.

Hamann, Brigitte. *Hitler's Vienna: A Dictator's Apprenticeship*. New York: Oxford University Press, 1999.

Hen, Józef. *Nowolipie Street*. DL Books, 2012.

Hilsenrad, Helen. *Brown Was the Danube: A Memoir of Hitler's Vienna*. New York: Thomas Yoseloff, 1966.

Hochstadt, Steve. *Exodus to Shanghai: Stories of Escape from the Third Reich*. New York: Palgrave Macmillan, 2012.

Holliday, Laurel. *Children in the Holocaust and World War II: Their Secret Diaries*. New York: Washington Square Press, 1995.

Hunter, Georgia. *We Were the Lucky Ones*. New York: Viking, 2017.

Kanter, Trudi. *Some Girls, Some Hats, and Hitler: A True Love Story Rediscovered*. New York: Scribner, 2012.

Kaplan, Paul M. *Jewish New York: A History and Guide to Neighborhoods, Synagogues, and Eateries*. Gretna, LA: Pelican, 2015.

Kennedy, John F. *A Nation of Immigrants*. New York: Harper Perennial, 2018.

Kluger, Ruth. *Still Alive: A Holocaust Girlhood Remembered*. New York: Feminist Press, 2012.

Krug, Nora. *Belonging: A German Reckons with History and Home*. New York: Scribner, 2018.

Lagnado, Lucette. *The Man in the White Sharkskin Suit: A Jewish Family's Exodus from Old Cairo to the New World*. New York: Ecco, 2007.

Lee, Erika. *America for Americans: A History of Xenophobia in the United States*. New York: Basic Books, 2019.

Levy, Debbie. *The Year of Goodbyes: A True Story of Friendship, Family, and Farewells*. New York: Hyperion, 2010.

Lindbergh, Charles, A. *The Wartime Journals of Charles A. Lindbergh*. New York: Harcourt Brace Jovanovich, 1970.

Luiselli, Valeria. *Tell Me How It Ends: An Essay in Forty Questions*. Minneapolis: Coffee House Press, 2017.

Mendelsohn, Daniel. *The Lost: A Search for Six of Six Million*. New York: Harper Perennial, 2013.

Morris, Jan. *Trieste and the Meaning of Nowhere*. Cambridge, MA: Da Capo Press, 2001.

Morton, Frederic. *Thunder at Twilight: Vienna 1913/1914*. Cambridge, MA: Da Capo Press, 2001.

Okrent, Daniel. *The Guarded Gate: Bigotry, Eugenics, and the Law That Kept Two Generations of Jews, Italians, and Other European Immigrants Out of America*. New York: Scribner, 2019.

Orgel, Doris. *The Devil in Vienna*. New York: Puffin Books, 1978.

Origo, Iris. *A Chill in the Air: An Italian War Diary 1939–1940*. New York: New York Review Books, 2017.

Pauley, Bruce F. *From Prejudice to Persecution: A History of Austrian Anti-Semitism*. Chapel Hill: University of North Carolina Press, 1992.

Peters, Olaf, ed. *Before the Fall: German and Austrian Art of the 1930s*. New York: Prestel/Ronald S. Lauder Neue Galerie, 2018.

Pinsker, Shachar M. *A Rich Brew: How Cafés Created Modern Jewish Culture*. New York: New York University Press, 2018.

Prochnik, George. *The Impossible Exile: Stefan Zweig at the End of the World*. New York: Other Press, 2014.

Rabinovici, Doron. *Eichmann's Jews: The Jewish Administration of Holocaust Vienna, 1938–1945*. Malden, MA: Polity Press, 2011.

Raggam-Blesch, Michaela. "The Anschluss Pogrom in Vienna," unpublished chapter from *The Shoah in Vienna: Memorial Topographies of a Destroyed Jewish Community, 1938–1945*. Translated by Tim Corbett. 2019.

Rosen, R. D. *Such Good Girls: The Journey of the Holocaust's Hidden Child Survivors*. New York: HarperCollins, 2014.

Rosner, Elizabeth. *Survivor Café: The Legacy of Trauma and the Labyrinth of Memory*. Berkeley, CA: Counterpoint, 2017.

Roth, Joseph. *The Radetsky March*. New York: Overlook Press, 2002.

Sands, Philippe. *East West Street: On the Origins of Genocide and Crimes Against Humanity*. London: Weidenfeld & Nicolson, 2016.

Silverman, Lisa. *Becoming Austrians: Jews and Culture Between the World Wars*. New York: Oxford University Press, 2015.

Snyder, Timothy. *Black Earth: The Holocaust as History and Warning*. New York: Tim Duggan, 2015.

Stanley, Jason. *How Fascism Works: The Politics of Us and Them*. New York: Random House, 2018.

Torberg, Friedrich. *Tante Jolesch or the Decline of the West in Anecdotes.* Riverside, CA: Ariadne Press, 2008.

Van Es, Bart. *The Cut Out Girl: A Story of War and Family, Lost and Found.* New York: Penguin Press, 2018.

von Rezzori, Gregor. *Memoirs of an Anti-Semite: A Novel in Five Stories.* New York: New York Review Books, 1981.

von Senger und Etterlin, Frido. *Neither Fear nor Hope: The Wartime Memoirs of the German Defender of Cassino.* New York: E. P. Dutton, 1964.

Vuillard, Éric. *The Order of the Day.* Translated by Mark Polizzotti. New York: Other Press, 2018.

Weyr, Thomas. *The Setting of the Pearl: Vienna Under Hitler.* New York: Oxford University Press, 2005.

Wiesel, Elie. *A Passover Haggadah: As Commented Upon by Elie Wiesel.* New York: Simon & Schuster, 2006.

Wildman, Sarah. *Paper Love: Searching for the Girl My Grandfather Left Behind.* New York: Riverhead, 2014.

Wistrich, Robert S. *The Jews of Vienna in the Age of Franz Joseph.* Liverpool, UK: Littman Library of Jewish Civilization, 1990.

Zweig, Stefan. *Chess Story.* Translated by Joel Rotenberg. New York: New York Review Books, 2011.

———. *The Collected Stories of Stefan Zweig.* London: Pushkin Press, 2013.

———. *The Invisible Collection: Tales of Obsession and Desire.* London: Pushkin Press, 2015.

———. *Messages from a Lost World: Europe on the Brink.* London: Pushkin Press, 2016.

———. *The World of Yesterday: An Autobiography.* Lincoln: University of Nebraska Press, 1964.

Selected Articles

Bencich, Marco. "Il Comitato di assistenza agli emigranti ebrei di Trieste (1920–1940): flussi migratori e normative." *Qualestoria* 34, no. 2, December 2006.

Corbett, Tim. "Once 'the Only True Austrians': Mobilising Jewish Memory of the First World War for Belonging in the New Austrian Nation, 1929–1938," in Madigan E., G. Reuveni, eds., *The Jewish Experience of the First World War*. London: Palgrave Macmillan, 2019.

———. "'Was ich den Juden war, wird eine kommende Zeit besser beurteilen': Myth and Memory at Theodor Herzl's Original Gravesite in Vienna" in *S.I.M.O.N. Shoah: Intervention, Methods, Documentation* 3, 2016.

Hödl, Klaus. "From Acculturation to Interaction: A New Perspective on the History of the Jews in Fin-de-Siecle Vienna." *Shofar: An Interdisciplinary Journal of Jewish Studies* 25, no. 2, 2007.

———. "'Jewish History' beyond Binary Conceptions: Jewish Performing Musicians in Vienna Around 1900." *Journal of Modern Jewish Studies*, 2017.

———. "'Jewish History' as Part of 'General History': A Comment." *Medaon 12, Magazin fur judisches Leben in Forschung und Bildung*, 2018.

Lamprecht, Gerald. "The Remembrance of World War One and the Austrian Federation of Jewish War Veterans," in Ernst, Petra, and Jeffrey Grossman, eds., *The Great War: Reflections, Experiences and Memories of German and Habsburg Jews (1914–1918)*.

Wyrwa, Ulrich. *Quest, Issues in Contemporary Jewish History, Journal of Fondazione CDEC*, no. 9, October 2016.

About the Author

JULIE METZ is the author of the *New York Times* bestselling memoir *Perfection*. She has written for publications including the *New York Times*, *Salon*, *Dame*, *Glamour*, and mrbellersneighborhood.com. Her essays have appeared in anthologies including *The Moment*, edited by Larry Smith, creator of Six-Word Memoirs. Julie has been a guest on podcasts including *Dear Sugars*, hosted by Cheryl Strayed and Steve Almond, and *Women of the Hour*, hosted by Lena Dunham, and she is the proud winner of a Literary Death Match, the competitive reading series founded by Adrian Zuniga. She lives with her family and two cats in the Hudson Valley.

BOOK
CLUB
FAVORITES

READER'S
GUIDE

EVA

AND

EVE

JULIE METZ

This reading group guide for *Eva and Eve* includes a note from the author, discussion questions, ideas for enhancing your book club, and a Q&A with author Julie Metz. The suggested questions are intended to help your reading group find new and interesting angles and topics for your discussion. We hope that these ideas will enrich your conversation and increase your enjoyment of the book.

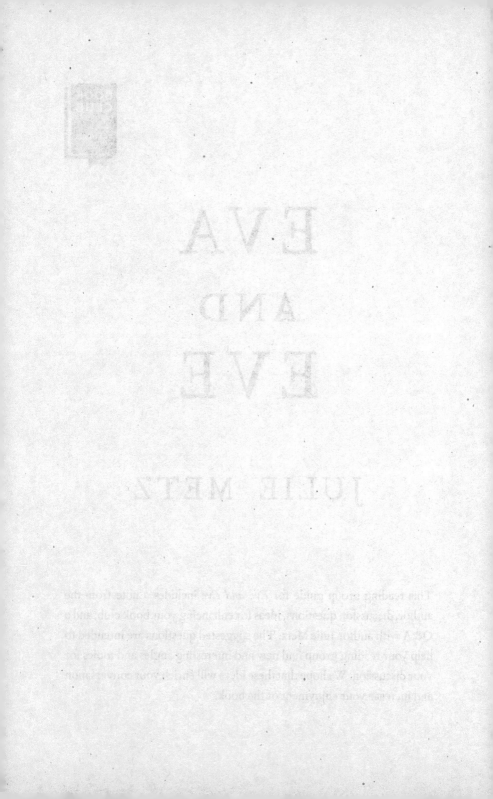

A Note from the Author

AFTER MY MOTHER, Eve, died, I inherited a stash of photos and paper documents, remnants from another lifetime. Like many children of Holocaust survivors, I knew only fragments of her early life. I was missing the thread that would stitch them together.

My mother's comfortable childhood in Vienna ended in March 1938, as Hitler's troops crossed the Austrian border. She told me and my brother a few stories, but they mystified me. In one, her father was saved from deportation because of an object used to package medicine, produced at his factory. It was made of paper, she told us, and shaped like a fan. How could a paper fan have saved her family?

In the drawer where my mother kept her perfumed slips and nightgowns, I found a small keepsake book from her childhood, the pages filled with inscriptions from relatives, teachers, and friends, many of whom did not survive. In this book my mother was named Eva. The book felt like a challenge, as if she'd left me clues to follow.

To find the missing threads, I traveled to Vienna to capture the sights and smells and flavors of my mother's childhood. With research and serendipity, I pieced together the story of Eva's survival and reinvention as Eve, made possible by helpers who will surprise you. I even found that paper fan. *Eva and Eve* is a memoir of a childhood lost, a family history found, and an immigration story for our time.

Topics and Questions for Discussion

1. *Eva and Eve* is an intimate exploration of one family's escape from Nazi-occupied Vienna. Do you have family members who lived through this time? How have you learned their stories?

2. For children and grandchildren of Holocaust survivors, there is often a silence around family stories of the Nazi era. This kind of silence exists around other sorts of family secrets and trauma. How would you go about researching your family's history?

3. In *Eva and Eve*, the author makes use of fictional devices in parts of the narrative. Why do you think she chose to do this, and do you think it is effective?

4. The Jews of Vienna, including the author's mother and grandparents, felt that they belonged to their city and would remain safe. Talk about why they felt this way, even with the rise of Hitler in neighboring Germany. Do you see any parallels to our time?

5. *Eva and Eve* introduces us to three sets of mothers and daughters. How would you describe your connection with your own mother? What aspects of her personality do you see in yourself? How do you think the author's relationship with her mother changes over the course of the book?

6. The Singer family's escape was the result of a combination of persistence and what seems like random good fortune. Or was it random? Talk about the role of brief encounters in your own life and how those changed your history.

7. For most of us in the United States, with the exception of Native Americans, our families came from somewhere else. What is your family's history in the United States? Did your family come by choice or as a result of persecution or enslavement? If by choice, what did they hope to find here? What did America mean to your ancestors, and what does it mean to you now?

8. The trauma of war and persecution can reverberate through generations. Do you have any experiences of this in your family?

9. *Eva and Eve* has a braided structure, interweaving the present and past. Talk about other books, films, or television shows with this kind of structure and how it works in storytelling.

10. The Holocaust is one of the most researched events in history. What do you think we can learn today from stories about the era of National Socialism in Germany and its occupied territories?

11. The persistence of anti-Semitism and racism in America has moved to the forefront of our national discussion. How would you envision a constructive and positive way to discuss these complex issues with friends, families, and your larger community?

12. In the book, the author describes her desire to reclaim Austrian citizenship, despite the anger her mother felt toward the country that had expelled her. She elaborated on this quest in a story she wrote for *Tablet* magazine, titled "A Daughter's Inheritance." How do you think the author's feelings about Austria change during the course of her research?

Enhance Your Book Club

Eva and Eve includes a bibliography of other books that shed light on the decades between the two world wars, the Holocaust, the fate of Vienna's Jews, and the history of anti-immigration movements in the United States. Below are author Julie Metz's brief summaries of seven of those titles.

The Hare with Amber Eyes: A Hidden Inheritance
Edmund de Waal

This moving memoir traces the history of a collection of netsuke, small Japanese carvings, through the author's family, the Ephrussi, from mid-nineteenth-century Paris to the present. At one point the collection was sent to a Viennese relative as a wedding gift and became entwined in the story of Vienna's Jews. I highly recommend the illustrated edition, filled with family photographs and documents.

Thunder at Twilight: Vienna 1913/1914
Frederic Morton

Many of us have little understanding of the forces that drew most of Europe into the First World War and laid the groundwork for the Second World War. This beautifully written account of the last two years of the Habsburg Empire brings to life the end of a faraway era, one that has nevertheless left its mark on our present day.

Behold, America: The Entangled History of "America First" and "The American Dream"
Sarah Churchwell

The subtitle of this book presents two eternal myths of the American experience. What readers discover is that these ideas have never been fixed, but instead have evolved over time, often manipulated to suit the needs of politicians eager to keep out the next wave of would-be Americans. "America First" was the slogan of a revived Ku Klux Klan in the 1920s and is now once again being used to advance a white nationalist agenda.

The Impossible Exile: Stefan Zweig at the End of the World
George Prochnik

During his lifetime, Stefan Zweig was a bestselling author and cultural icon in Vienna, his stories masterful studies of psychology and suspense. But he was also a Jew, and after Germany annexed Austria he was forced to flee. This book gives us a picture of the cultural world in which Zweig thrived. A meditation on the meaning of home, this biography helps us understand the trauma of exile that so many refugees experience.

The Order of the Day
Éric Vuillard

This riveting short book is as sharp as a knife. Vuillard describes two history-altering events: a 1933 meeting between Adolf Hitler and the German captains of industry who would go on to fund his rise to power, and the Anschluss, the arrival of Hitler's troops in Vienna on March 12, 1938, which changed the lives of Austria's Jews.

Hitler's Vienna: A Dictator's Apprenticeship
Brigitte Hamann

This is a portrait of the young man who wanted to be an artist but would eventually reinvent himself as the Führer in neighboring Germany. The book also presents a cultural history of Vienna, the city in which Adolf Hitler developed his racist ideas.

A conversation between the author and Caroline Leavitt,
New York Times **bestselling author of** *Pictures of You* **and**
With or Without You,
reprinted from carolineleavittville.com

Caroline Leavitt: What was the moment that haunted you into writing this particular book now?

Julie Metz: I like your use of the word *haunted*, because that is kind of what happened. My mother and I had a complicated relationship during our lives together, and that didn't end with her death. Shortly after she died, I discovered a keepsake book she'd kept hidden in the back of a drawer for decades. My father had never seen it, and they were married for fifty-four years. This keepsake book was one of the few personal possessions she was able to bring with her from Vienna when she and her parents fled Nazi persecution in March 1940. It was filled with inscriptions from childhood friends, relatives, and teachers, and I immediately wondered if those people had survived. It was clear to me that this secret book held a lot of grief and sorrow and also anger. My mother told only a few stories about her childhood. I began thinking about my mother as a ten-year-old in 1938 and the terror she lived through as a child as the family struggled to get to America. War leaves a mark on everyone it touches. There was no one left to tell me everything that had happened, so my research process started as a desire to fill in the spaces in the narrative. I am not a traditionally observant Jew, but two traditional questions surfaced: "If not me, then who? If not now, then when?"

CL: In reliving-through-writing your mother's story after her death, how did your relationship with her (since relationships don't necessarily end with death) change?

JM: In so many ways, my research and writing were part of my grieving process. The arc of grief can be long, especially where there are many unanswered questions. I wanted to understand my mother, to know her in ways she couldn't, or wouldn't, share during her life. At times I felt like she left me clues to follow. She'd saved all the family paperwork and photographs, and sometimes a document or photo would slip out just when I needed to see it. At times it truly felt like a séance. I untangled some mysteries and came to a place of deeper understanding and compassion.

CL: This book reveals how trauma can indeed be passed down through the generations. Do you see a way out of that?

JM: Writing about this time has helped me understand the legacy of war and persecution on generations that follow. I've met Bosnians and Serbians who have stories to tell about the genocide of the 1990s and how it carries into the present day. I've read about the aftermath of genocide in Rwanda. I've read two recent memoirs by Vietnamese refugees still living with the aftermath of the war there. I am not sure what the way out is, but since so many immigrants are fleeing situations of persecution and terror, I hope that there can be more compassion for the plight of people forced to leave their homes.

CL: What was your research like and what surprised you the most?

JM: I am not a trained historian, so I learned on the job. I had help from wonderful historians. . . . What amazed me was how many

1947: Where Now Begins
Elisabeth Asbrink

A brief and trenchant portrait of a year that encapsulates the violence of the war just ended and presages the conflicts we are grappling with to this day. We follow Nazis escaping to South America, the independence movement in India, political/religious conflicts in Palestine, philosopher Simone de Beauvoir's trip to Chicago, the changing lives of postwar women, and the onset of the Cold War.

historians are devoting their working lives to studying not just interwar Jewish culture generally, but specifically the world of Vienna's Jews. The city in those years was a cultural hub, and people migrated there from all over central Europe. I didn't realize how integrated Jews were in this city, and that despite periods of anti-Semitism, they felt at home. I'd always wondered why the Jews of Vienna didn't flee as soon as Hitler rose to power in neighboring Germany. They felt they were safe in Austria, that the hell that had begun in Germany couldn't possibly reach them. This was the tragedy. A group of people that had given so much—in music, literature, art, theater, science—were negated practically overnight.

CL: What's obsessing you now and why?

JM: Even after years exploring the interwar culture of Jewish life in Vienna, the world of my mother's childhood, I find that I'm not done yet. There are more stories to tell and I'm searching for them now.